ST. AUGUSTINE

THE GREATNESS
OF THE SOUL
DE QUANTITATE ANIMAE

THE TEACHER
DE MAGISTRO

Ancient Christian Writers

THE WORKS OF THE FATHERS IN TRANSLATION

EDITED BY

JOHANNES QUASTEN, S. T. D.
*Professor of Ancient Church History
and Christian Archaeology*

JOSEPH C. PLUMPE, Ph. D.
*Professor of New Testament Greek
and Ecclesiastical Latin*

The Catholic University of America
Washington, D. C.

No. 9

ST. AUGUSTINE

THE GREATNESS OF
THE SOUL

—◆—

THE TEACHER

TRANSLATED AND ANNOTATED

BY

JOSEPH M. COLLERAN, C. SS. R., Ph. D.

Professor of Philosophy
Mount St. Alphonsus Seminary
Esopus, New York

NEWMAN PRESS

New York, N.Y./Ramsey, N.J.

Imprimi Potest:
    Joannes M. Frawley, C.SS.R.
      Provincialis
        Brooklyni, N.Y., die 23 Septembris 1949

Nihil Obstat:
    Johannes Quasten, S.T.D.
      Censor Deputatus

Imprimatur:
    Patricius A. O'Boyle, D.D.
      Archiepiscopus Washingtonensis
      die 3 Octobris 1949

Library of Congress
Catalog Card Number: 78-62455

ISBN: 0-8091-0060-6

PUBLISHED BY PAULIST PRESS
Editorial Office: 1865 Broadway, New York, N.Y. 10023
Business Office: 545 Island Road, Ramsey, N.J. 07446

PRINTED AND BOUND IN THE UNITED STATES OF AMERICA

CONTENTS

ST. AUGUSTINE

THE GREATNESS
OF THE SOUL

Augustine, *Retractationes* 1. 8 (Maur.): In the same city (Rome) I wrote a dialogue in which many questions about the soul are raised and discussed: where it comes from, what sort of thing it is, how great it is, why it was united with the body, what results from its union with the body, what results from its departure. We discussed with particular care and thoroughness the question of its greatness. The purpose was to show, if we could, that actually it is not possessed of corporeal quantity, and yet has greatness of a kind. For this reason the entire book received its name from this one enquiry, so as to go by the title, *The Greatness of the Soul.* . . . This book begins as follows: "Seeing that you have plenty of leisure. . . ."

INTRODUCTION

To St. Augustine, especially in the earlier part of his career, the whole of "philosophy" consisted in the effort to arrive at a clearer knowledge of the nature of God and of the nature of the human soul.[1] A principal obstacle in the way of achieving these ends had been his inability, for a long time, to conceive of anything having reality and existence which was not corporeal:

> Because when I wished to think of my God, I knew not what to think of but bodies with bulk—for to my mind what was not such did not exist at all—this was the greatest and almost the only cause of my inevitable error.[2]

It was precisely this materialistic conception that led his brilliant mind to be ensnared by the absurd Manichaean teaching that there must be two primary substances, one good and the other evil; for he imagined evil to be a foul and misshapen material mass, and since a strange innate piety prevented him from attributing such a thing to the creation of God, he found it more logical to admit two infinite masses, one good and the other evil, essentially opposed to each other.[3] When that compromise settlement of his difficulties dissatisfied him, as was to be expected, he launched out into the sea of skepticism.[4]

Under the influence of St. Ambrose of Milan and of Manlius Theodorus, a Christian Platonist, he came to see that neither God nor the human soul could be material.[5] He then read the works of the Neoplatonists, especially of Plotinus, and gradually understood and appreciated that immaterial realities exist and are even more valuable than the material or corporeal as perceived by the senses.[6]

After his conversion to Christian truth and morality, Augustine showed a convert's zeal in impressing on the minds and hearts of others the truths that had liberated him from his earlier mental torment. It was natural that the rhetorician and teacher should discuss with his friends and communicate with his Christian contemporaries, the doctrines that meant so much to himself.

The question of the immateriality of the human soul he took up for extended treatment in the work *De quantitate animae*. This he wrote in the city of Rome, soon after his baptism and following the death of his mother: therefore, sometime during the latter part of 387 or the first half of 388 A.D.[7]

The enquiry took the form of a dialogue with Evodius, one of his closest friends, who had been born in Augustine's own native town of Tagaste, Africa, and who, after spending his youth as a soldier, worked for some time in civil service. Evodius was baptized a Catholic before Augustine, and immediately upon his conversion manifested the same intensity in his spiritual life as he had shown in his secular pursuits. He joined Augustine and the little group of relatives and friends at Milan shortly after Augustine's baptism; he had been one of the little community at Cassiciacum;[8] he was a source of comfort to his friend and the boy Adeodatus when Monnica died at Ostia;[9] and he made the return trip to Africa with Augustine and Nebridius. In Africa he was one of the first members of Augustine's monastic community at Tagaste, sharing the leader's enthusiasm for religious life and intellectual discussion. Besides his part in the *De quantitate animae*, Evodius was a disputant in the *De libero arbitrio*,[10] a dialogue on free will as the cause of moral evil;

this work was begun at Rome and finished in Africa after Augustine had become a priest at Hippo Regius. Evodius had accompanied Augustine from Tagaste to Hippo, and was a member of the monastery which Augustine founded there.[11] In the year 396 he was appointed Bishop of Uzala, near Utica. He continued his friendship with Augustine, corresponding with him on theological matters.[12]

In the present work Evodius proposes six questions regarding the human soul. The first two, which concern its origin and its characteristic quality, are treated quite summarily (1.2 - 2.3), while the last three, regarding the reason for the soul's union with the body, the result of that union, and the state of the soul when separated from the body, are practically brushed aside, with a bare suggestion of Augustine's views (36.81). The third question—*quanta sit anima?*—is the one that receives fullest consideration, and from it the dialogue takes its title, *De quantitate animae*.[13]

Augustine could speak of the "quantity" or "quantitativeness" of the soul only to insist that there is no quantity in it at all, except in the transferred sense of "virtual quantity," which is extent or degree of power. It is his contention that although the soul has no size and extension such as bodies have, yet it can be called "great" because of its abilities and capacities. It is true that when Evodius proposes the question *quanta sit anima?* he is intent on finding out not only the powers of the soul, but also the quantitative measurements he wrongly thinks the soul possesses;[14] and the Latin title quite adequately indicates this general problem as well as the specific conclusions on the greatness of the soul. But Augustine's main concern is with that greatness of power; for this he reserves his highest enthusiasm; and even the more protracted discussions of memory, skill, strength, sensation, and knowledge are made to serve as illustrations of the greatness of the soul.

Although the author, in rather typical fashion, draws out certain points at greater length than others, there is in this little book a more systematic and orderly development than in some of his other early works. From the very beginning (3. 4), he is sure of his position that the soul is not corporeal. His whole intent in discussing the question at all, is to defend his tenet against the objections raised by Evodius. Hence, the order of the treatise is determined by the order in which the arguments for the opposite opinion are presented. The structure of the book might be conveniently summarized:

1st Question: Origin of the soul (1. 2).

2nd Question: Characteristic of the soul (2. 3).

3rd Question: Greatness of the soul (3. 4 - 36. 80):

a) Distinction between dimensive and virtual quantity (3. 4)

b) Statement of thesis: There is no dimensive quantity in the soul (*ibid.*)

c) Negative argument: The fact that the soul lacks physical measurements does not imply that it cannot be a reality; example: justice (3. 4 - 4. 5)

d) Positive argument: The soul must be immaterial, to retain with its memory images of diverse bodies, and abstracted measurements (4. 6 - 15. 25)

e) Answers to objections:

1) Increase of virtue, knowledge, and skill does not indicate growth of soul, except in a metaphorical sense (15. 26 - 20. 34)

2) Increase of bodily strength does not indicate physical growth of soul (21. 35 - 22. 40)

3) Sensation in every part of body does not prove that the soul is extended (23.41 - 30.61)

4) Division of living things does not prove that the soul is extended (31.62 - 32.69)

f) Conclusion: Levels of greatness of the soul (33.70 - 36.80).

4th Question: Reason for union of soul and body

5th Question: Result of that union

6th Question: Result of separation

Not discussed at any length, but considered as implicitly and practically answered in the preceding (36.81).

In the course of his arguments to prove that the human soul is incorporeal, the Saint manifests his quite considerable mastery of the physical notions of his day,[15] and his interest in numbers and geometrical illustrations.[16] But he is at his best in describing the capacities and achievements of the human soul: his portrayal of the degrees or levels of its capability is rhetorically the most impressive and religiously the most fervent and inspiring part of the entire essay. The first level, and the lowest, is that of vegetative life, shared by man with the plants; the second, of sensitive life, common also to other animals. Of the distinctively human functions, the achievements of man in the various arts constitute the third level; these, Augustine observes, are glorious indeed, but still earthly in their scope and found even in men not worthy of genuine approbation. Moral perfection, still of the natural order, comprises the fourth level, and while this set of powers raises the soul to God, it has the drawbacks of the fear of death and the danger of relapse. There follows the stage—the fifth—in which the soul stabilizes itself in virtue and advances with tranquillity toward the contemplation of truth, the actual entrance into which, following purification, is the sixth degree of the soul's power. Finally, the very abode of the soul is reached in contemplative union of mind and heart with God. Augustine gives free rein to his enthusiasm as he outlines the details of these God-given capacities, and repeatedly goes over them. This extraordinary passage has been recognized by scholars as one of the chief sources of his theory of mysticism, as his *Confessions* contain the principal account of his mystical experiences.[17]

St. Augustine was never exclusively and professedly a "philosopher" in the accepted modern sense of one who studies, in a purely speculative way, the ultimate causes of things by means of unaided reason. He never confined himself to purely natural knowledge; he frequently began with truths of faith, which he tried to penetrate more deeply, and from the beginning of his writing apostolate he considered the authority of the Christian Faith the principal norm of truth.[18] Neither was he interested in speculation for its own sake; the purpose of knowledge was always the attainment of happiness by closer union with God.[19] As a means to that goal — which is rather mystical than philosophical, as we now use the latter word—he found the teachings of the Neoplatonists, particularly of Plotinus, suggestive and inspiring.[20]

In the present essay all his reasoning and arguing on the immateriality of the soul are directed toward the delineation of the steps that prepare the soul for complete mystical union. Here, too, there is evident and undeniable dependence on Plotinus, but at the same time there is clear evidence against the view, given great currency and support during the nineteenth and early twentieth centuries, that Augustine was really converted in 386 not to orthodox Catholic Christianity, but to Platonic philosophy.[21] Pages of this book, as of his other earlier ones, breathe an unmistakable Catholicity, quite alien to anything of which Plotinus ever dreamed. True, in the conception of sensation as an act of the soul alone,[22] in the contemplative procedure from the visible universe to the inner powers of the human soul and thence to God,[23] in the emphatic and almost exaggerated preference of the immaterial to the material,[24] there is undoubtedly a dependence on Plotinus and the other Platonists. But, whereas Plotinus holds emanation as the mode of origin of realities other than the Absolute, Augustine categorically affirms creation.[25] Plotinus apparently teaches the absorption of the purified soul into the Supreme Being; Augustine expressly excludes it.[26] Plotinus was ashamed of the human body;[27] Augustine, for all his emphasis on the immaterial element in man, sees a nobility in the human body because of the doctrines of the Incarnation of the Divine Word and of the bodily resurrection as taught in Christian revelation.[28] Whatever difficulties he has, speculatively, in conceiving the precise nature of the union of body and soul in man, Augustine, even at this early date, perceives that such a union is part of the beauty and order of the universe, which is due to God alone.[29] In fine, it can be said that though the philosophy is in good part the philosophy of Plotinus, there is more than philosophy here. There is unequivocal acceptance of Divine Revelation,[30] there is acknowledgment of the need of external help from God,[31] and there is the specifically Christian concept of love for all human beings as creatures of God.[32]

All philosophizing about quantity, about sense knowledge, memory, and physical laws, is to St. Augustine only a means of elevating the mind to the contemplation of God and of inciting the heart to a purer and warmer love of Him from whom we came and for whose glory we are made.

✦ ✦ ✦

The text followed in the present translation is that of the celebrated Maurist edition, reprinted in Migne's *Patrologia Latina* 32 (1845) 1035-1080. A convenient reprint of this text was offered by F. E. Tourscher, *De quantitate animae* (Villanova 1924).

Father Tourscher has also published a translation of the book, *The Measure of the Soul*, with accompanying Latin text (Philadelphia 1933). A later translation, by J. J. McMahon, under the title, *The Magnitude of the Soul*, appeared in the series: *The Fathers of the Church: Writings of Saint Augustine* 2 (New York, no date) 51-149.

LIST OF CHAPTERS

11

CHAPTER 1

Six questions about the soul. Whence does the soul come?

Evodius. Seeing that you have plenty of leisure, I would like you to answer some questions that I have. They are not, I think, unsuitable and inopportune. Frequently, you know, when I plied you with questions, you thought it well to put me off with that Greek saw which tells us not to seek what is beyond our powers. But in the present instance I do not think we ourselves are beyond our own powers. So, when I ask you about the soul, I do not deserve to hear: "Why concern ourselves with what is beyond our powers?"[1] but I deserve, so I hope, to be told what we are.

Augustine. State briefly what you would like to be told about the soul.

Ev. I shall do that. Having pondered over these points for a long time, I have them ready. I would like to know, then:

Where does the soul come from?
What sort of thing is it?
How great is it?
Why was it united with the body?
What results from its union with the body?
What results from its separation?

2. *Aug.* When you ask where the soul comes from, I must understand this in two senses. For when we ask where a man comes from, wishing to know what his native country

13

is, that is one thing; and asking him whence he is, meaning what he consists of—that is to say, of what elements and things he is composed—is another. Which of these do you want to know about, when you ask where the soul comes from? Do you want to know what is its native country, so to say, its homeland from which it has come here, or are you asking what its essence is?

Ev. As a matter of fact, I would like to know the answers to both questions; but which should be known first, I prefer to leave to your judgment.

Aug. I believe that the soul's proper abode, to put it that way, and its homeland, is God Himself by whom it has been created.[2] But its essence I cannot properly identify. For I do not think it comes from those common and familiar natures with which we come in contact by means of these our bodily senses. I do not think, for example, that the soul consists of earth, or of water, or air, or fire, or of all of these things together, or of any combination of them. If you were to ask me of what things that tree is composed, I would name those four very familiar elements, of which we must believe all such things are constituted; but if you were to go on and ask me what earth itself, or water, or air, or fire, is composed of, I would not be able to answer.[3] In the same way, when the question is, of what elements man is made up I am able to answer—of a soul and a body. Again, should you ask me about the body, I shall fall back upon those four elements. But when you ask about the soul, since it seems to be something simple and to have an essence all its own,[4] I shall be no less embarrassed then if you ask, as I said, what earth comes from.

Ev. I do not understand what you mean by stating that it has an essence of its own. You said it was made by God.

Aug. Just as I cannot deny that earth itself has been made by God, and yet I cannot say of what further bodies, so to speak, earth is composed. For earth is a simple body by the very fact that it is earth; and for that reason it is called an element of all those bodies that are made up of the four elements. It is not contradictory, therefore, to say both that the soul has been made by God, and that it has some distinctive nature of its own. And this distinctive nature, its very own, God Himself evidently has made, just as He has made the distinctive natures of fire, of air, of water, and of earth, so that all other bodies might be composed of all these elements.

CHAPTER 2

The characteristic of the soul: its likeness to God.

3. *Ev.* For the present, I accept your explanation of the origin of the soul, that is, that it comes from God. I shall give it a great deal of thought, and if I have any difficulty, I shall ask about it afterwards. Now, then, please explain what its nature is.

Aug. It seems to me that it is like to God. If I am not mistaken, it is about the *human* soul you are inquiring.

Ev. That is just what I would like you to explain: how the soul is like to God. For while we believe that God has no maker, you said before that the soul has God Himself for its Maker.

Aug. Well, so you think it was difficult for God to make something like Himself, although in the presence of so great a variety of images, you see that this is granted even to us?

Ev. But obviously the things we produce are mortal, whereas the soul that God makes is immortal, I think. But perhaps you think otherwise.

Aug. So you would have men make things on the same level that God makes them?

Ev. I would not say that, of course. But just as He in His immortality makes something immortal in the likeness of Himself, so, too, what we in our God-made immortality make in the likeness of ourselves ought to be immortal.

Aug. What you say would be correct, if you could paint a picture reproducing the image of what you believe to be immortal in yourself. But as it is, what you reproduce is a likeness of the body, which is certainly mortal.

Ev. How, then, noting that I cannot make anything immortal, as He can, am I like to God?

Aug. Just as the image of your body is not able to do what your body can do, so it is not surprising if the soul does not possess the same power as He in whose likeness it has been made.

CHAPTER 3

The greatness of the soul. Distinctions.

4. *Ev.* That, too, will do for the present. Tell me now, how great is the soul?

Aug. What do you mean by asking how great it is? I do not understand whether you are asking about the extent, so to say, of its width, or its length, or its solidity, or of all of these taken together; or whether you wish to know what it is able to do. For it is usual for us to ask how great Hercules was, that is to say, how many feet tall he was; and, again, how great a man he was, meaning the might and prowess that were his.

Ev. Regarding the soul, I should like to know how great it is in both senses.

Aug. But the former meaning cannot be applied to the soul, nor even be conceived with regard to it. For the soul is in no way to be considered as having length or width or, so to say, power of resistance. These are bodily properties, so it seems to me. We should thus be dealing with the soul in terms ordinarily used in speaking about bodies. Hence, too, the sacraments [5] carry the injunction that whoever desires to restore himself to the state in which he was made by God, that is, like to God, should contemn all corporeal things and renounce this whole world, which, as we see, is corporeal. There simply is no other way of saving the soul or of renewing it, or of reconciling it with its Maker. Therefore, if this is the purport of your question—"How great is the soul?"—I cannot answer it for you; but I can state definitely that it has no length, no width, no solidity, nor any of the properties generally looked for in measuring bodies. [6] And, if you wish it, I shall give you my reason for thinking so.

Ev. Yes, indeed, I want you to, and I am eager to hear it. For it seems to me that if the soul is none of these, it is practically nothing. [7]

Aug. First of all, then, if you will, I shall show you that there are many things which you cannot call nothing, although you cannot find in them any such extension as you are looking for in the soul. I wish you to see that not only is the soul not nothing, merely because you do not find in it length or any such thing, but that it is the more precious and the more estimable for having none of these properties. In the next place, we shall see whether it really has none of these properties.

Ev. Follow any order and method you wish. I am ready to listen and to learn.

CHAPTER 4

Even without bodily dimensions, the soul can be a reality.

5. *Aug.* Very good! But I should like you to answer my questions—perhaps you already know what I am trying to teach you: I take it that you do not doubt that this tree is not absolutely nothing?

Ev. Who would doubt that?

Aug. How about this? You do not doubt, do you, that justice possesses far greater excellence than this tree?

Ev. That is absurd—as if there were any comparison!

Aug. Very kind of you to agree with me. But now consider this. Since it is evident that this tree is so inferior to justice that you think there is not even ground for any comparison, and since you have acknowledged that this wood is, after all, something, would you have us believe that justice itself is nothing?

Ev. Who would be crazy enough to believe that?

Aug. Absolutely right! But perhaps you think this tree is something for the reason that it has height proper to itself and width and solidity, and that if you should take these properties away, it will be nothing.

Ev. So it seems.

Aug. Well, now, do you think that justice, which by your admission certainly is not nothing—which, in fact, is far more like to God and far more excellent than a tree—has length?

Ev. No, no. I could not conceive of justice as having length or width or any such dimension.

Aug. If, then, justice is none of these things, and yet not reducible to nothing, why do you think that the soul is nothing, unless it has length of some sort?

Ev. Stop—I have given up the idea that the soul would be nothing if it had no length or width or solidity. But you must realize that you have not yet stated whether it really has these properties or not. It may be that many things which lack these properties are really worthy of esteem; still, I do not think we have to admit without further argument that the soul belongs to this class.

6. *Aug.* I know that this problem remains to be solved, and I promised I would explain it in its turn. But because this is an extremely subtle problem and because it requires far different mental vision than we human beings ordinarily employ in the processes of our daily lives, I suggest that you content yourself to proceed the way I think you should be taken, and not to become tired on the roundabout route we have to follow, or to feel disappointed that you should arrive at the goal you wish to reach somewhat more slowly than you had expected. Now let me ask you first: do you think anything is a body which does not have, in proportion to its individual capacity, some length and width and third dimension?[8]

Ev. I fail to understand what you mean by "third dimension."

Aug. I mean that which enables us to conceive of the interior of a body, or to perceive it with the senses if the body is transparent, like glass. If you take this away from bodies, they cannot, in my opinion, be an object of the senses, nor can they be thought of at all as bodies.[9] I wish you would tell me what you think on this.

Ev. I have not the slightest doubt that all bodies must have these dimensions.

Aug. What about this—can you conceive of these three dimensions as existing anywhere except in bodies?

Ev. I do not see how they can exist anywhere else.

Aug. And therefore, you think the soul is nothing but a body?

Ev. If we grant that even the wind is a body, I cannot deny that the soul seems to be a body, for I think it is somewhat like that.

Aug. I grant you that the wind is a body the same as a current of air, were you to ask me about that. For we perceive that wind is nothing but the movement and agitation of the air about us. We can demonstrate this if we take a place where there is absolute calm and quiet, and wave a fan: even when we shoo flies we set the air in motion and we feel a puff. Now, when some unexplained movement of heavenly or earthly bodies causes this same thing to happen over a great area of the world, it is called wind, and it goes by various names according to the various directions it comes from. Or do you think otherwise?

Ev. No, I do not. What you say is acceptable to me. I did not say, however, that the soul is the same as wind, but somewhat similar to it.

Aug. Tell me first whether you think wind itself, which you have mentioned, has any length, width, and height. We shall then see whether the soul is somewhat on the same order: thus we can also find out how great it is.

Ev. Do you think it easy to find anything that has greater length and width and height than the air, which, when in motion, is wind, as you have just convinced me?

CHAPTER 5

The capacity of the soul.

7. *Aug.* You are right. Now, do you think that your soul is in your body, and nowhere else?

Ev. Yes, I do.

Aug. Is it merely inside the body, filling it out like a bag, or only on the outside, like a covering, or do you think that it is both inside and outside?

Ev. I think that which you mentioned last is correct. For unless it were inside, there would be no life under our skin; and unless it were outside, we could not—as we do—feel even a slight prick on the skin.

Aug. Why, then, ask any more regarding the greatness of the soul, since you see that it corresponds precisely to the dimensions of the body?

Ev. If that is a dictate of reason, I ask for nothing more.[10]

Aug. You are right in resting your inquiry with what reason teaches. But as to the reasoning just offered, does it seem quite valid to you?

Ev. In the absence of anything superior—yes. But in the proper place I shall inquire about something that really puzzles me: whether the shape the soul has remains the same when it leaves the body. I recall that I put this last among the questions to be discussed. But since it seems to me that the question of the number of souls pertains to quantity, I think that this should not be overlooked here.

Aug. There is something to be said for your opinion. But first, if you will, let us settle something that still disturbs me regarding the extension of the soul: thus I, too, shall learn something while you are being taken care of.

Ev. Ask questions as you please. This turn of making yourself a doubter really makes me doubt about what I had presumed to be already settled.

8. *Aug.* Tell me, please, do you not think that what is called "memory" is a word that stands for nothing?

Ev. Who could ever think that?

Aug. Do you think it pertains to the soul or to the body?

Ev. To doubt on this score would also be ridiculous. Why, it is not possible, is it, to believe or imagine that a body without a soul remembers anything?[11]

Aug. Well, now do you remember the city of Milan?

Ev. Yes, indeed.

Aug. Now that we have mentioned it, do you recall its size and characteristics?

Ev. I certainly do, and nothing more vividly and more completely.

Aug. Now then, since you do not see it with your eyes, you are seeing it in your mind.

Ev. That is right.

Aug. You also remember, I believe, how great a distance it is from us now.

Ev. Yes, I remember that too.

Aug. So you also see in your mind the distance separating the places.

Ev. Yes.

Aug. Therefore, since your soul is here where your body is, and does not extend beyond the dimensions of the body, as our previous reasoning demonstrated, how is it that it sees all those things?

Ev. I presume that this takes place through the memory; it is not because the soul is present in those places.

Aug. Then the memory retains images of those places.

Ev. So I suppose, for I do not know what is going on there at this moment; but certainly I would know it, if my mind reached out to those places and perceived what is transpiring there at the present time.

Aug. I think you are right. But surely, these images have to do with bodies.

Ev. It must be so. For city and countryside are nothing else than bodies.

9. *Aug.* Have you ever looked into tiny mirrors, or have you ever seen your face reflected in the pupil of another person's eye?

Ev. Yes, often.

Aug. Why does it appear much smaller than it actually is?

Ev. What else could you expect, than that it should be seen according to the size of the mirror?

Aug. Hence the images of bodies must appear small, if the bodies in which they are reflected are small.

Ev. Of course, they must.

Aug. Then, since the soul is in the same small space as its body, why is it that images so great can be represented in it that it can reproduce to itself cities and expanses of countryside and any other object of tremendous proportions? I would really have you give some further attention to what great objects, and how many objects, our memory contains; and, of course, these are all contained in the soul. What a profundity, therefore, what an amplitude, what an immensity must the soul have, to be able to accommodate these objects, although our previous demonstration seems to have shown that it has merely the same size as the body!

Ev. I have no answer for that, nor can I show adequately how all this puzzles me; and I really laugh at myself for having so hastily given assent to the previous argument restricting the greatness of the soul to the limits of the body.

Aug. So you no longer think that the soul is something on the same order as the wind?

Ev. Not at all. For even though the air, the flow of which is believed with good probability to constitute wind, may conceivably fill this entire world of ours, the soul is able to imagine within itself countless worlds of the same size and the same properties, and within what space it contains these images, I cannot possibly surmise.

Aug. See, then, whether it is not better, as I said before, to believe that the soul has neither length nor width nor height, just as you granted with regard to justice.

Ev. I should readily agree, if I were not even more at sea as to how it can receive all the countless images of such great expanses without any length and width and height of its own.

CHAPTER 6

The nature of length.

10. *Aug.* Perhaps we shall discover this, so far as it is possible to discover it, if we first make a thorough analysis of three things: length, width, and height. Accordingly, try your best to think of length which has not yet developed any width at all.

Ev. I cannot think of any such thing. If I should, for example, represent in my mind a spider's thread, than which our sight is accustomed to experience nothing more tenuous, I find that even in that thread there still is length over its full extent, and width and thickness. And however slight the width and thickness may be, yet I cannot deny that they exist.

Aug. Your answer is not entirely absurd. But, surely, when you realize that these three dimensions are present in the spider's thread, you seé them apart, and you know that they differ one from the other?

Ev. How could I help knowing that they differ? Otherwise, how could I see that none of them is lacking in this thread?

Aug. Now, then, by the same intellect by which you have differentiated them, you can also think of length alone, separated from the others, provided you do not set your mind on any bodily thing; for no matter what it may be, a body will have all of these dimensions. What I want you to think of now, is incorporeal.[12] For length taken alone can be grasped only by the mind; alone, it cannot be found in a body.

Ev. I understand.

Aug. Therefore, should you wish to cut that length— mentally, as it were—lengthwise, you see at all events that it cannot be done; if it were possible, width would also be present.

Ev. That is obvious.

Aug. Then, if you will, let us call that length pure and simple, a *line*. That is a term used by many scholars.

Ev. Call it what you wish. Names should cause me no trouble so long as the reality is made clear.[13]

11. *Aug.* Good! Not only do I agree with you, but I also advise you always to take a livelier interest in reality than in words. But as regards that line, which I think you really conceive correctly, if it is extended as far as possible from one end or from both ends, you see this can be done without limit. Or, does this tax the keenness of your mind too much?

Ev. I see it clearly, and with the greatest of ease.

Aug. Then you also see that if you do nothing but extend that line, no figure results.

Ev. I do not understand what you mean by "figure."

CHAPTER 7

Authority and reason.

Aug. For the present, I call that a figure in which some space is enclosed by means of one or more lines; for example, draw a circle, or connect four lines at their extremes, so that no end of any one line is unconnected with the end of another line.

Ev. I think I see now what you mean by "figure." But I wish I could see just as well where all this is leading to, or what you will do with this to give me the information I seek regarding the soul.

12. *Aug.* At the start I suggested to you and asked you to have some patience with our roundabout approach to this, and I now repeat my request. The problem we are dealing with is not a trifling one. It is not easy to solve. If possible, we want to grasp it clearly and settle it once and for all. It is one thing to believe on authority, another to have reason to back you. Reliance on authority offers you an excellent shortcut and eliminates toil. If that appeals to you, you may read a great deal which distinguished and inspired men have regarded as the essentials in this matter, and which they have offered as so many helpful hints, so to speak, to the unlearned—asking that they who could not be helped otherwise, either because their minds were too dull or too preoccupied, should believe them implicitly. As

a matter of fact, if such people—and their number is actually legion—wish to understand the truth by reason, they are very easily deceived by specious arguments and are so prone to fall for divergent and harmful opinions that they cannot slough them off at all; or it is only with the greatest difficulty that they free themselves from them. For these, therefore, it is best to put their trust in a first-class authority and to regulate their lives accordingly.[14] And if you think this the safer way, not only do I offer no objections, but I give my wholehearted approval. But if, on the other hand, you find you cannot restrain the eagerness with which you decided to arrive at truth by reason,[15] then you must be prepared to tread many long roundabout ways, with reason to guide you, that reason which alone deserves the name— right reason; and not only right reason, but reason with certitude, reason a total stranger to all semblance of falsity— granted, of course, that for man this is discoverable at all— so that no false or specious arguments can entice you away from it.

Ev. Henceforth I shall look for nothing with undue haste. Reason will be my guide and lead me where it will. As long as it brings me to my goal, I am satisfied.

CHAPTER 8

Symmetry in triangles.

13. *Aug.* God will grant this—He who with regard to such matters alone, or especially with regard to these, should be implored. But let us get back to the subject which I had begun. You know by now what a line is and what a figure is: tell me what I am asking you next, namely: do you think any figure can be drawn by extending a line at both ends or at either end, indefinitely?

Ev. I am sure it is quite impossible to do that.

Aug. What, then, must we do to draw a figure?

Ev. What but that the line in question be made finite and drawn in a circle so that its ends meet? I do not see any other possibility of enclosing a given space with one line: unless this is done, according to your definition of it, there will be no figure.

Aug. What if I wish to draw a figure by using straight lines? Can it be done with a single line?

Ev. Certainly not.

Aug. How about two lines?

Ev. It is not possible with two, either.

Aug. How about three?

Ev. Yes, that is possible.

Aug. It is quite clear to you, then, and you hold that when a figure is to be drawn with straight lines, it cannot be done with fewer than three. But suppose an argument from reason contradicted you on this: would it make you change 'his opinion?

Ev. Surely, if anyone could show me that this is false, my confidence in my ability to know anything would be shaken.

Aug. Well, now, tell me: how would you draw a figure with three lines?

Ev. By joining their extremities.

Aug. And where they join, an angle is formed—not so?

Ev. Yes.

Aug. And how many angles will this figure contain?

Ev. As many as there are lines.

Aug. And would you make the lines equal or unequal?

Ev. Equal.

Aug. What about the angles—are they all equal, or is

any one of them more acute or more
obtuse than the others?

Ev. They are also equal.

Aug. Is it possible for a figure consisting of three equal
straight lines to have unequal angles? Or is it impossible?

Ev. It is utterly impossible.

Aug. But suppose the figure consists of three straight
lines that are unequal: can the angles in
such a figure be equal or not?

Ev. They certainly cannot.

Aug. You are right. Now, will you tell me which figure
seems the more perfect and the more beautiful to you—
the one bounded by equal lines, or the one which has unequal lines?

Ev. Can there be any doubt that the one in which there
is greater equality is more perfect?

CHAPTER 9

Symmetry in quadrangles.

14. *Aug.* So you rank equality above inequality?

Ev. Certainly—who would not?

Aug. Now, take a look at the figure consisting of three
equal angles: what is opposite the angle, that is, what faces
each angle? Is it a line or an angle?

Ev. What I see is a line.

Aug. Well then, suppose you have angle opposite angle
and line opposite line: would you not admit that a figure
in which this occurs has greater equality?

Ev. I grant that, of course, but I quite fail to see how
that is possible with three lines.

Aug. Well, is it possible with four lines?

Ev. Quite possible.

Aug. Consequently, a figure consisting of four equal straight lines is more perfect than one consisting of three?

Ev. Yes, indeed, since it has greater equality.

Aug. And now, do you think that a figure consisting of four equal straight lines can also be drawn in such a way that not all the angles in it are equal? Or do you think it is impossible?

Ev. To me it seems possible.

Aug. How?

Ev. If two angles are obtuse and two acute.

Aug. Do you also see that the pair of acute angles face each other and the same is true of the two obtuse ones?

Ev. That is most manifestly true.

Aug. You observe, then, that here, too, equality is preserved as far as possible. For you obviously see that when you have a figure of four equal lines, either all your angles or at least pairs of angles are equal and the equal ones must be opposite each other.

Ev. Yes—that is my firm conviction.

15. *Aug.* Does it not impress you that even in these things there is a certain magnificent, unfailing justice?

Ev. How so?

Aug. Because we say, I believe, that justice is identical with equity; and equity seems to derive its name from some aspect of equality.[16] And as to the equity in this virtue, what is it but that each be permitted to have his own? And giving to each his own involves some sort of distinction. Or do you think otherwise?

Ev. That is clear—I am in complete agreement.

Aug. Well, do you think any distinction is present if all things are equal, with nothing at all to differentiate them?

Ev. Not at all.

Aug. Therefore, justice cannot be put into practice unless there is in its subjects a measure of inequality, so to say, and a measure of dissimilarity.

Ev. I understand.

Aug. Now then, though we admit a dissimilarity between the figures under discussion, that is to say, the one having three angles, the other four, while both have their lines equal: do you not think that a measure of justice reigns withal, in that the one which cannot have equality of opposites, does maintain an invariable equality of angles, whereas in the other which has such a perfect conformity of opposites, the law of angles admits a very considerable range of inequality? Here we have a fact that greatly impressed me, and I thought it well to ask you how this truth, this equity, and this equality appealed to you.

Ev. I see what you mean and I am fascinated.

Aug. To continue: seeing that you rightly prefer equality to inequality, and since, so it seems to me, there certainly is no one endowed with human understanding who would not do the same, let us, if you will, look for the figure which contains equality in the highest degree. Evidently, whatever it is, we shall doubtless prefer it to all others.

Ev. Very good. I am eager to know what it is.

CHAPTER 10

Relative symmetry in triangles and squares.

16. *Aug.* In the first place, then, tell me: do you think that of the figures to which we have given the consideration required, that one excels which consists of four equal lines and as many equal angles? As you observe, it has equality of lines and equality of angles. Besides, a thing we did not find in the figure enclosed by three equal lines, this figure has an equality of opposites; for, as you notice, line faces line and angle faces angle.[17]

Ev. It is just as you say.

Aug. Does it have the greatest possible equality, or do you think not? If it has, it would be useless for us to look for it elsewhere, as we had begun to do; if it has not, I would have you prove that to me.

Ev. I think it has; for where both angles and lines are equal, I see no possibility of finding inequality.

Aug. I dissent. For a straight line has perfect equality until it comes to angles. But when another line, coming sidewise,[18] meets it and forms an angle, do you not think that here we have inequality? Or does that part of a figure which is bounded by a line seem to you to correspond in equality or similarity with the part that is enclosed in an angle?

Ev. Not at all; and I am ashamed of not thinking twice. I drew my conclusion on observing the equality between the angles and between the sides; but, of course, the sides are very much different from the angles.

Aug. Take another very obvious indication of inequality. You must observe that in both cases the equilateral triangle and the square have a centre.

Ev. Yes, indeed.

Aug. Well, suppose we take this centre and draw lines to all the parts of the figures: Do you think the lines drawn are equal or unequal?

Ev. Unequal, of course. The ones we draw to the angles must be longer.

Aug. How many of these are there in the square, and how many in the triangle?

Ev. Four in the former, three in the latter.

Aug. And of all the lines, which ones are the shorter and how many are there in each figure?

Ev. The same number; namely, those drawn to the middle of the sides.

Aug. I think you are entirely right and there is no need of dwelling on this any further. It can serve our purposes. For you see, I think, that while in these cases we are in the presence of great equality, it is not yet perfect in every respect.

Ev. I see it all right, and I am most anxious to learn what figure it is that has the most perfect equality.

CHAPTER 11

Symmetry in circles. Definitions of point and sign.

17. *Aug.* What figure do you think, except the one whose boundary is consistently the same, with no angle interrupting its equality, and from whose centre equal lines can be drawn to every part of the boundary?

Ev. I begin to understand, I think. For you evidently are describing the figure which is bounded by one line, drawn in a circle.

Aug. You do understand. Now, then, consider this. The reasoning we went through a while ago has shown that a line is understood as having length alone, and does not connote any width, and, therefore, precludes dividing it lengthwise. Do you think any figure can be found without width?

Ev. No, indeed.

Aug. Well, can there be any width without length, however it be width alone,[19] just as we previously understood length without width? Or is this impossible?

Ev. I see that it is impossible.

Aug. You also see, if I mistake not, that width can be divided anywhere, whereas a line cannot be divided lengthwise.

Ev. That is evident.

Aug. Which, then, do you consider more estimable— that which suffers division, or that which does not?

Ev. That which does not, of course.

Aug. Therefore, you give a line preference to width. For if what is indivisible is to be preferred, we must also prefer what is less capable of division. But width can be divided anywhere, whereas length is divisible only crosswise, for it does not suffer division lengthwise. Therefore it is superior to width. Or do you disagree?

Ev. Reason compels me to admit just what you say.

18. *Aug.* Now let us study, if you will, whether there is anything in this calculation that cannot be divided in any way. If there is, it will be in that respect much more perfect than even our line. You see, of course, that a line can be intersected innumerable times. So I leave it to you to discover this indivisible thing.

Ev. I think that is indivisible which we were placing as

a centre in the figure, from which lines are drawn to the borders. For if it is divisible, it cannot be without length, or even without width. But if it has only length, it is not something from which lines can be drawn, but is itself a line. If, however, it also has width, it must have in addition, a centre from which lines are drawn to the extremities of its breadth. But reason rejects both these things. It must be this, therefore, which is indivisible.

Aug. You are right. But do you not think that that from which a line is drawn is quite the same, even though there is not yet any figure of which we consider it the centre? I mean, of course, the beginning of a line, that from which its length originates, and I would have you conceive of it as having no length whatever. For if you associate length with it, you fail completely to grasp the starting point of length.

Ev. It is quite the same.

Aug. This, then, which I see you do understand, is the most excellent of all the things described so far, and that because it admits of no division. When it is at the centre of a figure, it is called a "point." But if it is the beginning or the termination of one or more lines, or when in general it marks something that is to be understood as having no parts, without at the same time serving as the centre of a figure, it is called a "sign." [20] Therefore, a sign is a mark without parts; but a point is a mark fixed at the centre of a figure. Thus it happens that every point is also a sign, though obviously not every sign is a point. It seems important to me that we agree on this terminology: we shall not have to talk in too roundabout a manner in our discussion. Many, it is true, use the term "point" not for the centre of any figure, but only of a circle or a sphere; but we can dispense with all this attention to terminology.[21]

Ev. I agree.

CHAPTER 12

Important functions of sign and point.

19. *Aug.* You undoubtedly also see what important functions the sign has. A line begins with it and ends with it. We see that no figure can be drawn with straight lines unless the angle is closed by it. Further, wherever a line can be cut, it is cut through a sign, although a sign itself admits of absolutely no division. No line can be joined to another except it be present. Finally, though we have demonstrated that the circle because of its perfect symmetry, is to be considered superior to all other plane figures—we have so far said nothing about the third dimension—what else determines this symmetry than the point set in the centre? Here much could be said on the function of the point, but I limit myself and leave this to you for further development.

Ev. Very well, as you wish. If anything should not be clear, I shall not be slow to ask questions. But I see fairly well, I think, the extraordinary function of this sign.

20. *Aug.* Now, then, think this over: since you have grasped what a sign is, and what length is, and what width is, which of these do you think has need of any of the others, and to such a degree that it cannot exist without the other?

Ev. I see that width requires length, and that without length it escapes the mind entirely. Further, I grant that length does not need width for its existence, but without the sign it could not exist. It is obvious, however, that the sign can exist by itself and that it needs none of the others.

Aug. Yes, you are right. But give this a little more thought: can width really be divided from all directions, or, seen from a certain direction, is even it indivisible, although it admits of more division than a line?

Ev. I am sure I do not know how it could be indivisible.

Aug. I believe you just do not recall, for you really could not be ignorant of this. Let me remind you, then, in this way. Surely, in your idea of width you do not include any consideration of height.

Ev. You are absolutely right.

Aug. Well, then, let height be added to this width; and now tell me whether we have a new possibility of further all-around division.

Ev. That suggestion really makes me open my eyes. For I see now that it is capable of division, not only from above or from below, but also from the sides, and we have no dimension whatever impervious to division. Therefore, it is evident, too, that width cannot be cut with respect to those parts from which height is to rise.

21. *Aug.* Since, then, if I mistake not, you are familiar with length and width and height, I ask you whether there can be any height without the other two.

Ev. I see that you cannot have height without length; but it can get along without width.

Aug. Now, then, go back to your consideration of width, and, if in your mind you think of it as lying flat, so to speak, raise it upright on any one of its sides, as if you wished to draw it through the merest of chinks between closed doors. Do you still not understand what I have in mind?

Ev. I understand what you are saying, but not yet, perhaps, what you are after.

Aug. This, of course, that you tell me whether you think width raised up in that way has gone over into height and has now lost the name and description of width. Or does it still remain width, even though it has undergone this change of position?

Ev. I think it has become height.

Aug. Do you recall, I beg you, our definition of the third dimension? [22]

Ev. Certainly, I recall it and I am ashamed now of that answer. For even though width is raised up in that way, it does not permit a vertical division lengthwise. Hence we cannot associate with it any interior, though we may imagine a centre and terminal points. However, following your previous demonstration of the third dimension, as I seem to recall it, there is no height at all with which we cannot associate an interior.

Aug. You are right. And that is just what I wanted you to remember. Now, then, I would like you to answer whether you prefer what is true to what is false.

Ev. To have any further doubt about that would be incredibly foolish.

Aug. Tell me, then—if you will—is that truly a line which can be divided lengthwise? Is it a true sign which can be divided in any way at all? Or is it true width which, when it is raised upright, as we said, admits of vertical division down its length?

Ev. No, quite the contrary.

CHAPTER 13

*Knowledge of abstract quantities shows the soul is
immaterial. Definition of the soul.*

22. *Aug.* Now, then, have you ever seen with the eyes
of the body such a point, or such a line, or such width?

Ev. No, never. These things are not bodily.[23]

Aug. But if, by some sort of remarkable affinity of realities, bodily things are seen with bodily eyes, it must be that
the soul [24] by means of which we see these incorporeal things
is not a body, nor like a body.[25]   Or do you disagree?

Ev. Well, I now grant that the soul is not a body or anything like a body.   But just what is it? Tell me.

Aug. For the present, be sure it is settled that the soul is
without all such quantity as engages our attention at the
moment.   As to what the soul actually is, I am surprised
that you have forgotten that we discussed this topic previously.[26]   You must remember that the first question you
asked was where the soul comes from; and I recall that we
considered that question in two ways: first, we devoted to
the soul a regional inquiry, as it were; secondly, we in-
quired whether it was derived from earth, or fire, or any
other of the elements, or from all of them together, or from
a combination of some of them.   But on this problem we
agreed that there is no more sense in asking what the soul
is derived from, than in asking from what earth or any other
single element is derived.   For it must be understood that
although God made the soul, it has a certain essence of its
own, which is not composed of earth, nor of fire, nor of
air, nor of water; or we may be forced to the conclusion
that God gave earth its own exclusive individuality, but

failed to give to the soul that which makes it soul and nothing else.   But if you want a definition of the soul, and so ask
me—what is the soul?   I have a ready answer.   It seems to
me to be a special substance, endowed with reason, adapted
to rule the body.[27]

CHAPTER 14

The power of the immaterial soul.

23. And now give this your particular attention—the
question now at issue: whether the soul has any quantity
and, so to say, local extension.   Of course, precisely because
it is not a body—otherwise, as our previous reasoning
proved,[28] it could not perceive anything incorporeal—it
doubtless lacks the space by which bodies are measured. And
for this reason it is impossible to believe or conceive or
understand that the measure of the soul's greatness is of
that sort.   But if you wonder why the soul can retain in its
memory such great expanses of the sky, the earth, and the
sea, without having any bodily extension itself, that is a remarkable sort of power, but one which our previous conclusions make it possible for your mind to grasp, depending
on the acumen it applies.   For if, as already proved by
reason, there is no body that does not possess length, width,
and height, and if none of these can be in a body without the
other two; if, nevertheless, we have granted that the soul
can see even a mere line by some sort of interior eye—that
is, by the intelligence: this, I think, constitutes an admission that the soul is not bodily; more, that it is superior to
body.   Granting this, we have no reason, I think, to doubt
that it is also superior to a line.   For since those three di-

mensions must be in a body in order that it be a body,[29] it would be absurd if that which is superior to a body were not superior to all of these. But the line itself, which evidently is inferior to the soul, is superior to the other two dimensions, for the reason that it is less capable of division than those two. Moreover, those two dimensions become all the more divisible than the line, as they are extended into space; whereas a line has no extension other than length, and if that is taken away, there remains no extension whatever. Therefore, whatever is superior to a line must necessarily be without extension and unable to be divided and partitioned at all. It is to no purpose, then, so it seems to me, for us to make an effort to discover a quantity of the soul: there is none—admitting as we do that it is superior to a line. And if of all plane figures that is the most perfect which is drawn in a circle, and reason has shown that in it there is nothing more perfect and more important than the point, which no one doubts to be without parts:[30] why should it be surprising if the soul is not corporeal, nor extended in length, nor spread out in breadth, nor made solid by depth, and yet is present so effectively in the body as to control all the members of the body and serves as a pivot of action, so to speak, for all the motions of the body?

24. Again, the centre of the eye, which is called the "pupil," is nothing more than a certain point of the eye. Yet, it has such great power that from any elevated place it can see and survey half the sky, whose dimensions are beyond expression. Hence, it is not inconsistent with the truth to say that the soul is without all bodily magnitude as made up of those three different dimensions, even though it can form representations of any and all bodily magnitudes.[31] To few people, however, is it permitted to perceive

the soul by means of the soul itself, that is, in such a way
that the soul sees itself.[32] Moreover, it sees by means of
intelligence. And to this alone is it given to see that in the
sphere of reality there is nothing more potent and more
grandiose than those natures which it sees apart, so to say,
from bulk. And "bulk," by the way, is not an inept name
for bodily magnitude.[33] Indeed, if such were to be considered particularly estimable, then elephants would surely
have far greater intelligence than we. If someone bearing a
resemblance to them were to say that elephants have intelligence—I have been amazed to make the observation, though
I have observed that men often dispute even this point—
he would yet concede, I think, that a little bee has more
wisdom than an ass; and to compare them for size would
be worse than asinine.

Again, recalling what we were saying about the eye, who
does not see that the eye of the eagle is much smaller than
our own? Yet the eagle, soaring so far aloft that we can
scarcely make it out in broad daylight, has been known to
see a tiny hare hiding under a shrub and a fish beneath the
billows. Thus, even in regard to the senses, limited as they
are to the perception of things with body, bodily size con-
tributes nothing to the power of perception. This granted,
I ask: need we fear that the human soul, whose more perfect
and almost exclusive vision is reason itself,[34] by which the
soul endeavors to discover even itself—need we fear that it
is nothing, if the same power of reason should prove that the
soul, that is, itself, is without all magnitude by which a
thing is localized?

A certain greatness,[35] believe me, is to be attributed to
the soul, but not the greatness of bodily bulk. The realiza-
tion of this comes the more readily to those who approach
these subjects well-instructed, influenced not by a desire of

their own empty glory but by a religious love of truth; or who are now occupied with these problems, provided they, however poorly equipped they may have applied themselves to their inquiry, patiently and in all docility seek out good men and, so far as is permitted in this life, shun all familiarity with bodily things. And there is a certain Divine Providence, by which it cannot happen that the blessing of discovery should be withheld from religious souls who strive piously, chastely, and perseveringly to know themselves and their God—that is, to know the truth.[36]

CHAPTER 15

Objection: the soul grows with age.

25. But now, unless you have a difficulty still, let us leave this question and pass on to other problems. Perhaps in our discussion of those figures we went into greater detail than you had desired. You will see, however, provided you grant that our present disquisition profited somewhat by it, how valuable it will prove for the rest. For this kind of study trains the mind to perceive more subtle matters: thus it will not be dazed by their bright light, and, being unable to bear it, deliberately retreat to the very shadows it sought to escape. It also affords, if I mistake not, most solid arguments to dispel any doubt about what has been discovered and established—so far as it is permitted to man to track down such matters.[37] For my part, I have less doubt about these realities than I have about those which we see with these our bodily eyes, which always have to brook the opposition of watery discharges. Indeed, what would be less tolerable and harder to listen to, than to claim that we excel the brute animals because we have reason, and to admit, at the same time, that

it is with our bodily eyes that we see a given object which certain brute animals see even better than we do, and yet to insist that what we perceive directly by reason is nothing at all? [88] And if it be said that the latter object is quite the same as what the bodily eyes see, it would seem that absolutely nothing more unbecoming could be said.

26. *Ev.* I am delighted to follow you in this and I agree with you. Still, this makes me wonder: while it is so clear to me that the soul has no physical size that I see not the slightest objection to those arguments and see absolutely no reservation I should make, why is it, for one thing, that as the body grows with age, the soul also grows, or, at least, would seem to grow? Take little children: who would deny that they are not comparable in cleverness even to some of the brutes? Yet, who would doubt that as the children grow older, their reasoning faculty itself also develops a certain growth? Then, if the soul is diffused through the extent of its own body, how can it be without extension itself? But if it does not have such diffusion, how does it sense a stimulus on any and every part of the body?

Aug. What you are asking about is exactly what has often made me wonder also; therefore I am not unprepared—I give you the answer that I am wont to give myself. Whether it is the correct answer is for your reason to guide you in judging. Whatever its worth, I certainly cannot improve on it, unless perchance God should inspire me with something better in the course of our discussion. But let us proceed, if you will, in our usual manner: follow the lead of reason and answer your own questions. And, first of all, let us inquire whether the fact that with the advance of age man becomes more adapted to human convention and more and more versed in it, is a solid argument that the soul grows with the body.

Ev. Good—suit yourself. I, too, am all for that method of teaching and learning. I do not know why it is, but when I myself answer the questions I was putting without knowing the answer, the element of discovery becomes the more pleasant, not merely because of the fact ascertained, but also because of the interest aroused.

CHAPTER 16

Answer to objection: the soul progresses indepen-
dently of the body's growth.

27. *Aug.* Tell me, then, whether you think "bigger" and "better" are two distinct things, or one and the same, going under two different names.

Ev. I know that what we call "bigger" is one thing and what we call "better" is another.

Aug. Which of these two do you associate with quantity?

Ev. That, of course, which we call "bigger."

Aug. What about the case of the two figures and our admission that the round figure is better than the square? Is quantity responsible, or something else?

Ev. No, certainly not quantity; but that equality of which we treated before, is the reason for the superiority.

Aug. Now, then, weigh this: do you think virtue a sort of equality of life consistently in harmony with reason? For if in life one thing is out of harmony with another, we are, if I mistake not, more distraught than when some part of a circle is more or less distant from the centre than the other parts. Or do you think otherwise?

Ev. I agree, indeed, and I approve your description of virtue. For nothing is to be called or considered reasonable but what is true; and the one whose life is in all respects consonant with the truth is surely the only one, or at least eminently the one who lives a good and honorable life; and only the one who is so disposed is to be considered as having virtue and living by it.

Aug. Well said! But certainly you also see, I presume, that a circle is more like virtue than any other plane figure. Hence it is that we single out for special praise that verse of Horace's in which he describes a wise man as:

Strong and self-contained, all smooth and round.[39]

And that is well put. For you will find nothing among the treasures of the soul that shows greater all-around balance than virtue; nor among plane figures will you find anything with better balance than a circle. Hence, if a circle is superior to other figures, not because of its extent of space but because of its definite symmetry, how much more is virtue to be valued because it excels the other states of the soul, not by its greater tenancy of space, but by its approach to the divine in its balanced harmony with reason!

28. And when a child makes satisfactory progress, what is the measure of that progress, if not virtue? Do you not think so?

Ev. That is obvious.

Aug. You should not think, therefore, that the soul makes progress in the same way as the body, by growing larger with age. For it advances by making progress in virtue, whose beauty and perfection, we acknowledge, is derived not from greatness of size but from the great constancy that it has. And if "bigger" is one thing and "better" another, as you already stated, then whatever progress the soul makes with the advance in age and whatever proficiency it acquires in the use of reason constitutes, so it seems to me, not physical growth but an advance in excellence. Now, if the size of

the members were accountable for this, the taller and brawn-
ier a man is, the more prudent he would be; and that such
is not the case, I take it, you will not deny.

Ev. Who could deny that? Still, noting that you, too,
admit that the soul makes progress through the years, I
wonder how it happens that the soul, devoid of all quantity,
though it profits nothing from the size of the body's members, yet certainly does do so from the extent of time.

CHAPTER 17

Metaphorical growth of the soul.

29. *Aug.* Cease wondering, for here, too, my answer to
you will be along similar lines.

Plainly, the fact that many men of comparatively slight
and small physiques show themselves the intellectual su-
periors of some others who are veritable hulks of men, shows
that the size of members argues nothing for the soul. Similarly, because we see that many a young person is more
industrious and energetic than some of his elders, I do not
see any reason for thinking that the element of time elapsed
in the several periods of life causes souls to grow as it does
bodies. Indeed, even bodies, for which we own it to be
natural to grow and occupy more space in the course of time,
are often smaller, despite the fact that they are older; not
only in the case of the aged, whose bodies shrivel and become
smaller with the lapse of time, but even in the case of children, some of whom we observe to be shorter in stature than
others who are younger. If, then, periods of time, however
extended they may be, are not a cause of size even in bodies,
but this is entirely the work of the seminal element and of
certain natural factors, mysterious, indeed, and hard to iso-

late: how much less reason is there for thinking that the soul becomes longer over a long period of time, just because we note that it has learned much from continued experience?

30. But if you find it odd that we usually render the Greek word *makrothymia* with "long-suffering," it is well to note that many words are applied in a transferred sense from the body to the soul, as they are from the soul to the body. If Vergil, for example, spoke of a "wicked" mountain [40] and a "most just" earth [41]—which words, you notice, are transferred from the soul to bodies—what wonder, then, if conversely we speak of "longanimity," though actually only bodies can be long? Again, the virtue that is called "greatness of soul" is rightly understood to refer not to any space but to some force, that is, to a power and capability of the soul—a virtue all the more estimable, the more things it contemns. But we shall speak of this afterwards,[42] when we take up the question of the greatness of the soul, on the pattern of the question regarding Hercules—how great he was in the excellence of his deeds, not in the weight of his body. That distinction we made before.[43]

But here is the place for you to recall what we have already said in detail about the point, namely that reason set forth its paramount importance and its supreme dominance in geometrical figures. But do not importance and dominance indicate a certain greatness? Yet we found there is no extension in a point. Hence, when we hear or speak of the soul as being great or vast, we should think of it not as spatial, but as having power. Wherefore, if that is sufficient discussion of your first argument which found you holding the view that the soul grows with the age of the body, let us pass on to something else.

CHAPTER 18

Gradual acquisition of speech does not indicate material growth of the soul.

31. *Ev.* I do not know whether we have followed up all the problems that cause me real trouble, and it could be that some things escape my memory. Let us, however, take a look at one item that comes to mind now, the fact that a child does not speak in infancy, but does acquire the power as it grows up.

Aug. That is easy. For I believe it is apparent to you that everyone speaks the language spoken by people among whom he was born and brought up.

Ev. Everyone knows that.

Aug. Then imagine someone born and brought up in a place where people do not talk, but by nods and gestures signify the thoughts they have to express. Do you not think that he would do the same and would never talk, having never heard anyone speaking?

Ev. I wish you would not ask me about what cannot happen. How can I imagine such people or anyone being born among them?

Aug. Is that so? Did you not see at Milan a young man of most distinguished appearance and most charming manners, yet so mute and deaf that he could not understand others except by gestures and could not signify what he wished to communicate in any other way? The case is very well known. Again, I know of a certain man in the country who is the father, by a wife able to speak, of children all of whom, four, perhaps, or more—I do not recall exactly now—both male and female, are deaf-mutes. It was recognized that they were mute from the fact that they were unable to speak; and also deaf from the fact that they responded to no signs except by sight.

Ev. Yes, I know that first man well, and I believe you regarding the others I do not know. But why bring up these cases?

Aug. Because you stated that you could not imagine any-one being born among such people.

Ev. And I say the same thing now; for, if I am not mis-taken, you own that these were born among people who could speak.

Aug. I would not deny that, of course. But since we agree now that there can be some such people, I would like you to consider this. If a man and woman of this kind were to marry and by some chance became stranded in an isolated place where, however, they were able to live, and they gave birth to a child who was not deaf, how would that child con-verse with its parents? [44]

Ev. How do you think, but by returning signs with ges-tures in the same way as the parents gave them? But a little child could not do even that. So, my whole problem still remains. For what difference does it make whether what he acquires as his body grows, be speaking or making gestures, since both pertain to the soul, of which we do not want to admit that it grows?

32. *Aug.* Well, now it appears you also believe that when someone walks a tightrope, he has a more spacious soul than those who cannot do it.

Ev. That is different. Who would not see that this is an art? [45]

Aug. Why, I ask, an art? Because he has learned it?

Ev. Yes, that is it.

Aug. Why, then, if someone learns something else, do you not think that this, too, is an art?

Ev. I do not deny at all that whatever is learned also has to do with art.

Aug. Well, did not the child learn from his parents to make gestures?

Ev. He certainly did.

Aug. Consequently, you should admit that it is the result not of the growth of the soul, but of some art of imitation.

Ev. I cannot admit that.

Aug. Therefore, not everything that is learned has to do with art, as you had just now admitted.

Ev. Art does enter it.

Aug. Wherefore, he did not learn gesticulation, which you had also granted.

Ev. He did learn it; but that is not a case of art.

Aug. But you said a little while ago that learning is a case of art.

Ev. Very well, I give in: both speaking and making gestures, for the reason that we have learned them, are cases of art. But there are some arts that we learn by watching others, and other arts that are implanted in us by teachers.

Aug. Well, and which of these do you think the soul acquires by becoming larger? All of them?

Ev. Not all of them, I think, but only those of the first class.

Aug. Do you not think that ropewalking belongs to that class? For those who practice that art acquire it, I think, by observing others.

Ev. So I believe. Yet, not all who witness this and who watch carefully how it is done can master it; but only those who undergo instruction by masters of the art.

Aug. You are right, of course. And that is precisely the

answer I would give you regarding the art of speaking. Many Greeks, for instance, more frequently hear us speaking a language foreign to them than they witness the ropewalking artist; but to learn our language, they do exactly as we do when we wish to learn theirs, they often entrust themselves to teachers. That being so, I wonder why you wish to attribute to an increase of the soul the fact that people speak, but not the fact that some walk on ropes.

Ev. You are confusing these things somehow. For the one who entrusts himself to a teacher to learn our language already knows his own, which I think he learned because his soul grew; but when he learns a foreign language, I attribute that not to a growth of the soul, but to art.

Aug. Suppose the one who was born and brought up among mutes, later on and when he was already a young man, by coming among other people learned to speak when he had not yet learned any other language. Would you think his soul grew at the time he learned to speak?

Ev. I would never dare to say that. And now I give in to reason. I no longer think the fact that we speak argues for the growth of the soul. Otherwise I might be forced to admit that the soul acquires all the other arts also as the result of growth, and if I should say that, there would follow this absurdity, that the soul shrinks whenever it forgets something.

CHAPTER 19

The soul grows by learning.

33. *Aug.* You have a good understanding of the matter. And, to tell the truth, in a sense it is correct to say that the soul grows when it learns, and, conversely, that it is diminished when it forgets what it has learned; but in a metaphorical meaning of the words, as we showed before.[46] Just the same, we should be careful not to think of it as taking in a greater space, so to speak, when it is said to grow; rather, it has a greater potency to act when it is trained than when it is untrained. Still, it makes a great difference what it is that it learns, by means of which it somehow registers an increase.

In the body, indeed, there are three kinds of growth, but only one is necessary for achieving the natural harmony of its members. The second is a superfluous growth, which shows a measure of disharmony with the rest of the members of the body, whose health remains unimpaired; thus it sometimes happens that people are born with six fingers, and many other things; and these, when they are extremely abnormal, are called monstrosities. The third is an injurious growth which, when it occurs, is called a tumor. Here, too, the members are said to grow and actually occupy greater space, but at the expense of good health.

So, too, in the soul, there are certain natural growths, as it were, when it is said to develop growth from studies that are noble and tend to promote good and happy living. On the other hand, when we learn things that satisfy curiosity rather than need, although often enough they prove of practical value in a variety of cases, still they are superfluous and belong in the second category we set up. For example, if some flute player, like the one Varro[47] tells about, so charmed the hearts of the people that they made him king, the conclusion does not follow for us that we can find expansion of mind by cultivating that same art; no, no more than that we should desire to have abnormally large teeth simply because we had heard that someone armed with such teeth killed an enemy by biting him. Finally, there is that class of skills which is harmful in that it impairs the health of the soul. For example, by using the sense of smell and taste to act as a connoisseur of sauces, to know how to tell in what lake a fish was caught or to date a wine by vintage is a pitiable sort of skill. Such artistry does appear to promote the soul's growth. Actually, however, with the neglect of the mind it is wasted on the senses: the diagnosis given is that it has developed a tumorous or even consumptive condition.

CHAPTER 20

Innate knowledge in the soul?

34. *Ev.* What you say is acceptable to me and I am in agreement. Yet, I see a real problem in the fact that the soul in a new-born child to all appearances is utterly unskilled and without the use of reason. Why, if it is eternal, has it not brought some art along with it?

Aug. The question you are raising is an important one, an extremely important one; in fact, I am not sure there is any more important. It finds us holding opinions so diametrically opposed as to let you think that the soul has brought no art with it, whereas in my view it has brought all of them with it, and what is called learning is nothing else than re membering and recalling.[48]

But you realize, do you not, that this is not the right time to inquire whether such is actually the case? For the moment it is evidently our business to make clear, if possible, that the soul is not called small or great with regard to local dimensions. As to its eternity, if such there is, this we shall properly examine when we take up, to the extent that is possible, the fourth question you posed: why it was given to the body. Indeed, what difference does it make to the present quantitative consideration of the soul whether or not it always existed in the past or will always exist in the future, or whether it is now without knowledge and again possessed of knowledge? In fact, we have proved earlier that length of time does not explain magnitude even in bodies;[49] again, that it is a truism that skill can be utterly wanting to growth and at the same time be eminently present with the declining years. In addition, many other points were made which definitely show, I think, that the soul does not undergo expansion in proportion to the increase of the body brought on by the passing of time.

CHAPTER 21

Increase of physical strength does not indicate material growth of soul.

35. Let us examine, then, if you will, what there is to that other argument of yours, namely that the soul, which we claim has no extension, exercises the sense of touch throughout the whole extent of the body.[50]

Ev. I should be willing to go on to that, but for the fact that I think something ought to be said about strength. How is it that as the body grows in size with advancing age and lends increase of strength to the soul, the soul itself does not grow in extent? True it is, virtue is commonly associated with the soul, and strength with the body. Still, I would never divorce strength from the soul, noting, as I do, that in bodies without souls no strength is present. It is through the body, of course, that the soul uses its strength, as it does the senses; however, since these are functions of a living thing, who can doubt that both belong eminently to the soul? Therefore, since we see that growing children have greater strength than infants, and, again, that adolescents and youths increase in strength day by day until the process is reversed, and, as the body grows old, its strength wanes, this, so it seems to me, is a very definite indication that the soul grows with the body and then grows old with it.

36. *Aug.* What you say is not altogether absurd. But I always think of strength as coming not so much from the extent of the body or any advances in age, as from a certain training and a harmonious development of the body's members. To convince you of this, I ask you whether you think it a proof of superior strength if A walks a greater stretch than B, and ends up less fatigued?

Ev. I think so.

Aug. Why, then, if an increase in strength is due to advancing age and a simultaneous growth of soul, why is it that as a boy engaged in walking for the purpose of catching birds I could cover far greater distances without experiencing fatigue than when as a young man I devoted myself to other pursuits requiring more sedentary habits? Again, in the case of wrestlers, it is not the weight and size of the body that the trainers look for with critical eye, but bulging biceps, rippling muscles, and the entire proportion of the bodily figure, and it is rather from these that they make their appraisal of strength. But all these stand for little unless technique and practice go with them. It is, moreover, a common experience to witness men of giant frame bested by undersized opponents in moving or carrying weights, or even in wrestling. Indeed, who does not know that any one of your Olympic champions would be more quickly fagged out on the road than an itinerant peddler, whom the other could floor with one finger? Consequently, if we cannot speak even of all strength as being great in the same sense, but according as it proves superior in this or that regard; and if the contours and figures of bodies are what count most, not their size; and if the contribution made by practice is so important that it is quite generally believed that a man by taking up a little calf every day achieved that he could lift and hold it even after it had grown to be a bull, without noticing the increase in weight that it put on a little at a time—then the growth of strength with age is no indication at all that the soul has grown with the body.

CHAPTER 22

Whence greater physical strength?

37. But if animals with larger bodies have a greater measure of strength merely because they are larger, the reason is that by nature's law lighter masses yield to heavier ones. This holds true not only when by their own gravity they are borne toward their proper place, as for example, moist and earthen bodies fall toward the centre of the earth directly beneath them, whereas bodies composed of air and fire go upward—but it also happens when, against their own tendency, they are forcefully propelled by a foreign agent—

some mechanical device that hurls or shoots them or makes them rebound. Certainly, if you drop two stones of unequal size from a height, though you do this simultaneously, the larger one, of course, lands on the ground more quickly.[51] But if the smaller one is placed under the larger and so fastened that it cannot get away, it naturally yields and is brought down to the ground at the same time. Likewise, if the larger stone is thrown down from above while the smaller is tossed upward against it from below, then, when they meet, the smaller one necessarily rebounds and drops back. Lest you think that this happens for the reason that the lighter one was forced against its nature to go upward while the other was seeking its natural place with all the greater speed, imagine that the heavier one is hurled upward and meets the lighter which has been thrown toward the ground: you will still see the lighter one rebuffed and forced back skyward, but on the rebound falling in a different spot and thus coming down where there is nothing to obstruct it. Similarly, if both, not by a natural motion, but, let us say, by two men engaged in combat on the field, are thrown one against the other and strike together in mid-air, who would doubt that the lighter one would give way to the heavier in that direction from which the former was moving and to which the latter was directed? Such being the case, that is, though the lighter weights, as we said, yield to the heavier, still the measure of impetus by which they strike against each other is an important consideration. For if the lighter stone is hurled with greater impetus, for instance, when it is ejected by some powerful machine and strikes hard against a heavier one which was thrown with less force, or is already losing its velocity, although the lighter stone may rebound from the heavier, it nevertheless slows it up, or even, in proportion to impact and weight, drives it back.

38. Now that we have considered and understood this, so far as our present problem demands, see whether what is called strength in animals conforms to this reasoning. Plainly, no one can deny that the bodies of all animals are provided with a weight of their own. Now, wherever this weight, responding to the impulse of the soul, is brought to bear, it achieves much, depending on the amount in which it is present. But the soul's impulse uses the sinews like so many thongs to move the weight of the body. Dryness and moderate heat invigorate the sinews and render them more pliable; whereas rigidity that comes with moisture makes them sluggish and weak. Hence, in sleep the parts of the body become languid because, so physicians say and prove, it brings on coolness and moisture; and the energy evinced by people who have just been roused from sleep is weak indeed; and so it is that there is nothing weaker and more listless than people in a state of lethargy. But on the other hand it is an established fact that certain types of people who live in a delirious state and to whose nerve fibers the absence of sleep, or potent wine, or violent fever—that is, so many generators of heat—lend such abnormal pliability and endurance that they are able to struggle and do many things with greater strength than if they had health unimpaired, although their physiques are very much run down and made feeble by illness.

If, then, what is called strength is made up of an impulse from the soul and a sort of mechanism of the nerve sinews and the weight of the body, it is the will that gives the impulse; and this is intensified by hope or courage, but retarded by fear and far more so by despair; for in the case of fear, provided there is some underlying hope, generally a more energetic show of strength comes to the fore. A definite co-ordination of the body makes of it a smoothly-working machine; a well-balanced health keeps it in order, assiduous exercise makes it strong; weight is supplied by the substance of the members which age and nourishment build up, but which nourishment alone restores. The man who excels equally in all these respects has admirable strength; and to the extent that he lacks these things, one man is less strong than another. Often it happens, too, that a man, notwithstanding that he has slight weight of body to support him, by dint of persistent effort and by superior strategy bests another who is his superior in brawn. Again, sometimes there is so much of sheer bulk that even though it is used with negligible effort, it nevertheless crushes an opponent who puts forth a far more serious effort.

When, however, it is not physical weight nor muscular control that fails, but the will itself—that is, the soul—with the result that a stronger man is vanquished by another definitely weaker, because he has but a faint heart to offer for the courage of the other, I do not know whether this is to be credited to strength. If so, one might say that the soul has a reservoir of strength of its own, from which it derives added pluck or confidence. Here, we find, one man is equipped, another is not, and so it is seen how far superior the soul is to its body, even in regard to the activity it performs through the body.

39. And therefore, since an infant child has only the impulse to get something or get rid of it fully developed, whereas its muscles are untractable because of their recent formation and imperfect co-ordination, and are feeble on account of the flabbiness that predominates at that age, and are sluggish for lack of exercise; since, moreover, its weight is so slight that it does not exert any pressure worth mentioning even under the impact of something else, and is more

liable to receive than to inflict injury: who is there who, when he sees the years supplying all these deficiencies and is aware of the strength bestowed by them, would rightly and wisely infer [52] that the soul has grown, because it uses these things that develop more and more with the passage of time? Really, if such a person were to see small, light reeds shot from a loose-stringed bow which a youth hidden from view by a curtain is stretching as hard as he can, and he were to see the reeds going only a short distance and soon dropping to the ground; and if a little later he saw genuine arrows, weighted with iron, enlivened with feather vanes, and shot from a most stout bow and soaring high into the sky; and if then he were assured that both performances resulted from an equal effort by the same fellow—such a man, I say, would be capable of declaring that the fellow had grown and increased his strength in that brief span of time. And what statement could be more absurd than this?

40. Then, too, if the soul does grow, note how ill-advised it is to infer its growth from the strength of the body, and not to infer it from the store of its learning, seeing that it merely directs the former, while the latter is its exclusive possession. What is more, if we think the soul grows with the accession of strength, we must conclude that the diminution of strength results in its decrease. As a matter of fact, strength is diminished by old age, it is diminished by the effort of study; but it is in these periods that knowledge is acquired and developed. And it is utterly impossible that anything increase and decrease at one and the same time. Therefore, the fact of greater strength in greater age is no indication that the soul grows. Much more could be said; but if this satisfies you, I shall let well enough alone so that we may pass on to other matters.

Ev. I am quite convinced that greater physical strength is not owing to growth of soul. For, to say nothing of other pertinent reflections you made, the supposition that the soul grows by reason of insanity or bodily disease, while the body itself is reduced, is one that not even a crazy person makes, regarding whom everybody knows that his strength is far greater than a sane man ordinarily has. Hence it is most obvious to me that when we discover an extraordinary show of strength in anyone, it is the muscles that claim our admiration. Wherefore, please take up now the problem in which I am intensely interested: if the soul does not have a spatial magnitude commensurate with that of the body, why is it that it feels wherever the body is touched?

CHAPTER 23

Tentative definition of sensation. How sight operates.

41. *Aug.* All right, let us tackle that problem, as you wish, but you will have to give me much closer attention than you may think necessary. So, collect your wits as best you can and answer me what your idea of "sensation" is which the soul exercises through the body. For "sensation" is the proper term to use here.

Ev. I have always heard that there are five senses: seeing, hearing, smelling, tasting, and touching. I do not know what more to answer.

Aug. That division is very ancient and it is the usual popular presentation of it. But I would have you define what sensation itself is, so that all these may be included in one simple definition, and nothing else that is not sensation may be understood under it. However, if you cannot do this, I shall not press you. This one thing you can do—an(

that will be enough—you can either disprove or approve my definition.

Ev. With that method I shall perhaps not fail you, so far as I am able. But even that is not always easy.

Aug. Now then, listen: I think sensation is the soul's not being unaware of the body's experience.[53]

Ev. That definition satisfies me.

Aug. Stand by it as your own, then, and defend it while I disprove it briefly.

Ev. I shall defend it, all right, if you will stand by me; but if you do not, I am through with it already. Evidently you have good reason for deciding to refute it.

Aug. Do not rely too much upon authority, especially mine, which does not exist. Also, to quote Horace, "Have the courage to think for yourself,"[54] lest fear defeat you before an argument does.

Ev. I have no fear at all, no matter what the issue, for you will not suffer me to be in error. But begin if you have anything to say, lest I be worn out by delay rather than by your objections.

42. *Aug.* Tell me, then, what effect does your body undergo when you see me?

Ev. It does experience something, for, if I mistake not, my eyes are part of my body; and if they experienced nothing, how could I see you?

Aug. But it is not enough for you to prove that your eyes experience some effect, unless you also show me what they experience.

Ev. Well, what could it be but sight itself? For they see. If you were to ask me what a sick person experiences, I should answer, sickness; a lustful person, lust; a fearful person, fear; a joyful person, joy. Why, then, when you ask me what someone experiences when he sees, should I not answer that it is sight itself?

Aug. But a joyful person senses joy. Or do you deny that?

Ev. No, indeed, I agree.

Aug. I should say the same about the other emotions.

Ev. So should I.

Aug. But whatever the eyes sense, they see.

Ev. I should not say that at all. For who sees pain, even though the eyes often sense it?

Aug. Evidently you are concerned with the eyes. You are wide awake. See, then, whether, just as a joyful person senses joy by being joyful, so also one who sees senses sight by seeing.

Ev. Can it be otherwise?

Aug. But whatever the one who sees senses in the act of seeing, he must also see.

Ev. No, that does not follow. For, suppose he has a sensation of love when he sees: he does not see love, does he?

Aug. A very cautious and shrewd observation! I am glad you are not easily deceived. But now, note this: we agree that we do not see everything which the eyes sense, nor everything we sense in the act of seeing; but do you think that at least this is true—that we sense everything that we see?

Ev. Indeed, if I did not grant that, how could the fact that we see be called sensation?

Aug. Well, are we not also acted upon by everything of which we have a sensation?

Ev. That is right.

Aug. Then, if we have a sensation of everything we see, and if we are acted upon by everything of which we have a sensation, we are acted upon by everything we see.

Ev. I have no objection to make.

Aug. Therefore, you are acted upon by me, and I in turn am acted upon by you, when we see each other.

Ev. So I think, and for me this is an instant dictate of reason.

43. *Aug.* Take what follows, for I believe you would regard it as quite absurd and foolish if anyone should say that you are acted upon by a body, where that body which affects you is not present.

Ev. It does seem absurd, and I believe it is just as you say.

Aug. Well, now, is it not evident that my body is in one place, and yours in another?

Ev. Yes.

Aug. Just the same, your eyes have a sensation of my body, and if they have a sensation, they certainly are being acted upon; and they cannot be acted upon where that which acts is not present. Yet, your eyes are not there where my body is. Therefore, they are subjected to action where they are not present.

Ev. Well, I granted all those points which it seemed unreasonable not to grant; but this last which flows from the rest is so very absurd that I would rather own than I have made a rash concession somewhere along the line than admit that this conclusion is true. Not even in my sleep would I dare to say that my eyes have sensation where they are not present.

Aug. Then, see where you have dozed off. What would you have been too cautious to let slip by, if you had been as wide awake as you were a little while ago?

Ev. To be sure, that is what I am carefully retracing and reconsidering. Still, it is not quite clear to me that a concession should be regretted, except perhaps this, that our eyes have sensation when we see; for it is possibly sight itself that has the sensation.

Aug. Yes, that is it. Sight extends itself outward and through the eyes darts forth far in every possible direction to light up what we see. Hence it happens that it sees rather in the place where the object seen is present, not in the place from which it goes out to see. Therefore, it is not you that see, when you see me?

Ev. Who but a crazy person would say this? By all means—it is I who see, but I see by the emission of sight through the eyes.

Aug. But, if you see, you have a sensation. If you have a sensation, you are acted upon. And you cannot be acted upon at a place where you are not present. But you see me where I am. Therefore, you are acted upon where I am. But if you are not there where I am, I do not know at all how you dare to say that you see me.

Ev. I say that by means of sight, reaching out to that place where you are, I see you where you are. But that I am not there, I admit. Still, let us suppose that I were to touch you with a stick: I certainly would be the one doing the touching and I would sense it; yet I would not be there where I touched you. In the same way, because I say that I see by means of sight, even though I am not there, I am not thereby compelled to admit that it is not I who see.

44. *Aug.* Then you have made no rash concession. For your eyes can be defended in this way also: their sight is, as you say, like the stick. And your conclusion that your eyes see where they are not present, is not absurd. Or do you think otherwise?

Ev. It is just as you say, certainly. In fact, I now realize that if the eyes should see where they are present, they would also see themselves.

Aug. It would be more correct for you to say, not that they would see *also* themselves, but that they would see *only* themselves. For where they are, that is, the place they occupy, they alone occupy. The nose is not where they are, nor is anything else that is near them. Otherwise you would also be where I am, because we are near each other. Consequently, if the eyes were to see only where they are, they would see only themselves. But since they do not see themselves, we are compelled to agree not only that they can see where they are not, but even that they cannot see at all, except where they are not.

Ev. Nothing can make me doubt that.

Aug. Then you do not doubt that the eyes are acted upon where they are not present. For where they see, there they have a sensation, for seeing itself is a sensation, and to have a sensation is to undergo an action. Hence, where they have a sensation, there they are acted upon. But they actually see in another place than that in which they are.[55] Therefore, they are subjected to an action where they are not present.

Ev. I am surprised how I consider all this to be true.

CHAPTER 24

Criticism of the definition of sensation.

45. *Aug.* Perhaps you are right in thinking so. But tell me, please, do we see everything that we recognize by means of sight?

Ev. I think so.

Aug. Do you also believe that we recognize by means of sight everything we recognize by the act of seeing?

Ev. Yes, I believe that also.

Aug. Why, then, when we see only smoke, do we generally recognize that beneath it there is hidden fire which we do not see?

Ev. You are right. And now I do not think we see everything we recognize by means of sight, for we can, as you have shown, by seeing one thing, recognize another which is out of the range of sight.

Aug. Well, is it possible not to see what we sense by means of sight?

Ev. No, not at all.

Aug. Therefore, sense perception and recognition are two different things.

Ev. They are entirely different. For example, we have sense perception of the smoke which we see and from that we recognize that beneath it there is fire which we do not see.

Aug. You understand that correctly. But you surely see that when this happens, our body, that is, our eyes, are in no wise affected by the fire, but by the smoke which is all they see. For we have already agreed that to see is to have sensation, and to have sensation is to be acted upon.[56]

Ev. I grasp that and I agree.

Aug. When, therefore, as a result of an impression received by the body the soul is not unaware of something, this is not at once identifiable with one of the five senses mentioned; but this latter holds only when it is aware of the bodily experience itself. That fire, for example, is not seen nor heard nor smelled nor tasted nor touched by us; yet, the sight of smoke makes the soul aware of it. And, while this awareness is not called sensation, because the body is not affected by the fire, it is nevertheless termed recognition through sensation, because the fire is conjectured and established from an experience of the body, though the experience was something different, that is, the sight of a different reality.

Ev. I understand, and I see very well that this harmonizes with, and supports, that definition of yours which you gave me to defend as my own. ⸱ For I remember that you defined sensation as "the soul's not being unaware of the body's experience." [57] Therefore, the fact that smoke is seen we call a sensation, for by seeing the smoke the eyes experience it, and the eyes are parts of the body, and themselves are bodies; but the fire, of which the body had no experience at all, although its presence became known, we do not term an object of sensation.

46. *Aug.* I commend you on your memory and the intelligence that is yours to serve it. But your defense of the definition is tottering.

Ev. Will you tell me why?

Aug. Because you do not deny, I think, that the body undergoes some effect when we are growing, or when we become old. At the same time it is clear that we do not perceive it by any of the senses; and yet it does not escape the soul. Therefore, there is one effect on the body of which the soul is not unaware, though this cannot be called sensation. Plainly, by seeing those things to be larger which formerly we had seen smaller, and seeing men grown old who obviously had been young men and boys, we infer that our own bodies are undergoing some such change, even now while we are talking. Nor are we mistaken in this, I am sure; for I am more likely to make a mistake saying

that I *see* than saying that I *understand* that my hair is
growing now, or that my body undergoes constant change.
And if this change is an effect on the body, which no one
denies, and if we do not actually perceive it by the senses,
yet the soul is not unaware of it because we are not unaware
of it, then, as I said, the body undergoes an effect of which
the soul is not unaware, and yet it is not sensation. Wherefore, that definition which should include nothing which
is not sensation, is certainly defective, since it did include
this.

Ev. I see the only thing remaining for me to do is to
ask you to give another definition or to revise this one, if
you can; for in the light of your reasoning, perfectly convincing to me, I must own that it is defective.

Aug. It is an easy matter to correct this, and I want you
to try it. Take my word for it—you will do it, once you
grasp well where it is at fault.

Ev. There is no other possibility, is there, than that it
includes something that does not belong there?

Aug. How, then?

Ev. Because of the fact that the body ages, even in its
youth, it cannot be denied that it undergoes some change.
And when we know that, we have an experience of the body
of which the soul is not unaware. And yet it is imper-
ceptible to each and every sense; for neither do I see that
I am aging at this moment, nor do I perceive it by hearing,
or smelling, or tasting, or touching.

Aug. How, then, do you know it?

Ev. I infer it by reason.

Aug. On what arguments is your reasoning based?

Ev. On the fact that I see other people old, who, as I
now am, were once young.

Aug. Is it not by a sense faculty that you see them—one of the five?

Ev. Who denies that? But from the fact that I see them, I infer that I, too, am growing old, though I do not actually see it.

Aug. What words, then, do you think should be added to the definition to make it perfect, considering that sensation is present only when the soul is not unaware of an effect produced in the body, yet not in such a way that the soul recognizes it through another effect or through any other factor at all.

Ev. Kindly state that a little more clearly.

CHAPTER 25

Rules for definition. Application to definition of sensation.

47. *Aug.* I shall comply with your wish, and that the more willingly if you go slowly rather than hurry. At any rate, give me your complete attention, for what I shall say will be applicable in many respects.

A definition contains nothing less, nothing more than what is up for explanation; otherwise, it is in reality a bad definition. Now, whether it is free from such defects is determined by conversion; and that this is so, the following examples will make clearer to you. If, for instance, you were to ask me what man is, and I should give this definition: "Man is a mortal animal," you should not, just because what is said is true, approve it as a definition. But, by prefixing one little word, namely, "every," change the proposition and see whether the simple converse is also true; that is to say, whether, just as it is true that "every man is a mortal animal," it is also true that "every mortal animal is a man." When you find that this is not the case, you should reject the definition because of the fault that it includes something extraneous. For, not only man, but every beast as well, is a mortal animal. Hence, it is usual to complete this definition of man by adding "rational" to "mortal"; for man is a rational mortal animal; [58] and, just as every man is a mortal rational animal, so also every mortal rational animal is a man. The previous definition, then, was faulty because it included too much, applying to the beast as well as to man; the present one, embracing every man, and nothing besides man, is perfect.

Again, if it embraces too little, if, for example, you add "grammarian," it is likewise defective. For, even though every rational mortal animal that is a grammarian is a man, yet there are many men who are not grammarians and so are not embraced by this definition; and for this reason the statement in the first proposition is false, though its converse is true. For it is false that every man is a rational, mortal, grammarian animal but it is true that every rational, mortal, grammarian animal is a man. When, however, neither the statement of the proposition as such nor that of its converse is true, the defect obviously is greater than when only one is false. Take these two propositions: "Man is a white animal"; again, "Man is a four-footed animal." For, whether you say, "Every man is a white animal," or, "Every man is a four-footed animal," the statements are false, and the converse statements are also false. But there is this difference, that the first applies to some men, for a great many men are white; the second does not apply to any man, for there is no man who is a quadruped. For the present, you might learn these points testing definitions, how to judge of them in the proposition and in conversion. There are many other things of this kind offered in instructions, both verbose and vague, which I shall try to teach you by and by, at the right moment.

48. Now turn your attention to that definition of ours and, applying your added experience to a study of it, correct it. Well, we had discovered that while it was a definition of sensation, it included something besides sensation, and, therefore, was not true when converted. Perhaps it is true that every sensation is an effect on the body that does not escape the awareness of the soul,[59] just as it is true that "every man is a mortal animal." But just as it is false that "every mortal animal is a man"—for a beast is also that— so is it false that "every effect on the body that does not escape the awareness of the soul is a sensation," because our fingernails are growing now and the soul is not unaware of that, for we know it; yet we learn of it not by sensation but by inference. In the same way, therefore, as "rational" was added to the definition of man to make it exact, and the addition ruled out the beasts which had also been found included, so that we understand the definition in this form to embrace man only and all men—do you not think that our present definition requires some addition by which to exclude any foreign item it contains and to make it stand for sensation only and for all that is sensation?

Ev. Yes, I think so; but what addition can be made, I do not know.

Aug. Every sensation is certainly an effect on the body of which the soul is not unaware. But this proposition cannot be converted, because of that action on the body as a result of which it grows or shrinks, with our knowing it— that is, the soul is aware of it.

Ev. That is right.

Aug. Now, does the soul become aware of this through the action itself, or through something else?

Ev. Obviously, through some other factor. It is one thing to see that the nails are longer; another to know that they grow.

Aug. Since, then, growth itself is an action which we do not experience by any of the senses, while the increase in size which we do know by the senses is a result of the same action, but is not the action itself, it is obvious that we know such an action not through itself, but through something else. Therefore, if it were not through something else that the soul is aware of it, would it not be known by the senses rather than by inference?

Ev. I understand.

Aug. Why, then, do you hesitate regarding what is to be added to the definition?

Ev. I see now that sensation is to be defined thus: it is a bodily experience that of itself [60] does not escape the soul's awareness; for every sensation is just that, and each time you have that, you have, I believe, sensation.

49. *Aug.* If that is true, I admit the definition is perfect. But let us put it to a test, if you will, to see whether it is not shaky because of that second fault, as was the definition of man to which "grammarian" was added. You recall, of course, that it was said that "man is a mortal rational grammarian animal," and that this definition is faulty, because, though the converse of it is true, the orignal proposition is false. For it is false that "every man is a rational, mortal, grammarian animal," though it is true that "every rational, mortal, grammarian animal is a man." Wherefore, this definition is unsound for the reason that although it applies to

man alone, it does not apply to every man. And it may be that the definition we are boasting of as perfect, is like that. For, although the body's every experience directly entering the awareness of the soul is a sensation, still not every sensation is such. You may understand that in this way: brute animals have sense experience, and practically all of them have the use of the five senses, so far as nature has endowed them. You will not deny that, will you?

Ev. Certainly not.

CHAPTER 26

Do brute animals possess knowledge and reason?

Aug. Furthermore, you grant, do you not, that there is no knowledge [61] unless some reality is perceived and known by certain reason?

Ev. I grant that.

Aug. But a brute animal does not reason.

Ev. I grant that also.

Aug. Knowledge, therefore, does not apply to brute animals. But where there is awareness of something there you certainly have knowledge.[62] Therefore, brute animals have no sense experiences, if every sensation is bound up with a bodily experience of which the soul is directly aware. Yet, they do have sense experience, as was granted a little while ago. Why, then, do we hesitate to reject that definition, which has proved unequal to embracing all sensation, since, indeed, the sensation of brute animals is excluded?

50. *Ev.* I confess that I was deceived when I granted you that knowledge is present when something is perceived

by reason with certainty. For when you asked that question, I had only men in mind. I cannot, indeed, say that brute animals have the use of reason, nor can I deny them knowledge. Not to mention countless other examples, in my opinion the dog knew his master, whom, as the story goes, he recognized after twenty years.[63]

Aug. Tell me, I ask you, if two things were placed before you, one as an object to be attained, the other as the means of attaining it, which of these would you esteem more, and which would you prefer to the other?

Ev. Who could doubt that the object to be attained is the more estimable?

Aug. Now, then, considering that knowledge and reason are two distinct realities, do we attain to reason by knowledge, or to knowledge by reason?

Ev. The two of them, to my way of thinking, are so interconnected that it is by each that the other can be attained. For we could not attain to reason itself, unless we knew that we should attain to it. Therefore, knowledge came first, so that by it we might come to use reason.

Aug. What? Do we actually arrive at knowledge, which you say comes first, without reason?

Ev. Never would I say that; for that would be utterly unreasonable.

Aug. Therefore, it is by reason?

Ev. No.

Aug. By unreasonableness, then?

Ev. Who would say that?

Aug. By what means, then?

Ev. Without any means; knowledge, you know, is inborn in us.

51. *Aug.* It seems to me you have forgotten what we

previously agreed on, when I asked you if you thought that knowledge was present when there is some perception accompanied by certain reason. You answered, I think, that you thought this constituted human knowledge. But now you state that man can have some knowledge when he perceives reality without applying reason. Who would not see that nothing is more contradictory than these two assertions: that there is no knowledge unless some reality is perceived by certain reason, and that there is knowledge of something perceived without the use of reason? Hence, I should like to know which of the two you choose; plainly, it is utterly impossible that both be true.

Ev. I choose what I said just now. Yes, I must own that I granted the previous statement without thinking. When between the two of us we are trying to establish truth by the instrument of reason, and we do that by question and answer, how could we possibly reach the point at which a conclusion is drawn by reason, unless we had previously granted something? Moreover, how could a valid concession be made of what is not known? So, unless I previously knew something which this reason could use as a premise to lead on to something unknown, I would learn absolutely nothing by means of reason, nor would I call it reason at all. Therefore, it is pointless for you not to agree with me that prior to the use of reason there must be some knowledge in us which reason uses as a starting point.

Aug. Granted, and, as I agreed, I shall permit you to revise your opinion as often as you regret anything you conceded. But do not abuse this permission, I beg you; and do not let your attention flag the while I ask you questions; otherwise your continued careless concessions may make you doubt even about things granted with good reason.

Ev. Above all, go on to the remaining points. Although I shall do my best to be more alert—for I, too, am embarrassed that I should shift my opinion so often—still I will never be deterred from overcoming my embarrassment and correcting a blunder, especially if you give me a helping hand. Surely, the desire to be consistent should not make one espouse stubbornness.

CHAPTER 27

Reason and reasoning.

52. *Aug.* May that consistency come your way as soon as possible—I do like the sentiment you expressed. But now give your best attention to what I have in mind. I would like to know what difference you think there is between reason and reasoning.[84]

Ev. I cannot see a clear distinction between them.

Aug. Look at it this way, then. Do you think that a person who is already in his adolescence, or one who is in his manhood, or—to remove any ground for doubt—do you think that a wise man, as long as he is of sound mind, is in the uninterrupted possession of reason, in the same way that he enjoys physical health as long as he is spared disease and wounds? Or is it sometimes present, sometimes absent, the same as is the case with his walking, his sitting down, his talking?

Ev. A sound mind, I think, has the constant enjoyment of reason.

Aug. What about this? Given that it is by facts that are obvious and taken for granted, or by interrogating another or by correlating other facts that we arrive at the knowledge of some certain reality—do you think that we or wise men in general are doing this always?

Ev. No, not always. For no man, or no wise man, so it seems to me, is *always* seeking something by speculation either with himself or with someone else. For one who is in the process of seeking is still removed from discovery, and so, if he is forever seeking, he never makes a discovery. But the wise man has already discovered at least wisdom itself, not to mention anything else; and that is what he was seeking, perhaps by discussion, or in any other way he could, because he was in ignorance.

Aug. You are right. Here I would have you understand that this is not reason, when we are led on to something unknown by facts taken for granted and already known. For, as we have already agreed, this process is not always present in a sound mind; but reason is.

53. *Ev.* I understand. But why all this?

Aug. Because you stated a little while ago that I must agree with you that we have knowledge before reason, because reason proceeds from a basis in something known in leading us to something unknown. But now we have discovered that when this occurs, the operation should not be called reason; for a sound mind is not always performing that operation, although it always has reason. With rather good cause, though, the operation is called "reasoning." Thus, "reason" is in a sense mental sight, while "reasoning" would be reason's search, that is, the moving of that sight over the objects that are to be seen.[65] Hence, the function of the latter is to search, that of the former, to see. And so, when that sight of the mind which we call reason, is directed upon some object and sees it, that is called knowledge; but when the mind does not see, though it focuses its sight, that is called not-knowing or ignorance. For, too, not everyone who looks with his bodily eyes, sees—a fact we can most readily verify in the dark. This shows, I think, that looking and seeing are two different things. Applying the two to the mind, we call them reason and knowledge. But possibly you have some objection to make to this, or think that the distinction is not made sufficiently clear.

Ev. The distinction satisfies me more than I can say, and I am in hearty agreement.

Aug. Now, then, see whether you think we look in order to see, or see in order to look.

Ev. Here, indeed, not even a blind man would have a doubt that looking serves seeing, not vice versa.

Aug. It must be admitted, then, that seeing is to be valued more highly than looking.

Ev. Absolutely.

Aug. Therefore, knowledge, too, stands higher than reason.

Ev. I see that that follows.

Aug. Do you hold that brute animals are superior to, or happier than, human beings?

Ev. God forbid such awful folly!

Aug. Of course, you are right in shuddering at such an idea. Yet, the thought you expressed forces us to that conclusion, for you said that they have knowledge, but do not have reason. Man, however, has reason, and by this he arrives at knowledge only with great difficulty. But, granting that he achieves it with ease: of what use is reason to us that we should consider ourselves superior to brute animals, aware as we are that they have knowledge and that this was established as more estimable than reason?

CHAPTER 28

Brute animals have sensation, not genuine knowledge.

54. *Ev.* Yes, I am compelled either to deny that brute animals have knowledge, or to be quite satisfied that they be preferred to me, as they deserve. But please explain the significance of the story I brought up regarding Ulysses's dog,[66] for it was because it struck my fancy that I yelped so inanely.

Aug. What do you think is behind it except some power of sense perception, not of knowledge? As a matter of fact, many brute animals have keener sense perception than we, but this is not the place to go into the reason for that. In mind, however, and reason and knowledge God has placed us over them. The sense faculty they have, conjoined with the powerful force of habit, is able to discern the things that bring pleasure to souls such as theirs. Besides, this happens all the more easily because the soul of brute animals is more closely bound to the body; and it is to the latter that the senses belong which the soul uses for the life and enjoyment it derives from that same body. The human soul, however, because the instruments it uses, reason and knowledge—and it is with these we are concerned now—are far superior to the senses, makes itself independent, as far as it can, of the body, and gives first preference to joy experienced within; and according as it turns aside to the senses, the greater the likeness it gives man to beast. Hence it is that even whimpering children, the further they are from the use of reason, are that much quicker to recognize by sense even the touch and proximity of their nurses and will not bear the odor of others with whom they are not familiar.

55. Therefore, although here one thing led us to another, still I do like to spend some time on a discussion which serves to teach the soul the lesson that it must not fall back on the senses any more than necessity demands; but it should rather retire into itself, away from the senses, and become a child of God again. This is what it means to become a new man by putting off the old.[67] To undertake this is absolutely necessary because of the neglect of God's law: Sacred Scripture contains no greater truth, none more profound. I would like to say more about this point and tie myself down while I am, as it were, laying down the law to you, so that my one and only concern might be to render an account of myself to myself, to whom I am above all responsible,[68] and thus to become to God, as Horace says, like "a slave who is his master's friend."[69] This is an achievement that is utterly impossible unless we remake ourselves in His image, the image He committed to our care as something most precious and dear, when He gave us to ourselves so constituted that nothing can take precedence to us save He Himself.[70]

But to my mind this calls for action than which none is more laborious, none that is more akin to inaction, for it is such as the soul cannot begin or complete except with the help of Him to whom it yields itself. Hence it is that man's reformation is dependent on the mercy of Him to whose goodness and power he owes his formation.

56. But we must return to our subject. So, see whether you are now convinced that brute animals have no knowledge, and that the semblance of knowledge which strikes us in them is in its entirety merely the product of sense perception.

Ev. I am quite convinced; and if there is anything on this point that should be gone into more thoroughly, I shall

abide my time. At the moment I am anxious to know what
conclusion you are drawing from all this.

CHAPTER 29

The difference between knowledge and sensation.

Aug. What else do you think, but that our definition of
sensation which before included something or other besides
sensation, now is out of plumb because of the opposite defect, because it proved unable to accommodate every sensation? For brute animals have sensation but they do not have
knowledge. Now, whatever is not hidden is known;[71] and
everything that is known surely appertains to knowledge.
On all these points we have already agreed. Therefore,
either it is not true that sensation is an effect on the body that
does not escape the soul's awareness, or else brute animals
have no sensation, because they lack knowledge. We have,
however, granted that brutes have sensation. Therefore, that
definition of ours is defective.

Ev. I confess that I find no rejoinder to offer you.

57. *Aug.* Here is a further consideration that should
make us disown that definition even more. You recall, I
suppose, what we showed to be a third defect of a definition,
quite the worst fault of all—the case in which the definition
is false both ways, as, for instance, this one of man: "Man
is a four-footed animal." For whoever says and affirms that
every man is a four-footed animal, or that every four-footed
animal is a man, certainly is joking, or else he is crazy.

Ev. You are right.

Aug. Well, now, if this definition of ours should be diag-
nosed as laboring from that same defect, do you think there

is anything that should be more expeditiously rejected and banished in any consideration of the soul?

Ev. Who could deny that? But, if possible, this time I would prefer not to be detained so long again and to be plied with picayune questions.

Aug. No need to fear, our task is already done. Or, were you not already convinced from our discussion of the difference between brute animals and man that to have sensation and to have knowledge are two different things?

Ev. Yes, and thoroughly so.

Aug. Therefore, sensation is different from knowledge?

Ev. Yes.

Aug. And we do not have sensation through reason, but by means of sight, or hearing, or smell, or taste, or touch?

Ev. I agree.

Aug. And everything we know, we know by reason. Therefore, no sensation is knowledge; but whatever one is not unaware of belongs to knowledge. Hence, to be not unaware of something has nothing to do with sensation, any more than that a man can be correctly said to be a quadruped. Wherefore, this definition of ours, yours by adoption, stands convicted not only of having invaded another's domain and abandoned its own property, but of having had no ground whatever of its own to begin with, and of having grabbed from another all that it does hold.

Ev. What shall we do, then? Will you permit it to get off from court with this against it? I myself, it is true, gave it the best defense I could, but it was you who prepared the brief of the trial which deceived us. And even though I was not able to win the verdict, I gave my defense in good faith. That is enough for me. But you—what are you going to do, if you are charged with prevarication in court? For it was you who drew the definition into court to plead a brazen suit, and you then prosecuted it, forcing it to withdraw in shame.

Aug. There is no judge here, is there, to cause this definition or myself any fear? I had in mind to serve you in the manner of a retained attorney, to confute you in private for the purpose of instructing you, so that you would be prepared to present the defense when the case came up.

58. *Ev.* Then there is something you can say for this definition whose defense and protection you are rashly committing to me, regardless of my utter incompetence?

Aug. There certainly is.

CHAPTER 30

Sensation does not prove that the soul has physical extension.

Ev. And what is it, I beg you?

Aug. The fact that, although sensation and knowledge are two different things, the element of "not being unaware" is common to both, just as being an animal is common to man and the brute, even though enormous differences separate them. For whatever is apparent to the soul, either through the body's organism or through pure intelligence, of that it is not unaware. Sensation lays claim to the first; knowledge, to the second.

Ev. That definition, then, remains safe and established?

Aug. Yes, it does.

Ev. Where, then, was I led astray?

Aug. When I asked whether everything of which one is

not unaware is known.[72] You were not thinking when you answered in the affirmative.

Ev. What, then, would you have me say?

Aug. Not that knowledge is attained by the very fact that there is awareness of something, but only when awareness results from the function of reason; when, however, awareness comes through the body, that is called sensation, if a bodily experience of itself does not escape awareness. You must know that certain philosophers, and very keen minds at that, thought that not even what is grasped by the mind can be claimed for knowledge, unless what is grasped is held so tenaciously that the mind cannot be dissuaded from it by any argument.

59. *Ev.* What you say is most acceptable to me. But now that the essence of sensation has been treated most thoroughly, I think, let me suggest that we go back to that question which prompted us to undertake this explanation. Now, I had advanced as an argument to prove that the soul has precisely the same size as its body, the fact that it feels whatever is in contact with the body from the head to the tip of the big toe, no matter where you touch it. Here we were sidetracked to a definition of sensation—with no end of delays, though that may have been necessary. And now, if you will, let me see the fruit of all this labor.

Aug. Such there certainly is—very rich fruit too, for all that we were looking for has been realized. If sensation is a bodily experience that of itself does not escape the awareness of the soul [73]—a definition we discussed at greater length than you wished, in order that we might have a most firm grasp of it—you remember, then, do you not, that we found that the eyes exercise sensation where they are not, or, rather, that they are acted on where they are not? [74]

Ev. I remember.

Aug. If I am not mistaken, you also granted this, and you are not sorry now for having granted it, that the soul is far superior to, more powerful than, the body in its entirety.

Ev. I think to be dubious about that would be outrageous.

Aug. Listen. If the body can be acted on where it is not actually present, because of some adaptation to the soul —and we found that it is true of the eyes, in the act of seeing—are we to believe that the soul, to which the eyes owe this great faculty of theirs, is so coarse and sluggish as not to be aware of an experience of the body, if it is not actually present where that experience transpires?

60. *Ev.* That conclusion really strikes me, so forcibly, indeed, that I am completely stunned. I have no answer to give—I am completely lost. Yes, what shall I say? That this is not sensation when an effect on the body is taken directly into the awareness of the soul? What can it be, if it is not that? Shall I say that the eyes experience nothing when we see? That is most absurd. Shall I say that they make their experience where they are? But they do not see themselves, and where they are there is nothing but themselves. Shall I say that the soul is not more powerful than the eyes, when it is the soul that is the power of the eyes? Nothing would be more foolish. Or should one say that more power is involved in experiencing an effect where something is present than where it is not present? But if that were true, sight would not be superior to the rest of the senses.

Aug. Let us suppose that the eyes experience, where they are, a blow or something falling into them or a mucous infection. The soul is not unaware of this. The experience given is not called sight, but touch. What is more, the eye could be affected in this way even in the case of a dead body, with no soul present to become aware of such effects. But as to the eye's experience which it can have only when the soul is present, namely the experience of sight, this experience it has only where it is not. Who would not see from this that the soul is not contained in any place? For the eye, which is a body, experiences only that outside the pale of its own physical whereness which it would never experience without the soul."[75]

61. *Ev.* What, then, shall I do, I ask you? Can it not be established by such arguments that our souls are not in our bodies? And if such is the case, is it not true that I do not know where I am? For who can take away from me the fact that I myself am my soul?

Aug. Do not lose your head—take courage! You see, a thought and consideration such as this invites us to enter into ourselves and, to the extent that is possible, separates us from the body. As for your supposition that the soul is not contained in the body of a living person, although it may seem absurd, there have been some very learned men who held that view,[76] and I think there are some even now. However, you realize yourself that the question is a most delicate one, and to solve it the mind's wits must be made to function at their best. Right now let us see what further argument you would adduce to prove that the soul has length or breadth or anything like that. As to that argument from the sense of touch, you realize that it is not favored by truth: there is nothing in it to prove that the soul is diffused throughout the whole body, as is the blood. Or, if you have nothing further to propose, let us see what remains.

CHAPTER 31

Does vivisection prove that the soul has quantitative coextension with the body?

62. *Ev.* There would be nothing further, did I not recall how we used to marvel when we were boys, at the way the tails of lizards would continue to wriggle when we had cut them off from the rest of the body. That this movement is possible without a soul I cannot convince myself at all. Neither do I understand how it can be that the soul is without spatial dimensions when it can be cut off piecemeal along with the body.

Aug. I might answer that air and fire are both kept in a body made of earth and moisture, by the presence of the soul, so that there is a blending of all four elements; that when, with the departure of the soul, the air and fire escape upward and free themselves, they agitate those little segments, and that the more violently, the fresher the wound through which they instantly rush forth; that then the activity diminishes and finally ceases, while what is escaping becomes less and less and ultimately disappears entirely. But this is an explanation which is discredited by what I took in with my own eyes—an observation coming to me so late as to seem almost incredible, but one that demands my credence just the same.[77]

When we were in the Ligurian countryside recently, those boys of ours[78] who were with me at the time pursuing their studies, noticed, while lying on the ground in a shady spot, a many-footed little animal creeping along— a good-sized worm, I would say. It is commonly known, yet I had never observed in it what I shall report here. One of the boys cut the animal in half with the broad end of a stylus he happened to have with him; whereupon both parts of the body moved away from the cut in opposite directions with as swift movement of the feet and with as much energy as if they had been two distinct animals of the same kind. Dumbfounded by the curious sight and eager for an explanation, they excitedly brought the two live segments to where Alypius [79] and I were sitting. We, too, not a little fascinated, observed the segments running all over the tablet wherever they could. And when one of them was touched by the stylus, it turned itself toward the place of the pain, while the other, sensing nothing, went about its own motions away from the first. What is more, to see how far this could go, we made the experiment of cutting the worm—they were really worms now— into a number of segments. They would all move about and about, so that if we had not done this to them and had the fresh wounds not been visible, we might have supposed that these things had been separately born, and that each was living an independent life.

63. But what I said to those boys when they eyed me with fixed attention, I hesitate to tell you now. We have already proceeded so far that unless I give you a different answer, one which is supported as plausible by my case, all this mental exertion of ours, supported by all this discussion, may appear to have collapsed because one little worm bored through it. I told the boys to stay right at their studies as they had begun, and in this way they would come at the proper moment to inquire into these matters and learn about them, if the subject warranted it. But if I wished to explain the discourse I had with Alypius as the boys went away, when the two of us, each to the best

of his ability, racked our brains making conjectures and finding new problems, we would have to devote many more words to this than we have given to the present discussion from its beginning, with all its circumlocutions and digressions.

But I shall not keep from you what I think. If at that time I had not yet possessed a great deal of information [80] about the body, about place, time, and motion—all questions which provoke most keen and abstract discussion because of their being involved in this very topic of ours—I should have been inclined to yield the palm to those who say that the soul is corporeal. Hence, to the best of my ability, I warn you—and warn you again—not to run headlong and heedlessly to the writings or discussions of spellbinders, people who rely too much on the senses of the body: you must first set straight and steady the steps that lead the soul to God's presence. Otherwise your studies and efforts will accomplish only that they will divert you more readily than will static ignorance, from that peaceful sanctum of the mind to which the soul in its present life is a stranger.

64. Now, witness a reply to the difficulty, which, I see, has upset you very much. It is not the strongest but is the simplest explanation of many; nor is it the most convincing to me personally, but it is the best choice I could make for your own case.

Ev. Do give it to me as quickly as you can.

Aug. First, I want to state this: if the reason why these phenomena occur in the division of certain bodies proves especially hard to fathom, we must not promptly lose our heads over this one fact so as to put down as false all that previously seemed to you clearer than light. For it may be that the explanation of this fact escapes us because it is beyond human comprehension; or, if someone does know the explanation, it is impossible for us to question him; or, again, our own mental capacity is such that he could give us no satisfaction if we did ask him. Now, it is not right, is it, that whatever we have acquired as solid knowledge and which we concede to be truth indubitably established, should be dropped, wrested from us merely because it is contradicted? No, on the contrary, if those points which in your replies you granted as absolute certainties remain as convincing as before, there is no reason for having a childish fear of this little worm, even though we cannot account for the multiplicity of its lives.

If, for instance, you had positive and undeniable proof that someone is a respectable person and you discovered him among a gang of robbers whom you were pursuing, and if by some chance he were to drop dead before you could question him, you would, even though the matter were never cleared up, retain the conviction that there was some reason—any reason at all—for his associating and living with criminals, rather than that criminal complicity should have been involved on his part. Now, it has been demonstrated to you by so many arguments which we set forth before and which you yourself approved without the slightest hesitation, that the soul is not contained in place [81] and for this reason has no quantity such as we observe in bodies. Why, then, do you not simply take for granted that there is some cause why certain animals, when cut up, continue to live in all the separate parts, though that cause is not that the soul can be dissected with the body? And if we do not succeed in discovering that cause, is it not better to keep on seeking the true explanation than to accept one that is false?

CHAPTER 32

*Analogy of the word to show that the soul is
inextended and indivisible. The soul and
number. The soul's greatness.*

65. *Aug.* Let me ask you next whether you think that
in the words we use there is a difference between the
sound itself and what the sound signifies?[82]

Ev. I think they are both the same.

Aug. Tell me, then, whence does that sound come when
you speak?

Ev. Who could doubt that it comes from me?

Aug. So, the sun comes from you when you mention
the sun?

Ev. You asked me about the sound, not about the
reality itself.

Aug. Sound, then, and the reality signified by sound
are two different things. But you said they are both the
same.

Ev. Very well, I grant now that what signifies the sun
and the reality which is signified are different.

Aug. Then tell me whether, knowing this language,[83]
you could mention the sun in speaking, if the meaning of
" sun " did not precede the sound.

Ev. No, not at all.

Aug. Well, suppose that before the word leaves your lips,
intent on its proper enunciation, you were to pause in
momentary silence: does not that remain in your thought
which another is about to hear vocally expressed?

Ev. Obviously.

Aug. Now then, even though the sun as such is of tremendous size, can the notion you have of it in your thought before you utter it, possibly be regarded as having length or breadth or any such thing?

Ev. Of course not.

66. *Aug.* Well now, tell me: when the word springs from your mouth, and I, upon hearing it, think of the sun which you were thinking of before you uttered the word and while you uttered it, and which perhaps both of us are thinking of now—does it not seem to you that the word, so to speak, received from you the meaning which it was to convey to me through the instrument of my ears?

Ev. It does seem so.

Aug. Then, since a word consists of sound and meaning, and the sound has to do with the ears and the meaning with the mind, do you not think that in a word, just as in some living being, the sound is the body and the meaning is, as it were, the soul?

Ev. To me the similarity is most striking.

Aug. Now consider whether the sound of a word can be divided into letters, while its soul—that is, its meaning—is indivisible; in fact, it is the meaning which, as you said a moment ago, appears to have neither length nor breadth in our thought.

Ev. I agree completely.

Aug. Now this: when that sound is divided into its several letters, do you think it keeps the same meaning?

Ev. How can the individual letters mean the same as the word which results from their union?

Aug. But when the dismemberment of the sound into its letters results in the loss of its meaning, you do not suppose, do you, that anything else has occurred than the departure of the soul from a torn body? Is it not as if some word's death has taken place?

Ev. Not only do I agree, but so enthusiastically that nothing in this discussion has given me greater delight.

67. *Aug.* If, then, this illustration has made it sufficiently clear to you how the soul can remain undivided when the body is cut up, see now how the several segments of a body can live without the soul having been divided. Now, you have already granted, and correctly, I think, that the meaning, the quasi-soul of the sound in the utterance of a word, cannot possibly be divided in itself, although the sound, its quasi-body, can actually be divided. We saw that in the case of the word "sun," division of the sound left no remnant of meaning in any of its parts. And so, when the body of the sound had been dismembered, we considered those letters simply as dead members, that is, devoid of meaning. Consequently, if we should strike upon some word which after undergoing division can still retain some meaning in its several parts, you would have to own that in this instance dismemberment did not result in complete death, as it were, for you will be confronted with the fact that the members, considered separately, have meaning of a sort and continue to have the breath of life, so to speak.

Ev. I grant that entirely and I ask you to give an example of such a sound.

Aug. Here is one. When I look in the vicinity of the sun—we spoke of that word a while ago—Lucifer meets my eye. When this word is split between the second and third syllable, the first part when pronounced—"*Luci*"[84]—certainly has some meaning; and so there is life in more than half of the word's body. The remaining part also has a soul, for this is what you hear when you are told to bring something. How could you obey if someone were to tell you "*Fer codicem*"[85] if *fer* had no meaning? When "*Luci*" is prefixed to this, the word is "*Lucifer*" and it signifies a star; but when that is taken away, it still has some meaning and thus, as it were, retains life.

68. But since it is space and time in which all things perceived by the senses are contained, or rather, which they contain, then what we perceive by the eyes is divided by space; what we perceive by the ears is divided by time. For instance, just as that worm as a whole occupied more space than any part of it, so a greater span of time is taken up in saying "*Lucifer*" than if one were to say only "*Luci.*" Hence, if this latter "lives" in virtue of its meaning, in the diminution of time brought about by the division of that sound, while the meaning itself was not divided—for not the meaning, but the sound, was extended in time— then we should judge in the same way of the worm with its body cut to pieces: that, although a part, by the simple fact that it is a part, lives in a smaller space, still the soul is not at all divided, nor has it been reduced in a reduced space, notwithstanding that it simultaneously dominated all the members of the whole living body, when they were extended over a larger space. The soul, you see, occupied not space, but the body which it controlled. It is quite like to that meaning which, without being extended in time, yet animated, as it were, and integrated all the letters of the word with their individual pauses and durations.—Let this illustration suffice you for the present, I ask you. Yes, I see, you do like it. At all events, a really thoroughgoing discussion of this matter, one in which justice is done not on the basis of illustrations, which as often

as not prove fallacious, but on the basis of realities themselves—this is something you must not look for at this time.
The fact is, this long discourse must be brought to a close.
Moreover, there are many other matters in which you are
deficient. Your mind must first be trained in them to give
you the insight and perspicacity to understand most clearly
whether what certain very learned men say is actually
true: namely, that the soul can in no way be divided in
itself; but that this is possible by reason of the body.[86]

69. Now let me tell you, if you will—rather, let me assist
you to an appreciation of how great the soul is, not in regard
to extension in space and time, but in regard to its power
and capacity. If you remember, we proposed that distinction some time ago.[87] As to the number of souls, however,
—seeing that you thought this relevant to the problem in
hand—I do not know what answer to give you.[88] I would
be more inclined to say that the question should not be
brought up at all or at least that you should postpone it for
the time being rather than that I should say that number
and multitude have no connection with quantity, or that
I am presently equal to the task of solving such an involved
problem for you. For if I should tell you that there is only
one soul, you will be at sea because of the fact that in one
it is happy, in another unhappy; and one and the same
thing cannot be both happy and unhappy at the same time.
If I should say that it is one and many at the same time,
you will smile; and I would not find it easy to make you
suppress your smile. But if I say simply that it is many,
I shall have to laugh at myself, and it will be harder for
me to suffer my own disapprobation than yours. Listen,
then, to what I promise you will be worth hearing—though
it may tax the energies of both of us or either of us to the

extent that you may want to decide not to go to this trouble.

Ev. I yield to you completely, and I am eager that you give me an explanation, one which I can follow, of what greatness there is in the soul.

CHAPTER 33

The seven levels of the soul's greatness. Its significance in the body, its significance to itself, its significance before God.

The First Level of the Soul [89]

70. *Aug.* Oh, would that the two of us could put our questions on this topic to a man of great learning—not only that, but one of great eloquence, too; yes, to one wise and perfect in every respect! What efforts he would make to explain, by statement and proof, what the soul means to the body, what it means to itself, what it means before God, to whom it is very near, provided it is perfectly undefiled, and in whom it finds its supreme and complete perfection! But now, since I have no one else to do this for me, I venture this—not to fail you. This, at all events, will be my reward, that while I endeavor to explain to you, untutored as I am, what powers the soul has, I may confidently experience what powers I myself have. But from the start let me rid you of any far-flung and boundless expectations you may have. Do not think that I shall speak of every soul, but only of the human soul, which should be our only concern, if we have concern for ourselves.

In the first place, then, as anyone can easily observe, the soul by its presence gives life to this earth- and death-

bound body.[90]   It makes of it a unified organism and maintains it as such, keeping it from disintegrating and wasting
away.   It provides for a proper, balanced distribution of
nourishment to the body's members.   It preserves the
body's harmony and proportion, not only in beauty, but
also in growth and reproduction.   Obviously, however,
these are faculties which man has in common with the
plant world; for we say of plants too, that they live, we see
and acknowledge that each of them is preserved to its own
generic being, is nourished, grows, and reproduces itself.

The Second Level of the Soul

71. So, go up another level and see what power the soul
has in the senses, which offer a plainer and clearer understanding of what life is.   Of course, we should pay no attention to a certain kind of utterly crude perversion which
is more wooden than the very trees it takes under its wing,
and which believes that the vine suffers pain when a grape
is plucked and that such things not only feel it when they
are cut, but even that they see and hear.   Of this impious
error [91] this is not the place to speak.   Now, then, following
the scheme I proposed, look at what power the soul has in
the senses and in the entire nobility of the higher living
organism, by reason of which we cannot possibly belong in
the same category with things which are held down by
roots.

The soul directs itself to the sense of touch and through
it feels and distinguishes hot and cold, rough and smooth,
hard and soft, light and heavy.   Then again, it distinguishes countless varieties of savors, odors, sounds, and
shapes, by tasting, smelling, hearing, and seeing.   And in
all these the soul seeks and selects whatever suits the nature

of its own body; it rejects and shuns what is unsuited. At certain intervals it withdraws itself from the senses, and, by giving them time off, so to say, gives their activities an opportunity to recuperate their strength, the while it lumps together in manifold combinations, and mulls over, the images of realities it has taken in through the senses; and all this constitutes sleep and dreams.

Frequently, too, it takes advantage of the mobility present to delight in making gestures and unusual motions, and without effort it sets the parts of the body in harmony. For sexual union it does what it can, and by companionship and love it strives to forge two natures into one. It cooperates not merely to beget offspring, but also to foster it, to protect and nourish it. It attaches itself by habit to things among which the body acts and by which it sustains the body, and from these, as if they were of its own constitution, it is reluctant to be separated; and this force of habit which is not terminated even by separation from the realities themselves and by the passing of time, is called memory. But again, no one denies that the soul can produce all these effects even in brute animals.

The Third Level of the Soul

72. Advance, then, to the third level, which belongs to man exclusively. Think of memory, not of things that have become habituated by repeated acts, but of the countless things that have been attained and retained by observation and illustration [92]—all the arts of craftsmen, the tilling of the soil, the building of cities, the thousand-and-one marvels of various buildings and undertakings, the invention of so many symbols in letters, in words, in gesture, in sound of various kinds, in paintings and statues; the lan-

guages of so many peoples, their many institutions, some new and some revived; the great number of books and records of every sort for the preservation of memory and the great concern shown for posterity; the gradations of duties, prerogatives, honors, and dignities, in family life and in public life—whether civilian or military—in profane and sacred institutions; the power of reason and thought, the floods of eloquence, the varieties of poetry, the thousand forms of mimicries for the purpose of entertainment and jest, the art of music, the accuracy of surveying, the science of arithmetic, the interpretation of the past and future from the present. These things bear the mark of greatness [93] and they are characteristically human. But here we still have a capacity shared by both the learned and the unlearned, by both the good and the wicked.

The Fourth Level of the Soul

73. Take hold now and swing yourself onto the fourth level, which goodness and all true worth call their home. Here it is that the soul ventures to take precedence not only over its own body, acting some part in the universe, but even over the whole body of the universe itself. The goods of the world it does not account its own, and comparing them with its own power and beauty, it keeps aloof from them and despises them. Hence, the more the soul turns to itself for its own pleasure, the more does it withdraw from sordid things and cleanse itself and make itself immaculately clean through and through. It steels itself against every effort to lure it away from its purpose and resolve. It shows high consideration for human society and desires nothing to happen to another which it does not wish to happen to itself. [94] It submits to the authority and the

bidding of wise men and is convinced that through them God speaks to itself. Yet, this performance of the soul, noble as it is, still requires strenuous effort and the annoyances and allurements of this world engage it in a mighty struggle, bitterly contested. In this work of purification there is an underlying fear of death, sometimes not strong, but sometimes all-pervading. It is scarcely present when one has a very vigorous faith that—and to see the truth of this is granted only to the purified soul—all things are so governed by the great providence and justice of God that death cannot come as an evil to anyone, even though someone may inflict it with evil intentions. But on this level there is a great fear of death, when, on the one hand, confidence in God's justice is so much the weaker the more anxiously one seeks for it; and when, on the other hand, corresponding to the lack of tranquillity in the presence of fear, there is a greater lack of understanding; for tranquillity is absolutely necessary for the study of matters shrouded in mystery.

Further, as the soul in the course of its progress realizes more and more, what great difference there is between its state of purity and its state of defilement, the greater is its apprehension that when it has sloughed off this body, God may find it less endurable than it finds itself when defiled. There is, moreover, nothing more difficult than to fear death and to refrain from the allurements of this world in a degree commensurate with the jeopardies involved. Yet, so great is the soul that it can do even this, by the help, of course, of the goodness [95] of the supreme and true God— that goodness which sustains and rules the universe, that goodness by which it has been brought about not only that all things exist, but that they exist in such a way that they cannot be any better than they are. [96] It is to this divine goodness that the soul most dutifully and confidently commits itself for help and success in the difficult task of self-purification.

The Fifth Level of the Soul

74. When this has been accomplished, that is, when the soul will be free from all corruption and purified of all its stains, then at last it possesses itself in utter joy and has no fears whatever for itself nor any anxiety for any reason. This, then, is the fifth level. For it is one thing to achieve purity, another to be in possession of it; and the activity by which the soul restores its sullied state to purity and that by which it does not suffer itself to be defiled again are two entirely different things. On this level it conceives in every way how great it is in every respect; and when it has understood that, then with unbounded and wondrous confidence it advances toward God, that is, to the immediate contemplation of truth; and it attains that supreme and transcendent reward for which it has worked so hard.

The Sixth Level of the Soul

75. Now, this activity, namely, the ardent desire to understand truth and perfection, is the soul's highest vision: it possesses none more perfect, none more noble, none more proper. This, therefore, will be the sixth level of activity. For it is one thing to clear the eye of the soul so that it will not look without purpose and without reason and see what is wrong; it is something else to protect and strengthen the health of the eye; and it is something else again, to direct your gaze calmly and squarely to what is to be seen. Those who wish to do this before they are cleansed and healed recoil so in the presence of that light

of truth [97] that they may think there is in it not only no goodness, but even great evil; indeed, they may decide it does not deserve the name of truth, and with an amount of zest and enthusiasm that is to be pitied, they curse the remedy offered and run back into the darkness engulfing them and which alone their diseased condition suffers them to face. Hence, the divinely inspired prophet says most appositely: *Create a clean heart in me, O God, and renew a right spirit within my bowels.* [98] The spirit is "right," I believe, if it sees to it that the soul cannot lose its way and go astray in its quest for truth. This spirit is not really "renewed" in anyone unless his heart is first made clean, that is to say, unless he first controls his thoughts and drains off from them all the dregs of attachment to corruptible things. [99]

The Seventh Level of the Soul

76. Now at last we are in the very vision and contemplation of truth, which is the seventh and last level of the soul; and here we no longer have a level but in reality a home at which one arrives via those levels. What shall I say are the delights, what the enjoyment, of the supreme and true Goodness, what the everlasting peace it breathes upon us? [100] Great and peerless souls—and we believe that they have actually seen and are still seeing these things—have told us this so far as they deemed it should be spoken of. [101] This would I tell you now: if we hold most faithfully to the course which God enjoins on us and which we have undertaken to follow, we shall come [102] by God's power and wisdom to that supreme Cause or that supreme Author or supreme Principle of all things, [103] or whatever other more appropriate appellative there may be for so great a

reality. And when we understand that, we shall see truly
how *all things under the sun are the vanity of the vain.*[104]
For "vanity" is deceit; and "the vain" are to be understood
as persons who are deceived, or persons who deceive, or
both. Further, one may discern how great a difference
there is between these and the things that truly exist;[105]
and yet, since all the other things have also been created and
have God as their Maker, they are wonderful and beautiful
when considered by themselves, although in comparison
with the things that truly exist, they are as nothing. Then
shall we acknowledge how true are the things we have
been commanded to believe, and how excellently we have
been nurtured in perfect health by Mother Church,[106] and
how nourishing is that milk which the Apostle Paul de-
clared he gave as drink to children.[107] To take such food
when one is fed by a mother is most proper; to do so when
one is already grown would be shameful; to refuse it when
needed would be regrettable; to find fault with it at any
time or to dislike it would be wicked and impious; but to
discuss it and communicate it in kindness betokens a wealth
of goodness and charity.

We shall also see such great changes and transformations
in this physical universe in observance of divine laws, that
we hold even the resurrection of the body, which some
believe with too many reservations and some do not believe at all, to be so certain that the setting of the sun is no
greater certainty to us.[108] Then, indeed, shall we contemn
those who ridicule the assumption of human nature by the
almighty, eternal, immutable Son of God as a warranty and
as first fruits of our salvation, and His birth from a Virgin,
and the other marvels of that historic account.[109] We shall
contemn them for acting like boys who, when they see an

artist painting with other pictures set up before him so that he can follow them closely, cannot believe it possible to draw a man unless the painter looks at another picture.

Furthermore, in the contemplation of truth, no matter what degree of contemplation you reach, the delight is so great, there is such purity, such innocence, a conviction in all things that is so absolute, that one could think he really knew nothing when aforetime he fancied he had knowledge.[110] And that the soul may not be impeded from giving full allegiance to the fullness of truth, death—meaning complete escape and acquittal from this body—which previously was feared, is now desired as the greatest boon.

CHAPTER 34

God alone surpasses the soul.

77. You have heard how great is the power and capacity of the soul. To recapitulate briefly: just as we must acknowledge that the human soul is not what God is, so we must confidently hold that among all the things He has created there is nothing closer to God.[111] Therefore, it has been the divinely inspired and categorical teaching of the Catholic Church that no creature is to be adored by the soul (I prefer to use the very words by which these things were taught me),[112] but that He alone is to be adored who is the Creator of all things that are, from whom all things come, by whom all things are made, in whom all things exist;[113] that is, the unchanging Source, unchanging Wisdom, unchanging Love, one God, true and perfect, who never was not, never will not be, never was other, never will be other than He is. Nothing is more hidden than He,

nothing more present. To find where He is is difficult; but to find where He is not is more difficult still.[114] Not all can be with Him, and no one can be without Him. And if there is any greater mystery that we human beings could mention of Him and if we could do more in a way quite proper and due—let such mention be made.

It is this God alone, then, who is to be adored by the soul, without reservation and without confusion. Clearly, whatever the soul adores as God, it necessarily considers more excellent than itself; and neither the earth, nor the seas, nor the stars, nor the moon, nor the sun, nor anything at all that can be touched or seen with our eyes, nor even heaven itself, invisible to us, are to be considered superior to the nature of the soul. In fact, reason proves conclusively that all these things are far inferior to a single soul, if lovers of the truth will but muster the courage to follow its leadership with great constancy and devotion over paths that prove rugged for being little traveled.

78. But if there is anything further in the universe besides objects which are known by the senses and which, in short, occupy space—and we have said that the human soul is superior to all such things—if, I say, there are other creatures made by God, some are less excellent than the soul, some are equal to it: the soul of a brute animal, for instance, is less excellent, that of an angel, equal;[115] but better than the soul, there is nothing. And if at any time any of these is better, that is the result of the soul's sin, not of its nature. Still, sin does not make the human soul so inferior that the soul of a brute animal is to be preferred to it or even compared with it. Hence, God alone is to be adored by the soul, since He alone is its Maker. But man, no matter who he may be, and be he ever so wise and

perfect, or any soul at all endowed with reason and bliss
supreme, is at most to be loved and imitated; and deference
is to be shown it in keeping with its merit and proper rank.
For *the Lord thy God shalt thou adore, and Him only shalt
thou serve.*[116]

Let us realize, however, that as far as is possible and
commanded, we must give assistance to souls of our own kind
struggling in error, and realize, too, that when this is done
properly, God is acting through us. And let us not arrogate
anything to ourselves as our own, deceived by a desire of
empty glory, for by this one evil we are plunged from the
heights to the depths. And let us hate, not those who are
crushed by vices, but the vices themselves; not sinners, but
just sins. We should indeed be willing to help everyone,
even those who have harmed us or wish to harm us or wish
at least that harm befall us. This is true religion, this is
perfect religion, this alone is religion; and it is through this
instrument that reinstatement with God has to do with the
greatness of soul which we are examining and which makes
it worthy of freedom. For He frees from all things whom
it is most useful for all to serve, and to be content in whose
service is perfect freedom—the only freedom.

But I see that I have almost overstepped the limits of my
plan and, without stopping for questions, spent all this time
talking about a great many things. I do not regret it, however. For although these truths are scattered through all
the many writings of the Church, and though we may
therefore seem to have synopsized them to excellent advantage, still, they cannot be clearly understood unless one
takes a determined stand on the fourth of those seven levels,
and, preserving piety[117] and acquiring the fitness and
strength to perceive them, examines all these truths one by
one, giving them his greatest care and his best judgment.

For each one of these levels has a distinct excellence of its own; and these levels we would do better to call *acts.*

CHAPTER 35

Various names for the levels of the soul.

79. In fact, our inquiry concerns itself with the power of the soul, and conceivably the soul can put all these things into *action* simultaneously; though it may appear to the soul itself that it is actually doing only what it does with difficulty, or, at least, with fear. For, obviously, it performs such an action with greater care than the rest. Now, then, to serve the purpose of instruction, let us, following the ascending order, call the first act vitalization; the second, sensation; the third, art; the fourth, virtue; the fifth, tranquillity; the sixth, initiation; the seventh, contemplation.[118] They can also be designated in this way: (acts) "concerning the body"; "through the body"; "about the body"; "toward itself"; "in itself"; "toward God"; "in God."[119] The following, too, is possible: (acts performed) "excellently concerning another thing"; "excellently through another thing"; "excellently about another thing"; "excellently in the presence of an excellent thing"; "excellently in an excellent thing"; "excellently in the presence of Excellence"; "excellently in Excellence."[120]

You may ask questions about any of these afterward, if further explanation seems to be called for. Here I wanted to employ these several designations that you might not become confused and, therefore, reject the one or the other, seeing that one uses a terminology or even division different from the other. As a matter of fact, the same realities can be correctly and accurately labeled and divided in countless ways;

in the presence of so much choice each one simply uses the one he considers most suitable.

CHAPTER 36

Order in the universe. What true religion is. The remaining questions about the soul.

80. The supreme and true God, then, by the inviolable and changeless law by which He rules everything He has created, makes the body subject to the soul, the soul subject to Himself, and thus all things subject to Himself. There is no act at all in which He leaves the soul to itself either to punish or reward it. For He has judged it to be the height of excellence that everything that exists be precisely as it is; that there be such order in a graded arrangement of nature that when we consider the whole universe no flaw of any kind should offend our sensibilities;[121] and that every punishment and every reward of the soul should always make some contribution measuring up to the beauty and order proper to all things. The soul, it is true, has received free will, and those who try to discredit that by baseless arguments are so blind that they do not even realize that it is by their own free will that they are uttering such inanities and impieties. Yet, the gift of free will is such that no matter what the soul undertakes with it, it does not disturb any part of the divine order and law. It is a gift coming from the Lord of all creation, who is wise and whose power cannot be made to yield.

But to see these things as they should be seen is given to only a few, and no one is rendered fit for this except by true religion. And true religion is that by which the soul binds itself again to the one and only God and reconciles itself to Him from whom it had torn itself away, as it were, by sin.

Accordingly, in that third act, religion grips the soul and begins to be its guide. In the fourth, it purifies it. In the fifth, it reforms it. In the sixth, it initiates it. In the seventh, it nurtures it. And in one case this transpires quite quickly, in another, somewhat slowly, according to one's capacity of love and merits. But, no matter how those in whom He works out His designs may wish to respond, God always attains His purpose with perfect justice, with absolute propriety, and with the greatest beauty.[122]

And again, the question of what advantages the consecration even of infant children may have, is a very difficult one; we must, however, believe that it has some advantage. Reason will solve this when the proper time for studying the problem comes. True, I have been proposing a host of other problems for you to take up in due course, rather than to have you learn them by instruction. This procedure will prove especially profitable, if you will make your inquiries with piety as your guide.

81. Considering all this, who has cause to complain that the soul was given to the body to control and direct it, since a system of order in the universe better than this which shows so much divine greatness, is an impossibility? Or who would think of inquiring how the soul is affected in this corruptible and frail body,[123] seeing that it has justly been thrust with it into death as a result of sin,[124] and that virtue enables it to raise itself up even in this life? Or what it will be like after this life of the body, knowing that the penalty of death must surely remain while sin remains, but that virtue's and piety's reward is God Himself, that is, Truth itself?

Now, then, if you will, let us finally conclude this long discussion and devote our efforts to fulfilling the laws of God with all religious care.[125] There simply is no other escape from the great evils involved. But if anything I have said is not as clear as you would like it, do make a mental note of it and bring it up some other time when opportunity offers. And He who is over us, the Teacher of all, will not fail us when our study has Him for its object.

Ev. As for me, I was so stimulated by this talk of yours, that I thought it wrong to interrupt it. And if you think this the proper place to conclude the discussion, and if this summary treatment of those three remaining questions is what you had in mind to give now, I shall abide by your decision. At the same time, I shall make it my constant concern to strike the opportune time—since you are so preoccupied—and also to make myself more fit for the investigation of these matters which are so important.

THE TEACHER

Augustine, *Retractationes* 1. 12: During the same period of time [as that in which *De Gen. cont. Manichaeos* and *De musica* were written] I wrote a work entitled *The Teacher*. In it the discussion centres around the problem and its solution: that there is no teacher other than God who teaches man knowledge, which is also in accord with what is written in the Gospel—*One is your teacher, Christ.* This book begins as follows: "What do you think we purpose to do when we speak?"

INTRODUCTION

A short and relatively minor work, the *De magistro* of St. Augustine might seem almost lost in the bulk of apologetic, theological, pastoral, and polemic treatises that constitute his contribution to Christian thought and literature. Far from being passed over unnoticed, however, it became one of the most influential of his earlier writings. In the most fertile theological period of the Middle Ages it was made the subject of commentary and discussion,[1] while even in our own day it has been studied rather extensively as a suggestive source of truth in philosophy, in pedagogy, and in the discussion of problems regarding the meaning and value of language.[2]

Augustine wrote this book at Tagaste, Africa, in the year 389, two years after his baptism and shortly after his return from Italy.[3] Cast in the form of a dialogue, it is a report of an actual conversation with his son Adeodatus, who, though only sixteen years of age, manifested talent and precocity similar to his father's. The Saint testifies that the thoughts ascribed to the boy were actually expressed by him:

> Thou hadst fashioned him well. When he was only fifteen years of age, he already excelled many grave and learned men in talent. . . . There is a book of ours, entitled *The Teacher;* in it he converses with me. Thou knowest that all the thoughts expressed in the person of the one discussing with me are his own, although he was only sixteen years of age. . . . The talent he showed filled me with awe.[4]

It is not certain whether Adeodatus died in that same year—

389—or the year following. If the former date is correct, it may well be that Augustine intended the present dialogue as a monument to his son.[5]

Like most conversations, *The Teacher* is spontaneous in expression and irregular in construction. Interruptions, corrections, repetitions abound. Indeed, the Saint, intent on training and sharpening his son, occasionally seems to mislead him deliberately. As in most of Augustine's writings, profound and challenging thoughts, couched in engaging rhetoric, blend with arguments that sometimes become specious and tenuous and with explanations frequently too repetitious to escape the charge of being somewhat boring.

Despite its apparent looseness of structure, the book is nevertheless not a careless or amateurish product. A clear pattern can be discerned, which it might be well to set out in summary form:

A) Introduction:

    a) Purpose of speech: to teach or remind (1. 1-2)

    b) Words are signs (2. 3-4)

B) First proposition, stated provisionally: Nothing can be made known without a sign, except actions which one is not performing when a question is asked (3. 5-6)

C) Parenthetical Clarifications:

    a) Signs signify:

        1) other signs, either reciprocally or not (4. 7-6. 18)

        2) realities that are not themselves signs (4. 7 f.)

    b) The need of reflecting on the thing signified, not on the word (8. 21-24)

    c) Realities more important than signs (9. 25-28)

D) First Proposition, stated definitely: No teaching, i.e., communicating one's judgments, without signs (10. 29 f.). However, the essences of certain natural phenomena and of human actions may be known without intentional signs (words) in proportion to spectator's intelligence (10. 32)

E) Second Proposition: Even words are not the reason for our attaining truth—i.e., *not even with words do we teach.* (10. 33-35; 12. 39-40; 13. 45)

F) Conclusion: Men cannot teach one another. *God is the only teacher of men.* (11. 38; 14. 45 f.)

G) Corollary: Function of words: to admonish or prompt us to seek the truth within us (11. 36; 14. 46)

The thesis of the work, then, is that it is only God who is the ultimate cause and reason for the acquisition of truth by man when he learns. The extensive analysis of signs and of their import, which constitutes the bulk of the book, is intended by the author to emphasize the necessity of using signs, and, at the same time, their inadequacy, at least so far as the truth and certainty of our knowledge are concerned. As words have no power to make us know physical realities unless we have previously had some experience of those objects through the senses, so, Augustine argues, words cannot make us "see" intelligible realities within the mind. That can be brought about only by the power and wisdom of God.[6] Thus is manifested the truth of our Lord's words, *One is your teacher, Christ.*[7] Again, as physical light is necessary that we may perceive corporeal realities, so the divine wisdom must 'illumine' the human mind,[8] verifying St. John's description of Christ as *the true light that enlightens every man that cometh into the world.*[9]

This celebrated doctrine of the "Interior Teacher," also called "internal light,"[10] had been suggested by Augustine before,[11] and was to thread through his more mature works,[12] although its most explicit presentation is in the *De magistro*.

The Saint himself makes clear that it was in the writings of the "Platonic philosophers" that he found suggestions of the intimate contact of God with the human soul, and of the "illumination" of the intellect by God:

> And I read there . . . that the soul of man, though it gives testimony of the light, is nevertheless not itself the light; but the Word of God, God Himself, is the true light that enlightens every man coming into the world.[13]

Plato, whom Augustine considered the most gifted and most reliable of the ancient philosophers,[14] had compared the principle of intelligence with the light of the sun, and intellectual knowledge with the body's vision:

> You are aware that when the eyes are directed toward the objects on which the light of day is no longer shining . . . they see dimly and are almost blind, lacking clearness of vision. . . . But when they look at objects on which the sun is shining, they see clearly. . . . Then consider the mind in the same way: when it contemplates that which is illumined by truth and being, it perceives and understands it clearly; but when it turns toward that which is shadowy—that which begins and ceases to be—it has only opinion, it begins to blink, changes its opinions constantly, and seems to lack understanding. . . . Now, that which imparts truth to the objects known, and the power of understanding to the knower, call it the Idea of the Good and conceive it as the cause of knowledge and of truth so far as it is known. . . .[15]

This "Idea" in Plato's explanation not only renders reality intelligible, but also is the reason for all reality in things.

Plotinus, considered by Augustine to be a second Plato,[16] amplified this notion. He taught that the Supreme Being —he calls it *The One*—transcends all changeable things of our experience and is an absolute and incomprehensible being.[17] This God is absolutely simple, admitting of no composition of essence and attributes,[18] and no divisibility of itself into inferior substances.[19] To account for the multiplicity of finite things, Plotinus postulates that *The One* diffuses itself unconsciously by emanation.[20] Although he conceives the emanation as in some way necessary, he nevertheless does not admit a pantheistic identification of the emanations with the principle, nor any impairment in the principle; strictly speaking, neither necessity nor freedom can be attributed to the transcendental *One*. The first emanation is *The Mind* (Νοῦς), which is the image of the Supreme Being; it is an "illumination," both in the sense that it proceeds from *The One* like rays from the sun, and in the sense that it is essentially cognoscitive both of itself and of *The One*.[21] In *The Mind* are all the "ideas" or archetypes of lower things;[22] from it directly emanates a "world soul" which, being an abode of forces, contains in itself, and gives rise to, all principles of activity, including the human soul. Some of these forces deteriorate and become matter. This latter is the least perfect manifestation of the Absolute and one which has for its internal principle a second and derivative world soul, the φύσις.[23] In man, who is partly spiritual and partly material, the prime duty is to overcome the material which tends to separate him from *The One*. Again, by means of knowledge which is attained by the illumination of the Νοῦς, the soul purifies itself and prepares itself for eternal and ecstatic union with the Supreme Being.[24]

Objectionable though some features of this doctrine must be to a Christian—notably, emanation rather than creation as an explanation of the origin of contingent being—it nevertheless offered some fertile suggestions which Augustine could borrow and apply in an analogical way to Christian doctrine. For *The One* of Plotinus he substitutes God the Father, and for *The Mind*, the Divine Word, the Second Person of the Blessed Trinity.[25] Whereas Plotinus attributes intelligence to man because his soul comes from the "world soul," Augustine maintains that man possesses eternal truths because he is created by, and therefore reflects the perfections of, the Divine Intelligence. Like Plotinus, Augustine holds that the clarity of intellectual perception depends largely on moral rectitude.[26]

But Augustine's principal inspiration for his doctrine of divine "illumination" comes from the Scriptures. In the writings of St. Matthew, St. John, and St. Paul he found the seeds of his teaching that the Son of God is the cause and pattern of all created truth, and the light of all intellects, which, in their actual understanding, depend on God and are illuminated by Him.[27] He considers Christ as a "Light," and that in a proper sense, not in the metaphorical one according to which He is called "a rock."[28] This is not to deny that the notion of "illumination" is a metaphor, but only to insist that the name "Light" is attributed primarily and essentially to God and extended by application to created things, such as the sun, because of their participation in the perfections of God.[29]

Since Augustine did not describe clearly and precisely just how this "illumination" operates, there have been various conflicting interpretations. Malebranche claimed that he derived from Augustine his doctrine that the soul attains its concepts by seeing the divine ideas, or the attributes of God, so far as they are imitable by creatures.[30] Some medieval theologians, and with them, E. Portalié, hold that Augustine teaches a production of concepts directly by God, so that He is to be understood as imprinting

on our intellects a representation of reality, thus fulfilling
directly the function that Aristotelians ascribe to the agent-
intellect.[31]   E. Gilson thinks that the doctrine of the "Interior Teacher" or "internal light" is proposed as an explanation not of the mode of obtaining concepts, but of
the ultimate source and guarantee of the truth of self-
evident judgments.[32] Several Thomists maintain that God,
in Augustine's explanation, "illumines" the intellect very
indirectly, by creating in man a power or "internal light"
that is the equivalent of the abstractive intellectual faculty,
the agent-intellect, of Aristotle and St. Thomas.[33]   The fact
is that some of Augustine's expressions may be interpreted as
indicating a created, natural, intellectual light. Refuting the
Platonic doctrine that the ability to answer questions on matters which one has never studied is due to the acquisition of
knowledge in a previous existence, he states:

> We ought rather to believe that the nature of the intellectual
> mind is so constituted that it sees those things which by the dis-
> position of the Creator are connected with intelligible realities in
> the natural order, in a sort of incorporeal light of a unique kind
> (*quadam luce sui generis incorporea*), just as the eye of the body
> sees the objects within its range in this physical light, a light to
> which it was created susceptible and properly suited.[34]

St. Thomas understands that light as being "of the *same*
kind*" as the intellect, and therefore natural and created:
the agent-intellect.

Because of the variety of ways in which Augustine speaks
of it in different works, the nature of the "internal light"
will probably never be settled to the satisfaction of all, although certain opinions, such as that of Malebranche, can
be definitely excluded.[35]   It seems, however, that in so far as
the *De magistro* alone is concerned, "illumination" is offered directly and primarily as an explanation of the cause

and guarantee of the truth of our judgments. In this book
" to learn " means " to come to an absolutely true and certain
knowledge." If a hearer judges the testimony of a speaker
to be false, or if he does not know the truth after the other has
spoken, he is considered by Augustine not to have *learned*.[36]
His purpose is to bring out that all truth has its foundation
in God, and that all knowledge of truth, to explain which
the pagan philosophers had had recourse to mythical and
perverse doctrines of the pre-existence of human souls, or
of demi-gods controlling intelligence, owes its existence and
reliability to the triune God of revelation, the eternal Truth.

The references in the earlier parts of the treatise to
derivation of ideas of things from the mere sight of things
and from the sound of words, are only preliminaries leading
up to the point that words do not give absolute certainty.
Besides, the Saint does not make a clear-cut distinction here
between the bare act of knowing the essence of things and
the act of judgment whereby the intellect predicates that
essence of the concrete thing seen. When he finally intro-
duces the doctrine of the "teacher" and of the "light," it is
in relation to the problem of truth and certainty.

There is a Platonic influence, but not a perfect resemblance to Plato's and Plotinus's doctrines, in the central
teaching of the De magistro; so, too, there is a dependence,
along with an essential change, in the view that what is
called "teaching" is really only "reminding."

It is a fact that by deft questioning one can direct even
unlearned persons to give correct conclusions on matters
of mathematics or other sciences, regarding which they have
never thought before. Furthermore, even abstruse and profound truths that we find expressed in a book often appear
so obvious, on consideration, that we feel we have known

them before. These facts so impressed Socrates that he maintained that the truth resides internally within the mind, so that no one "teaches" or "gives" truth; and the aim of his method of instruction, the dialogue, was to draw out that truth, to "deliver" it. He considered himself a "spiritual midwife," whose task it was to help others to express their mental conceptions and then to examine and criticize them, in order to determine whether they were worth the labor of delivery.[37] The method and the defense of it are well presented by Plato. But the latter attempted to explain this phenomenon by maintaining that the soul began its present state of existence with the body, with a store of "innate" ideas, acquired in a previous existence.[38] Hence, what is called "learning" is literally only remembering.

Whether Augustine ever admitted the pre-existence of the human soul is not entirely clear;[39] it is at least certain that he later reprobated it.[40] The doctrine of the "Interior Teacher" and the "internal light" also seems to render such a view unnecessary. Nevertheless, in the De magistro and even in his later works he consistently speaks of teaching as "reminding," and of what appears to be learning, as "remembering." For beyond the sense faculties Augustine conceives of a storehouse of knowledge, a sort of "belly of the mind,"[41] in which are conserved the images of things perceived by the senses, which we afterwards properly recall. But since by contemplation and internal reflection we can know spiritual realities, the soul itself, and unchangeable principles whereby we judge statements as true or false, the Saint considers the knowledge of these also as being in the same storehouse, which he calls the "memory."[42] Since the soul is not continually aware of all this knowledge explicitly, it can, under the influence of God's "illumination," bring it to light from that "memory" in which it was latent. Thus it is said to recall or remember it. When one had been conscious of that knowledge before and afterwards forgot it, we all speak of the revival as "remembrance"; if the notions and principles had never been previously discerned clearly, the act of penetrating, understanding, and applying them is what it is generally called "learning," but Augustine insists that it is also "a sort of remembering." [43] He expressly defends the notion of a "memory of the present." [44] Thus it is that he can use the terminology of Plato, without sharing the complete doctrine of Plato. He merely uses as synonyms the words "learn," "think," "recall," because they all designate acquiring knowledge from the Interior Teacher. His "memory," then, may be said to be at least partially equivalent to what would now be called the "unconscious" or the "subconscious." [45]

Consistently with the thinkers he admired and with his own position as expressed elsewhere,[46] Augustine's philosophizing in the De magistro is directed toward the attainment of happiness, which as a Christian he knew could be found only in God.

He will teach us, to know and love whom is happiness of life, and this is what all proclaim they are seeking, though there are but few who may rejoice in having really found it (14. 46).

The ultimate purpose of this treatise is, therefore, practical and ascetical, and was achieved in the case of Adeodatus who acknowledges (ibid): "I shall now, with His (Christ's) help, love Him the more ardently, the more I progress in learning. . . ." This, characteristically, is what St. Augustine seeks to achieve in all the readers of his works. For him knowledge must lead to love.

✶   ✶   ✶

The present translation was made from the text published by the Benedictine Monks of St. Maur as reprinted by J. P. Migne, *Patrologia Latina* 32 (Paris 1845) 1193-1220.

The following modern translations may also be noted:

Bassi, D., *Sant' Aurelio Agostino, Il maestro, La vera religione* (Corona Patrum Salesiana, Series latina 11, Turin 1941), with the Benedictine text, 1-125.

Guzzo, A., *Aurelio Agostino: Il maestro* (La nostra scuola 33, Florence 1927).

Leckie, G., *Concerning the Teacher and On the Immortality of the Soul by St. Aurelius Augustine* (New York 1938) 1-56.

Thonnard, F. J., *De magistro, De libero arbitrio* (Bibliothèque augustinienne, Paris 1941), with the Benedictine text, 7-121.

Tourscher, F., *The Philosophy of Teaching, a Translation of St. Augustine's De Magistro* (Villanova 1924). Tourscher also published a Latin text for schools—Villanova 1924.

LIST OF CHAPTERS

CHAPTER 1

The purpose of speech.

Augustine. What do you think we purpose to do when we speak?

Adeodatus. As far as occurs to me at this moment, we intend either to teach or to learn.

Aug. One of these is clear to me, and I agree with you: obviously, when we speak we do wish to teach. But as to learning—how does that enter in?

Ad. Well, how do you think, but by asking questions?

Aug. Even in that case, as I understand it, we intend to do nothing else than to teach. For, I ask you, do you put questions for any other reason than to teach the one you interrogate, what it is you wish to know?

Ad. You are right.

Aug. So you see that our purpose in speaking is solely to teach.[1]

Ad. No, that is not clear to me. For if speaking is nothing more than uttering words, I notice we do that when we sing. And since we often sing when we are alone, with no one present to learn, I do not think we wish to teach anything.

Aug. Yes, but I think there is a kind of teaching which functions by reminding—an important kind, indeed, as the theme of our discussion will bring out.[2] But if you do not think that we learn when we remember and that one does not teach when he reminds, I make no objection; and let me agree, for the present, to two reasons for speaking:

either to teach, or to remind others or ourselves; and the latter is what we do even when we sing, do you not think so?

Ad. Not entirely. For it is very seldom that I sing to remind myself; I do so only for the pleasure I get out of it.

Aug. I see your point. But you are, of course, aware that what pleases you in song is a certain rhythm of sound. Since this can be added to words or taken from them, is not speaking one thing, and singing another? Song, as you know, is produced by flute and harp; again, the birds sing; and sometimes we, too, hum musical sounds without words, which can be called song, but not speech. Is there anything here you would take exception to?

Ad. No, nothing.

2. *Aug.* You hold, then, that speech originated for the sole reason of teaching or reminding?

Ad. So I would hold, did it not strike me that when we pray, we certainly do speak; and—there is the rub—it is not right to think that God should be taught by us or that we should remind Him of anything.

Aug. You are unaware, I take it, that the only reason for our being commanded to pray *in closed inner rooms*[3]—by which term is meant the sanctum of the mind—is that God does not need to be reminded or taught by our speech in order to grant us what we desire. One who speaks gives an external sign of what he wants by articulated sound. But God should be sought and prayed to precisely in the silent depths of the rational soul, which is called "the inner man"; for here is where He wished His temples to be. Have you not read in the Apostle: *Know you not that you are the temple of God and that the Spirit of God dwelleth in you?* [4] and, *Christ dwells in the inner man?* [5] And have you not noticed this in the Prophet: *Speak in your hearts and lament on your couches; offer the sacrifice of justice, and hope in the Lord?* [6] Where do you think the "sacrifice of justice" is offered but in the "temples" of the mind and on the "couches" of the heart? And the place for sacrifice is also the place for prayer. Wherefore, there is no need of speech—that is, of vocalized words—when we pray, except perhaps to manifest the mind, as the priests do, not that God may hear, but that men may hear and, by being reminded, may with one accord dedicate themselves to God. Or do you regard this differently?

Ad. I am in complete agreement.

Aug. It does not strike you, then, that when the supreme Teacher taught His disciples to pray, He taught them certain things to say? Apparently, what He did was only to teach us how we ought to speak when we pray. [7]

Ad. That causes me no trouble at all. For He did not teach them words, but realities by means of words. Thus they were to remind themselves to whom to pray and what to pray for when they offered their prayers in the sanctum of the mind, as you have said. [8]

Aug. A sound interpretation! I believe you notice at the same time that even when a person merely strains his mind toward something, although we utter no sound, yet because we ponder the words themselves, we do speak within our own minds. So, too, speech serves us only to remind, since the memory in which the words inhere, by recalling them, brings to mind the realities themselves, of which the words are signs.

Ad. I understand and follow you.

CHAPTER 2

Words are signs. Can meanings of words be shown only by using words?

3. *Aug.* Do we agree, then, that words are signs? [9]

Ad. Yes.

Aug. Now, can a sign be a sign unless it signifies something?

Ad. No.

Aug. How many words are there in this verse:

If nothing from this great heaven-doomed city remain? [10]

Ad. Eight.

Aug. Then there are eight signs?

Ad. Yes.

Aug. I presume you understand this verse.

Ad. Quite well, I think.

Aug. Tell me what each word signifies.

Ad. I see what "if" signifies, but I find no other word to indicate its meaning.

Aug. Whatever the word signifies—do you at least know where it exists?

Ad. It seems to me that "if" signifies doubt, and where is doubt but in the mind?

Aug. I grant that for now. Go on to the rest.

Ad. "Nothing" can signify only what does not exist.

Aug. Perhaps you are right—only I cannot agree with you because of your admission a while ago that nothing is a sign unless it signifies something. Now, the non-existent certainty cannot be something. Therefore, the second word in this verse is not a sign because it does not signify anything;

and we were mistaken in agreeing that all words are signs, or that every sign signifies something.

Ad. Really, you are pressing that too far. Just the same, it would be quite stupid for us to utter a word if we had no meaning to attach to it. Yet I believe that in speaking with me now you are not just emitting sounds, but that by each sound issuing from your lips you are giving me a sign so that I may understand something. Hence, you should not utter those two syllables when you speak if you do not mean anything by them. But if you see that they are necessary to convey something and that we are taught or reminded when they strike our hearing, then you do really see what I want to say but cannot explain.

Aug. What are we to do, then? Shall we, instead of saying that this word signifies a thing which does not exist, rather say that it signifies some state of the mind when it sees no reality, yet finds, or thinks that it finds, that the reality does not exist?

Ad. That may be precisely what I was struggling to explain.

Aug. Then—however that may be—let us go on, before a most absurd situation overtakes us.

Ad. What can that be?

Aug. That "nothing" detain us and we be delayed.

Ad. That surely would be ridiculous. Yet I see that somehow it could happen. Yes, I see clearly that it has happened!

4. *Aug.* We shall have a clearer understanding of this sort of confusion in its proper place,[11] God willing. Now get back to that verse and try your best to explain what the other words in it signify.

Ad. The third is the preposition "from," for which we can, I think, say "of."

Aug. I am not asking you to substitute for one word quite familiar another equally familiar having the same meaning —if, indeed, it has the same meaning—but let us grant that for the present. Undoubtedly, if the poet had said, not "from this great city," but "of this great city," and if I asked you what "of" means, you would say "from," since here you would have two words, that is, signs, signifying, as you think, the same thing. But what I am looking for is that one single thing, whatever it is, which is signified by those two signs.

Ad. It seems to me that some sort of separation from a thing in which something had been, is signified; and that this is said to be "from" the former, be it that that former thing no longer remains, as in the present verse where a city no longer remains, though some Trojans could be "from" that city; or be it that it does remain, for instance, when we say that traders "from" Rome are in Africa.

Aug. Granted that this is so, and let me not enumerate how many exceptions to this rule of yours can be found: just the same, you can readily see that you have explained words by words—that is, signs by signs—and what is quite familiar by what is equally familiar. But I would like you to show me, if you can, the realities themselves of which these are signs.

CHAPTER 3

Can anything be made known without a sign?

5. *Ad.* I am astonished that you do not know, or rather pretend not to know, that what you wish cannot be accomplished at all by any replies of mine. For we are holding a discussion, and in so doing we cannot give answers except

in words. But here you are looking for realities which, whatever they may be, certainly are not words, and yet you
yourself, too, are using words to ask for them. Therefore,
you must first ask for them without words, if you want me
to answer on the same terms.

Aug. You are within your rights, I admit. Yet if I should
ask you what the three syllables signify when the word *paries*
["wall"] is pronounced, could you not point it out with your
finger, so that, by your showing me and without your using
any words, I could directly see the thing itself of which
this three-syllable word is a sign?

Ad. I admit that can be done, but only in regard to
nouns that signify bodies, and when those bodies are
present.

Aug. We do not call color a body, do we? Do we not
rather call it a quality of a body?

Ad. Yes.

Aug. Why, then, can it, too, be pointed out with the
finger? Or do you also add to bodies the qualities of bodies,
so that the latter, when they are present, can be manifested
equally well without words?

Ad. When I mentioned bodies, I meant all corporeal
things; that is, everything in bodies that can be known by
the senses.

Aug. But think this over—should you not also make some
exceptions here?

Ad. Good advice! For I should have said, not all corporeal things, but all visible things. I admit, of course, that
sound, odor, savor, weight, heat and other properties that
pertain to the senses other than sight, although they cannot
be known by the senses unless they are in bodies, and therefore are bodily, nevertheless cannot be indicated by pointing
the finger.

Aug. Have you never seen people holding a sort of conversation with deaf persons by means of gestures, and the deaf themselves also using gestures to ask questions or to answer them, to communicate or indicate most, if not all, of their wishes? When this is done, surely not only visible objects are manifested without words, but also sounds and savors and all the other things of this sort. Yes, actors in the theatres, too, present and enact entire stories, for the most part by employing pantomime without words.[12]

Ad. I have nothing to say against that, except that not only I but even the pantomimist himself would be unable to show you, without using words, what that "from" means.

6. *Aug.* Perhaps you are right. But let us suppose that he can. You do not doubt, I presume, that whatever that action of the body would be by which he would try to show me the reality that is signified by this word, it would not be the reality itself, but a sign of it. Therefore, he, too, though not using a word for a word, will still be indicating a sign by a sign—meaning that the monosyllable "from" and the gesture will signify some one thing, which is what I would like to have shown me without a sign being made.

Ad. How, I ask you, is it possible to do what you want?

Aug. In the same way that it was possible with regard to the wall.

Ad. Not even that, so our step-by-step reasoning has made clear, can be shown without a sign. For obviously the pointing of the finger is not the wall, but a sign by means of which the wall can be seen. I see nothing, therefore, that can be made known without signs.

Aug. What if I were to ask you what walking is, and you were to get up and walk? Would you not be using the reality itself, rather than words or any other signs, to teach me?

Ad. I admit that is so, and I am ashamed that I did not see what is so evident. From this thousands of other things now occur to me, which can be shown directly and not through signs, such as eating, drinking, sitting, standing, calling, and countless other things.

Aug. Well, tell me now, if I, completely ignorant of the meaning of this word, were to ask you what walking is, while you were walking, how would you teach me?

Ad. I should walk somewhat faster, so that following your question some new element would suggest it to you; and at the same time I would be doing only what had to be shown.

Aug. Do you not know that walking and hurrying are two different things? One who walks does not by that fact hurry. And one who hurries does not necessarily walk; for we speak of hurrying in regard to writing and reading, and countless other things. Hence, if after my question you were to do more hurriedly what you happened to be doing, I would think walking is the same as hurrying, for that is the new element you would have added; and I would for this reason be misled.

Ad. I admit that we cannot manifest a thing without a sign, if we are asked about it while we are in the act of doing it. For if we add nothing, he who puts the question will think that we are unwilling to show him, and that, ignoring him, we are merely continuing to do what we were doing before. Should he, however, ask about things that we are able to do, but does not ask while we are actually doing them, we can, by doing it after he puts his question, show what he is asking about, by means of the reality itself rather than by a sign—unless he chances to ask me what speaking is, while I am speaking. For then, whatever I should say to teach him—speak I must; and pursuing my course from there, I shall teach him until I make plain to him what he wants to know, without departing from the reality itself which he asked to have shown him, and without looking for signs to manifest it, other than speech itself.[13]

CHAPTER 4

Are signs manifested by means of signs?

7. *Aug.* Very keen, indeed! Now then, see whether we agree that those things can be demonstrated without signs which we are not performing when we are asked about them, and yet are able to perform at once, or which perchance are themselves signs when we perform them. When, for example, we talk, we make signs, and for that reason we speak of "signifying."

Ad. We agree.

Aug. When, therefore, certain signs are asked about, signs can be manifested by means of signs. But when a question concerns realities which are not signs, they can be manifested either by performing them after inquiry, if they can be performed, or by giving signs by which attention can be directed to them.

Ad. That is right.

Aug. Now, in this threefold classification let us, if you will, consider that group in which signs are manifested by means of signs. For words are not the only signs, are they?

Ad. No.

Aug. It seems to me, then, that in speaking we signify by words either words themselves or other signs, as when we say "gesture" or "letter"—for the things signified by these two words are still signs; or we signify something else which is not a sign, as when we say "stone"—a word which is a sign, since it signifies something, but what is signified is not, in turn, a sign. The latter class, however—that is, the class of words which signify things that are not signs— does not pertain to the topic we have proposed for present discussion. For we have undertaken to consider that class in which signs are manifested by signs, and here we found two divisions in it, seeing that by means of signs we teach or bring to mind either the same signs or different signs. Do you not think so?

Ad. It is obvious.

8. *Aug.* Then tell me to which sense word-signs pertain.

Ad. To hearing.

Aug. What about gestures?

Ad. To sight.[14]

Aug. What if we find words in writing? Are they words, or are they not more correctly to be understood as signs of words? To be a word, it must be uttered in an articulate vocal sound with some meaning; but the voice cannot be perceived by any other sense than hearing. Thus it is that when a word is written a sign is presented to the eyes, and this brings into the mind what pertains to hearing.

Ad. Yes, I agree.

Aug. I presume you also agree that when we say "noun"[15] we signify something.

Ad. Indeed, we do.

Aug. What, then?

Ad. Evidently, that which anything is called, as "Romulus," "Rome," "virtue," "river," and countless other things.

Aug. Those four nouns do not signify any realities, do they?

Ad. They certainly do.

Aug. There is no difference between these nouns and the realities which they signify?

Ad. Indeed, there is a great difference.

Aug. I should like you to tell me what it is.

Ad. This above all, that the former are signs, the latter are not.

Aug. Is it agreeable to you that we term "signifiables"[16] those things which can be signified by signs and yet are not signs, just as we call those things "visibles" which can be seen? Thus in what follows we shall be able to discuss these things more conveniently.

Ad. Certainly, I agree.

Aug. What about this? Those four signs which you cited a little while ago, are they signified by no other signs?

Ad. I am surprised that you think I have already forgotten that we found that things written are to things spoken as signs of signs.

Aug. Tell me what difference there is between them.

Ad. The former are visibles, the latter, audibles. As to this last word, why not use it[17] if we have decided to use "signifiables"?

Aug. I am all for it, and I like it. But once again I ask you, can these four signs be signified by no other, audible sign, the same as you bethought yourself of the visible ones?

Ad. This, too, I recall was said a little while ago. For I answered that "noun" signifies something, and I brought those four under this signification, and I know that both "noun" and these nouns when uttered by the voice, are audibles.

Aug. What, then, is the difference between an audible sign and the audible things signified, which in turn are signs?

Ad. Between what we call "noun" and these four things that we have included under its signification, I see this difference: the former is an audible sign of audible signs, whereas the latter, while being audible signs, nevertheless signify not signs, but realities that are sometimes visible—like Romulus, Rome, river—and sometimes intelligible, such as virtue.

9. *Aug.* That is it exactly. Now, you know that all things uttered by the articulate voice with some signification are called words?

Ad. I know that.

Aug. Therefore, a noun is also a word, because of course we see that it is uttered with some meaning by the articulate voice. And when we say that an eloquent person uses choice words, he evidently also uses nouns; and when the slave in the play of Terence replied to his aged master:

> Propitious words, prithee [18]—

the latter had also used many nouns.

Ad. I agree.

Aug. Then you grant that the two syllables which we utter in saying *verbum* ["word"], also signify "noun," and that, therefore, "word" is a sign of "noun."

Ad. I grant that.

Aug. I would like you to answer this also. Since "word" is a sign of "noun," and "noun" is a sign of "river," and "river" is a sign of a reality which can be seen directly: now, just as you have told me the difference between this reality and "river" which is its sign, and between this sign and "noun" which is the sign of this sign, tell me what you think is the difference between the sign of "noun," which we found to be "word," and "noun" itself, of which it is the sign?

Ad. I see this difference: those things which are signified by "noun" are also signified by "word," for as "noun" is a word, so also "river" is a word; whereas not all the things that are signified by "word" are also signified by "noun." For example, both that "if" which is at the beginning of the verse you quoted, and this "from" which led us to these matters over a long route of discussion, under the guidance of reason, are words but not nouns. And there are many such examples. Therefore, since all nouns are words but not all words are nouns, I think the difference between "word" and "noun" is obvious, that is to say, between the sign of that sign which does not signify any other signs, and the sign of that sign which does in turn signify other signs.

Aug. You grant that every horse is an animal, yet that not every animal is a horse?

Ad. Who could doubt that?

Aug. Then the difference between "noun" and "word" [*verbum*] is the same as the difference between "horse" and "animal." Perhaps, though, you may be dissuaded from assenting by the fact that we speak of *verbum* in still another sense ["verb"], signifying those words that are conjugated through the tenses, as for instance: "I write, I wrote," "I read, I read," which obviously are not nouns.[19]

Ad. You have voiced exactly the misgivings I had.

Aug. Do not let that disturb you. For we call "signs" in general all those things which signify anything, and among them we also find words. So, too, we speak of "military signs," and they are properly called signs. Words do not belong to this class.[20] Yet, if I were to tell you that just as every horse is an animal but not every animal is a horse, so, although every word is a sign, not every sign is a word, you would, I think, not hesitate to agree.

Ad. Yes, I understand, and I quite agree that there is the same difference between the general term "word" and "noun" that there is between "animal" and "horse."

10. *Aug.* You also know that when we say "animal," this three-syllable noun, vocally expressed, is one thing and what is signified is another?

Ad. I have already granted that regarding all signs and things signifiable.

Aug. You do not think, do you, that all signs signify something other than what they are themselves, just as the three-syllable word "animal" does not signify what it itself is?

Ad. Certainly not. For example, when we say "sign," that signifies not only other signs, whatever they are, but also itself; for it is a word, and all words are certainly signs.

Aug. Well, when we say *verbum* ["word"], does not something similar occur in the case of this dissyllable? For if this dissyllable signifies everything that is expressed by the articulate voice with some meaning, it itself is also included in this class.

Ad. That is so.

Aug. Further, is it not the same with "noun"? For it signifies nouns of all genders, and "noun" itself is a noun of the neuter gender. If I should ask you what part of speech "noun" is, could you correctly answer anything but "a noun"?

Ad. You are right.

Aug. Therefore, there are signs which include themselves in the things they signify.

Ad. Yes.

Aug. When we say *coniunctio* ["conjunction"], do you think that this four-syllable sign is a case in point?

Ad. Not at all. The things it signifies are not nouns; but it is itself a noun.

CHAPTER 5

Reciprocal signs.

11. *Aug.* You have been very attentive. Now see whether there are signs which have reciprocal signification, meaning that as one is signified by another, so the latter is signified by the former. To illustrate, there is no such relationship between the quadrisyllable present in saying *coniunctio* ["conjunction"] and what is signified by it, as when we say "if," "or," "for," "for surely," "unless," "therefore," "because," [21] and the like. For these are all signified by that one word, but that one four-syllable word is not signified by any of them.

Ad. I see; and I would like to know which signs have reciprocal signification.

Aug. You do not know, then, that when we say "noun" and "word" we express two words?

Ad. Yes, I know that.

Aug. But you do not know that when we say "noun" and "word" we express two nouns?

Ad. I know that, too.

Aug. Then you know that as "noun" is signified by "word," so "word" is signified by "noun." [22]

Ad. I agree.

Aug. Can you tell me the difference between them, other than that they are written and pronounced differently?

Ad. Perhaps I can, for I see that it is the same as I stated a little while ago. When we say "words," we signify everything expressed by the articulate voice with some meaning. Hence, every noun and "noun" itself when spoken is a word. But not every word is a noun, although when we say "word" we have a noun.

12. *Aug.* What if someone should state to you and show that as every noun is a word, so every word is a noun? Could you find any difference between them besides the different sounds of the letters?

Ad. I could not, nor do I think there is any difference at all.

Aug. What if all things expressed by the articulate voice with some meaning are both words and nouns, but are called words for one reason, and nouns for another? Will there be no difference between a noun and a word?

Ad. I do not understand how.

Aug. At least you understand this: that everything colored is visible, and everything visible is colored, although these two words have distinct and different meanings.

Ad. I do.

Aug. What, then, if in like manner every word is a noun and every noun is a word, although these two nouns, or two words, that is to say, "noun" and "word," have a different meaning?

Ad. I see now that it can happen; but how it happens is something I look to you to explain.

Aug. You are aware, I suppose, that everything expressed by the articulate voice with some meaning, both strikes the ear that it may be heard, and is committed to memory that it may be known.

Ad. I am aware of that.

Aug. Then there are two things that occur when we express something with the voice as described.

Ad. Yes.

Aug. What if words receive their name from one of these, and nouns from the other—that is, *verba* ["words"] from *verberare* ["strike"] and *nomina* ["nouns"] from *noscere* ["know"] so that the first has come to be called such from its connection with the ears, while the second had to do with the mind? [23]

13. *Ad.* I shall grant that when you show how we can correctly call all words nouns.

Aug. That is easy. For I believe that you have learned and hold that a "pronoun" is so called because it can stand *for* a noun, though it denotes a thing with less complete signification than does the noun. In fact, I think that was the definition you used to recite to the grammar teacher: "A pronoun is a part of speech which, when used for a noun, signifies the same thing, though less perfectly." [24]

Ad. I remember—that is correct.

Aug. You see, then, that according to this definition pronouns serve only for nouns and can be used in place of them alone. For example, when we say "this man," "the king himself," "the same woman," "this gold," "that silver"— "this," "himself," "same," "this," and "that" are pronouns; "man," "king," "woman," "gold," and "silver" are nouns, and these give a fuller signification to the objects than do the pronouns.

Ad. I see and agree.

Aug. And now mention a few conjunctions—make your own choice.

Ad. *Et* ["and"], *que* ["and"], *at* ["but"], *atque* ["and"].

Aug. All these that you have mentioned, do they not seem to you to be nouns?

Ad. Not at all.

Aug. But at least you think I spoke correctly when I said: "All *these* that you have mentioned"?

Ad. Yes, indeed. And now I realize how admirably you indicated that I did express nouns; for otherwise one could not correctly speak of them as "all these." But still I am afraid you seem to me to have used a correct expression only because I cannot deny that these four conjunctions are also words, meaning that you could correctly refer to them as "all these" because it is correct to say "all these words." But if you ask me what part of speech "words" is, I can only reply "a noun." Wherefore, it is perhaps to this noun that your pronoun is added, to make your expression correct.

14. *Aug.* Keen enough, but you are deceived. In order to be undeceived, note with increased keenness what I shall say, if indeed I am able to say it as I wish. For treating of words by means of words is as complicated a business as interlocking and rubbing the fingers of one hand with the fingers of the other, where it is scarcely discernible, except by the one doing it, which fingers are itching and which are relieving the itch.

Ad. I am all attention, for that analogy has aroused my interest.

Aug. Surely, I am pronouncing words, and they consist of letters.

Ad. Yes.

Aug. Then—to use in preference to all others that authority which is dearest to us—when the Apostle Paul says: *There was not in Christ "is" and "is not," but "is" was in Him,*[25] I do not think it is to be held that the three letters which we pronounce when we say *est* ["is"] were in Christ, but rather what is signified by those three letters.

Ad. You are right.

Aug. You understand, then, that he who said *"is" was in Him* meant nothing else than "what was in Him is called 'is.'" Thus, if he had said "virtue was in Him," he certainly would be taken to have said only "what was in Him is called 'virtue'": we should not think that the two syllables pronounced when we say "virtue" were in Him, but what is signified by these two syllables.

Ad. I understand and follow.

Aug. Further, you understand, too, that it makes no difference whether one says "it is called 'virtue'" or "it is named 'virtue'"?

Ad. That is clear.

Aug. Therefore it is just as clear, that it makes no difference whether one says "what was in Him is called 'is'," or "is named 'is.'"

Ad. I see no difference here either.

Aug. Do you also see by now what I wish to show you?

Ad. To tell you the truth, not yet.

Aug. So you do not see either that a noun is that by which anything is named?

Ad. Clearly—I see that nothing is more certain.

Aug. Therefore, you see that "is" is a noun, because what was in Him is named "is."

Ad. I cannot deny it.

Aug. But if I were to ask you what part of speech "is" is, I think you would say, not that it is a noun, but that it is a verb, although our reasoning has shown that it is also a noun.

Ad. It is exactly as you say.

Aug. You no longer hesitate to admit, do you, that other parts of speech are also nouns in the same way, as we have shown?

Ad. I do not hesitate to admit it, since I acknowledge that they signify something. But if you should ask what the several things they signify are called—that is, named—I could answer only that they are those parts of speech which we do not call "nouns" but which, as I see it, logic constrains us to call such.

15. *Aug.* Are you not apprehensive that there might be someone who could discredit this reasoning of ours by saying that we should attribute to the Apostle authority regarding realities, not regarding words, and that, therefore, the foundation of this argument is not so solid as we think? He could say that possibly Paul, though scrupulously correct in his manner of life and in his teaching, nevertheless lacked such correctness when he stated, *"is"* was in *Him*—especially since he himself acknowledges that he is *rude in speech.*[26] Tell me, how are we to refute such a person?

Ad. I have no reply to offer, and I suggest that you find a recognized master in word lore, that rather by his authority you may accomplish what you are after.

Aug. So you think that in the absence of authorities less cogency attaches to simple reasoning, by which we prove that something is signified by all the parts of speech; that, consequently, something is designated; and if it is designated, it is named; if named, it certainly is named by a noun. We have here a fact which finds most ready substantiation in the various languages. Everybody sees, for example, that if you ask what the Greeks have for what we call "who?" the answer is *tis*; what the Greeks have for what we call "wish," the answer is *thelo*; what the Greeks have for what we call "well," the answer is *kalos*; what the Greeks have for what we call "writing," the answer is *to gegrammenon*; what the Greeks have for what we call "and," the answer is *kai*; what the Greeks have for what we call "from," the answer is *apo*; what the Greeks have for what we call "alas," the answer is *oi*. And so it is seen that regarding all these parts of speech I have just enumerated,[27] such an interrogator would be speaking correctly, which would not be possible unless they were nouns. Wherefore, seeing that by this reasoning we can dispense with an appeal to the authority of any of the eloquent to establish that the Apostle Paul spoke correctly, what need have we of looking for anyone to bolster our opinion?

16. But lest someone too slow of comprehension or some supercritic still refuse to give in, and claim that we should give assent only on the authority of those who are universally acknowledged legislators of words: in the Latin language is there anyone who is the peer of Cicero? Now, in those celebrated orations of his, the so-called "Verrines," he expressed the preposition *coram* ["before"] as a noun, unless the passage actually has it as an adverb.[28] It may be, however, that I do not understand that passage very well, and some other occasion may put some other interpretation on it, either by myself or by another; but there is an argument which, I think, admits of no reply.

As you know, the most eminent masters of argumentation teach that a noun and a verb constitute a complete sentence which may be said to be true or false. The same Tullius somewhere calls that sort of thing a "proposition."[29] And when the verb is in the third person, they say the nominative case must be used with it; and they are right, for if you consider with me, for instance, the expressions "a man sits" or "a horse runs," you recognize, I think, that they are two propositions.

Ad. I recognize that.

Aug. You see that in each there is a noun: in the one,

"man," in the other, "horse"; and a verb: in the one, "sits," in the other, "runs"?

Ad. Yes, I do.

Aug. Consequently, if I should say only "sits," or "runs," you would rightly ask me "who?" or "what?"—and I should answer "a man," or "a horse," or "an animal," or anything else that would restore the noun to the verb and complete the proposition, that is, such a sentence as can be said to be true or false.

Ad. I understand.

Aug. Note what follows. Suppose we see something at a distance and are uncertain whether it is an animal or a stone or something else; and suppose I should say to you, "Because it is a man, it is an animal." Would I not be speaking rashly?

Ad. Yes, absolutely. But certainly it would not be rash for you to say, "If it is a man, it is an animal."

Aug. You are right. Accordingly, the "if" in your statement pleases me and it pleases you; but in my statement the "because" displeases both of us.

Ad. I agree.

Aug. Now see whether these two sentences are complete propositions: "'If' pleases"; "'Because' displeases."

Ad. Yes, they certainly are.

Aug. Very well, now tell me which are the verbs here, and which the nouns.

Ad. I see the verbs are "pleases" and "displeases." But the nouns—what else are they than "if" and "because"?

Aug. Therefore, it has been proved to satisfaction that these two conjunctions are also nouns.

Ad. Yes, indeed.

Aug. Can you by yourself bring this out with regard to the other parts of speech, according to the same norm?

Ad. Yes.

CHAPTER 6

Signs that signify themselves.

17. *Aug.* Then let us proceed. To begin with, tell me whether, as we have found that all words are nouns and all nouns are words, you think that all nouns are vocables[30] and all vocables nouns?

Ad. Indeed, apart from the different sound of the syllables, I see no difference between them.

Aug. For the moment I have no objection to make to that, although there are those who distinguish between them also with regard to the meaning; but there is no need of considering their opinion now. You must note, however, that we have now come to those signs which signify each other reciprocally, with no difference between them except the sound, and which signify themselves along with the other parts of speech.

Ad. I do not understand.

Aug. Then you do not understand that "noun" is signified by "vocable" and "vocable" by "noun," so that there is no difference between them except the sound of the letters, so far as "noun" in the general sense is concerned? We also speak, of course, of a "noun" in a special sense, as one of the eight parts of speech[31] not including the other seven.

Ad. I understand that.

Aug. Well, that is what I said: "vocable" and "noun" signify each other reciprocally.

18. *Ad.* I grasp that, but I am asking what you meant when you said: "they signify themselves along with other parts of speech."

Aug. Has not our previous reasoning shown us that all the parts of speech can be called both nouns and vocables, that is, that they can be signified both by "noun" and "vocable"?

Ad. Yes.

Aug. Well, then, if I should ask you what you would call "noun" itself—that is, that sound expressed by two syllables [*nomen*], would you not correctly answer me, "a noun"?

Ad. Yes.

Aug. The quadrisyllabic sign which we express when we say *coniunctio* ["conjunction"] does not signify itself in the same way, does it? For this noun cannot be counted among the things it signifies.

Ad. Exactly.

Aug. That is what I meant when I said that "noun" signifies itself along with the other things it signifies; and the same, you can see for yourself, also holds of "vocable."

Ad. An easy matter now. But here it strikes me that *nomen* is used in both a general sense and a special sense, but that "vocable" is not ranked among the eight parts of speech. Therefore I think that besides the difference of sound, the two differ in this respect also.

Aug. What about *nomen* and *onoma*—do you think there is any difference between them other than the sounds which also distinguish the Latin and Greek languages?

Ad. No, indeed, I see no other difference here.

Aug. We have considered, then: signs which also signify themselves, signs with reciprocal signification, signs whose range of signification applies also to another, and signs whose

11 9

sole difference lies in their sound. This fourth class we have just now established; the previous three we understand as applying to both "noun" and "word."

Ad. Yes, precisely.

CHAPTER 7

Summary of the preceding chapters.

19. *Aug.* Now I would like you to review the results of our discussion.

Ad. I shall do it as well as I can. First of all, as I recall it, we devoted some time to the question of why we speak. We found that we employ speech in order to teach or to remind. Even when we ask questions, we have in mind only to teach the one asked what we wish to hear; and as to singing, what we appear to do in it for pleasure, is not properly speech. When we pray to God whom we cannot presume to teach or remind, the function of our words is either to remind ourselves or to make us remind or teach others.

Then, when it had been made sufficiently clear that words are only signs, and that things which do not signify anything cannot be signs, you quoted a verse; I was to show what each word meant. The verse was:

If nothing from this great heaven-doomed city remain.

Although the second word is extremely familiar and most obvious, still we could not determine what it signifies. When I suggested that it is not given a place in speech without a purpose, but that by using it we teach something to the hearer, you replied, it is true, that possibly this word serves the purpose of indicating the state of mind when it has found, or thinks it has found, that something it seeks does not exist; but then, to the accompaniment of a witticism you sidetracked I know not what unfathomable element in the problem, and put off the explanation to another time; and do not think that I have forgotten your obligation!

Then, when I tried my best to explain the third word in the verse, you kept on insisting that I show you not another word with the same meaning, but the thing itself signified by the words. And when I said that we could not do that in verbal discourse, this brought us to those things which are indicated to such as ask about them, by pointing with the finger. In my opinion this applied to all corporeal things, but we found that this was so only of visible things.

From there we came, somehow or other, to the deaf and the pantomimists, who by means of gesture and without uttering a sound signify not only what can be seen, but also many other things and practically everything that we express in speech. Still, we found that gestures too, are signs. Then, again, we began to look for a method of indicating without any signs the realities themselves signified by means of signs: demonstrably, a wall and color and everything visible indicated by pointing the finger are actually indicated by means of some sign. Here I made a mistake, stating that nothing like that could be found. We finally agreed that those things can be manifested without a sign which we are not in the act of doing when we are asked about them and which we are able to do after inquiry. But speaking does not belong to that class, for we saw clearly enough that if we happen to be speaking when we are asked what speaking is, it is easy to manifest that by means of speech itself.

20. This made us realize that either signs are the means of manifesting signs, or signs are the means of manifesting other things which are not signs, or again, that even without

a sign things can be manifested if we can perform them upon inquiry. And of these three we undertook to consider and discuss the first more thoroughly. This discussion made it plain that there are some signs which cannot in turn be signified by those signs which they signify, as when we use the quadrisyllable *coniunctio* ["conjunction"]; and that there are other signs which can, as when we say "sign" we also signify "word," and when we say "word" we also signify "sign," for "sign" and "word" are two signs and also two words. It was further shown that in this class in which signs signify each other reciprocally, some are not equally applicable, some are equally applicable, and some are identical in meaning. For example, the disyllable heard in pronouncing *signum* ["sign"] signifies absolutely everything by which anything is signified; but when we say "word," that is a sign not of all signs, but only of those which are uttered by the articulate voice. Hence it is evident that although *verbum* ["word"] is signified by *signum* ["sign"] and vice versa—that is, the first pair of syllables is signified by the second and the second pair is also signified by the first —nevertheless greater applicability attaches to *signum* than to *verbum*; that is to say, the former pair of syllables signifies more things than does the latter.

But "word" in its general sense is the equivalent in applicability of "noun" taken in a general sense. In fact, so our reasoning has shown us, all the parts of speech are also nouns, because pronouns can be added to them, and of all of them it can be said that they name something, and there is not one of them which cannot constitute a complete proposition by having a verb joined to it. But although "noun" and "word" have an equal range of applicability by reason of the fact that whatever is a word is also a noun, yet their applicability is not identical. For it was argued with sufficient probability that they are called "words" for one reason, and "nouns" for another. Indeed, the former of these was found to denote a striking on the ear, and the other a mental remembrance, as can be gathered from the fact that in speaking we very correctly say: "What is the name of this thing?" when we want to commit a thing to memory; but we are not accustomed to say: "What is the word of this thing?"

We found, however, that *nomen* and *onoma* not only have the same range of applicability, but are identical in meaning; beyond the different sound of the letters, there is no difference between them.

Oh, yes,—I forgot concerning the class in which signs signify each other reciprocally, that we found no sign which does not signify itself along with other things.

I have recalled these points as well as I could. Now it is for you whom I consider to have said nothing in this discussion which was not founded on positive knowledge, to see whether I have given a good, orderly summary of them.

CHAPTER 8

The practical value of such discussion. The necessity of directing attention to realities signified.

21. *Aug.* You have adequately recalled from memory everything I wanted. In fact, I must acknowledge to you that I now see these distinctions more clearly than when the two of us resorted to inquiry and discussion to dig them out of ever so many hiding places.

But what destination do I have in mind to reach with you over this circuitous route? This is hard to say just now.

Maybe you think we are just dillydallying and diverting our minds from serious matters by turning to childish problems, or that the practical result we are after is but slight or mediocre. Or if you surmise that this discussion will issue in something important, you desire to know even now what it is, or at least to hear it mentioned. But I would have you believe that I have not intended any cheap comedy [32] in this conversation—for even though we may play with words, still that is not to be considered in a childish sense—and that what we are giving our thoughts to is of no slight or ordinary profit; though, if I say that there is a happy life, and that everlasting, to which I desire that God—that is, Truth itself [33]—may lead us by stages suited to our weak step, I am afraid I shall appear ridiculous for having set out on this great journey by considering not the realities themselves which are signified, but only the signs. So then, you will pardon me if I play this prelude with you, not to do any play-acting, [34] but to exercise the powers and keenness of our minds and so prepare ourselves not only to bear, but also to love the warmth and light where the blessed life reigns. [35]

Ad. Do go on as you have begun: I shall never think of belittling what you think worth saying or doing.

22. *Aug.* Very well, let us, then, consider that division in which signs signify not other signs, but those things we call signifiable. And first tell me whether man is man.

Ad. But now you are perhaps joking.

Aug. Why so?

Ad. Because you think it necessary to ask me whether man is anything but man [*homo*].

Aug. I suppose you would think that I was again poking fun at you if I should also ask whether the first syllable of this noun is other than *ho-* and the second other than *-mo*.

Ad. I certainly would.

Aug. But when those syllables are joined, you have *homo* —or will you deny that?

Ad. Who could deny that?

Aug. I ask you, then, whether you are these two syllables conjoined?

Ad. Not at all. But I see what you are driving at.

Aug. Tell me, then, to save me from appearing offensive to you.

Ad. You think the inference is that I am not a man.[36]

Aug. Well, do you not think so too, since you grant the truth of everything we have said before, from which this follows?

Ad. I shall not tell you what I think until I first hear from you whether in your question about man being man you were asking about those two syllables or about the reality itself which they signify.

Aug. Do you rather answer in what sense you have taken my question. For if it is ambiguous, you should have guarded against that first, and not answered until you found out in what sense I put the question.[37]

Ad. But why should this ambiguity embarrass me, when I have given the answer to both questions? For man is certainly man: obviously, those two syllables are nothing more than those two syllables; and that which they signify is nothing but what it is.

Aug. Cleverly said, indeed. But why have you understood in both senses only this one thing mentioned, "man," and not the other things we have referred to?

Ad. How can you prove that I did not understand the others in the same way, too?

Aug. Not to mention other considerations, if you had understood that first question of mine entirely from the standpoint of the sound of the syllables, you would have made no answer to me. For you could have been under the impression that I was not even asking a question. Actually, however, when I pronounced three words, the middle one of which I repeated, asking "whether man is man" [*utrum homo homo sit*], you took the first and last words not as the signs which they are, but according to the realities signified by the signs. And this is already obvious from the mere fact that you immediately decided with absolute confidence that my question should be answered.

Ad. You are right.

Aug. Why, then, did you choose to take merely the one found in the middle, both according to the way it sounds and according to what it signifies?

Ad. Look, I now take the whole thing only from the standpoint of what is signified. I agree with you that we cannot carry on a conversation at all, unless at the sound of the words the mind is directed to the realities of which the words are signs. So, show me now how I was deceived by that inference whose conclusion is that I am not a man.

Aug. No, rather let me ask you the same questions again, so that you yourself may discover where you have erred.

Ad. Fine!

23. *Aug.* I shall not repeat my first question, because you have already answered it. Now, then, consider carefully whether the syllable *ho-* is nothing further than *ho-*, and whether *-mo* is nothing further than *-mo*.

Ad. That is all I see here.

Aug. See also whether man [*homo*] results from combining the two.

Ad. That I should never grant. For we determined, and rightly so, that when a sign is expressed we should give attention to what is signified, and from the consideration of that to grant or deny what is said. But as to those syllables, pronounced separately, we have owned that they are just sounds for the reason that they are expressed without any signification.

Aug. Therefore, it is your opinion and your firm conviction that in answering questions one should have regard only for what is signified by the words?

Ad. I do not see why that should be debatable so long as words are words.

Aug. I would like to know how you would refute the man we frequently hear about in jokes, who concluded that a lion issued from the mouth of another with whom he was having an argument. As you know, he asked whether what we say issues from our mouth, and the other could not deny it. Then he contrived, as he could easily do, to make the man use the word "lion" in the course of the conversation. When that happened, he began to taunt him and heckle him for apparently having vomited up so horrible a beast, though he was not such a bad fellow at all; and that simply because he had acknowledged that whatever we say comes out of our mouth, and because he could not deny that he had said "lion."

Ad. Indeed, it would not be difficult to refute that clown. I would not grant that whatever we speak of comes out of our mouth. The things we speak of, we signify; and what comes forth from the mouth of the speaker is not the reality signified, but the sign by which it is signified. The exception is when it is the signs themselves that are signified,[38] a class we treated a little while ago.

24. *Aug.* Thus you would, indeed, be well guarded against him. Nevertheless, what answer would you give me if I ask you whether "man" is a noun?

Ad. What, but that it is a noun?

Aug. Well, when I look at you do I see a noun?

Ad. No.

Aug. Do you want me to tell you, then, what follows?

Ad. Please do not. For I myself realize that it follows that I am not "man," since when you asked me whether "man" is a noun, I answered that it is. As a matter of fact, we had already agreed to grant what is asked or deny it, according to the reality which is signified.

Aug. Just the same, it seems to me that it is not without some advantage that you tumbled into this answer. For it was the law of reason itself which is imparted to our minds [39] that got the best of your caution. If I should ask, for instance, what man is, you would perhaps answer, "an animal." But if I should ask what part of speech "man" is you could not answer this correctly except by saying "a noun." Wherefore, though it so happens that "man" is both a noun and an animal, the former is said from the standpoint of being a sign, the latter, from the standpoint of the thing which it signifies. And so, should anyone ask whether "man" is a noun, I would answer simply that it is; for he indicates sufficiently that he wishes to be understood as speaking of "man" as a sign. But if he should ask whether man is an animal, I should with much greater alacrity give an affirmative answer. For, plainly, if without mentioning either "noun" or "animal," he should ask simply what man [*homo*] is, the mind would quickly pass on, by force of that accepted rule of language, to what is signified by the two syllables, and the answer would simply be "an animal"; or even the whole definition would be given—"a mortal rational animal." [40] Do you not think so?

Ad. Yes, absolutely. But when we grant that "man"

is a noun, how shall we avoid the all too odious conclusion, that we are not men?

Aug. How do you think but by making clear that the conclusion does not correspond to the sense in which we agreed with the one who put the question? Should he, however, acknowledge that he draws the conclusion from the other sense, there is no reason at all to be hesitant; for why should I be afraid to admit that I am not "man" [*hominem*], namely, that I am not those three syllables?

Ad. Nothing could be more true. Why, then, should the mind take offense when someone says, "So, you are not 'man,'" since, according to what we granted nothing truer could be said?

Aug. Because as soon as those words are pronounced, I cannot but think that the conclusion has reference to what is signified by these two syllables, and that by reason of the rule which naturally has dominance, namely, that when signs are heard the attention is directed to the realities signified.

Ad. I agree with you.

CHAPTER 9

The relative value of reality, the knowledge of it, and its signification.

25. *Aug.* Now, then, I would like you to realize that realities signified are to be esteemed more highly than their signs. For whatever exists for the sake of something else must be inferior to that for whose sake it exists—unless you think otherwise.

Ad. It seems to me one should not be too hasty in giving assent to this. For example, when we say "filth," I think this noun is far superior to the reality it signifies. For what offends us when we hear that word, does not apply to the sound of the word itself. In fact, by the change of one letter, the noun *coenum* ["filth"] becomes *coelum* ["heaven"]; but we see what a great difference there is betwen the realities signified by these nouns. Therefore, I should certainly not attribute to this sign what we loathe in the reality which it signifies; and hence I rightly prefer the former to the latter, for we prefer hearing the sign to coming in contact with the reality by any of the senses.

Aug. You have really been on your guard. It is false, then, that all realities are to be valued more highly than their signs?

Ad. So it seems.

Aug. Tell me, then, what purpose was in the mind of those who labeled this vile and detestable thing with a name? Would you approve or disapprove them?

Ad. I do not venture approval or disapproval. I do not know either what was in their mind.

Aug. Can you at least determine what intention you have when you pronounce this name?

Ad. Yes, indeed. I wish to signify that I have in mind to teach or remind the one with whom I am speaking, a thing which I think he should learn about or be reminded of.

Aug. Well, this teaching or reminding, or the being taught or reminded, which you suitably express by this noun, or which is expressed to you—should that not be considered of greater value than the name itself?

Ad. I grant that the knowledge that results from this sign is to be considered superior to the sign; but I do not think that therefore this holds for the reality itself.

26. *Aug.* In our opinion, then, even though it may be false that all realities ought to be considered superior to their signs, it is nevertheless not false that everything that exists for the sake of something else is inferior to that for whose sake it exists. Certainly, the knowledge of filth for the sake of which the name "filth" has been conceived, is to be esteemed more highly than the name itself, which, as we have established, is in turn superior to filth. For the only reason why that knowledge has been considered superior to the sign with which we are concerned, is that the latter demonstrably exists for the sake of the former and not vice versa. It is like the case of a glutton and, as the Apostle says, *worshipper of his belly* [41] who stated that he lived to eat. A temperate man who heard him protested and said: "Would it not be much better to eat to live?" [42] This he assuredly said in conformity with that same rule. [43] For the only reason the glutton gave displeasure was that he so depreciated the value of his own life as to consider it inferior to the pleasure of his palate, saying that he lived for the sake of food. And the other man rightly deserved praise for the simple reason that, understanding which of those two things served as a means toward the other, and, therefore, was inferior to the other, he gave the reminder that we should eat to live rather than live to eat. So, too, if some talkative wordmonger were to say, "I teach in order to talk," you and any other person who judges of things as they should be judged, might answer: "Man, why do you not rather talk in order to teach?"

If this is where the truth lies, and you know it to be so, you realize indeed how much less value is to be credited to words than to that on account of which we use words; and this the more as the use of words is itself to be considered superior to words. Words exist that we may use them; but we use them for the purpose of teaching. Just as teaching is superior to talking, so talking is superior to words. Therefore, instruction " is far superior to words. But I am anxious to hear what objections you may want to make.

27. *Ad.* I agree, of course, that instruction is superior to words. But whether some objection cannot be made against the rule according to which everything that exists for the sake of something else is inferior to that for whose sake it exists, I do not know.

Aug. This is something we can treat more opportunely and more thoroughly at some other time. For the present what you concede is sufficient for what I am striving to prove. You grant, at any rate, that knowledge of realities is more valuable than the signs of realities. It follows, then, that the knowledge of the realities which are signified is to be preferred to the knowledge of their signs. Do you not think so?

Ad. I did not grant, did I, that the knowledge of realities is superior to the knowledge of signs? I said only that it is superior to the signs themselves. Therefore, I have my misgivings about agreeing with you on this point. For what if, as the name "filth" is preferable to the reality it signifies, so also the knowledge of this name is to be preferred to the knowledge of that reality, even though the name itself is inferior to that knowledge? There are, to be sure, four things here: the name, the reality, the knowledge of the name, and the knowledge of the reality. Wherefore, just as the first excels the second, why may not the third excel the fourth? But even if it does not excel it, there is no need of considering it inferior, is there?

28. *Aug.* It is with real admiration that I note how you have upheld what you have granted and explained what

you have thought. But you understand, I suppose, that the trisyllabic noun pronounced when we say *vitium* ["vice"] is better than what it signifies, although the knowledge of the noun itself is far inferior to the knowledge of vices. Hence, though you may distinguish those four things and reflect on them—name, reality, knowledge of the name, and knowledge of the reality—here we rightly put the first before the second. For example, when Persius says,

But he is besotted by vice [45]—

the noun "vice" put in the poem did not debase the verse, but even gives it an artistic effect, whereas when the reality itself which is signified by this noun is present in anyone, it does debase him. But we note that the third thing does not excel the fourth in the same way; rather, the fourth excels the third. For the knowledge of this noun is inferior to the knowledge of vices.

Ad. Do you think this knowledge is preferable, even when it makes greater wretches of men? For among all the pains devised by the cruelty of tyrants and inflicted by their passion, it is this that the same Persius ranks first—the one that tortures men who are forced to acknowledge vices they cannot avoid.[46]

Aug. In the same way you could deny that the knowledge even of virtues is to be preferred to the knowledge of the noun "virtue." For, obviously, to see virtue and not to have it is a torment; and that is just what the same satirist hoped tyrants would be punished with.

Ad. May God avert such folly! Now I understand that it is not knowledge itself with which the best instruction of all[47] fills the mind, that is to be blamed. But those should be regarded the greatest of all unfortunates, and I think Persius thought the same, who are so diseased that such a potent remedy will not relieve them.

Aug. You are right. But what difference does it make to us what the opinion of Persius is? We are not subject to the authority of the poets in such matters. Besides, if the one sort of knowledge is to be preferred to the other, it is not easy to explain that in this case. I am satisfied with what we have established: that the knowledge of realities which are signified, even though it may not be superior to the knowledge of signs, is at all events superior to the signs themselves. So let us now analyze more and more thoroughly that class of realities which we said can be indicated by themselves, without the use of signs, such as speaking, walking, sitting, lying down, and the like.[48]

Ad. I recall what you are referring to.

CHAPTER 10

Is teaching possible without signs? Words themselves do not make us know realities.

29. *Aug.* Do you think that all actions which we are able to perform the moment we are asked about them, can be manifested without a sign, or would you make any exception?

Ad. Considering this whole class over and over again, I still find nothing that can be taught without signs, except perhaps speaking, and possibly teaching, if someone should inquire what teaching itself is. For I see that whatever I may do, following his inquiry, to make him learn, he does not learn from the reality itself which he desires to have shown to him. For example, if anyone should ask me what walking is, while I am not, as was said, engaged in anything or while I am doing something else, and I should try to teach him what he is asking about, without a sign, by promptly starting to walk, how am I to avoid having him think that just the amount of walking I have done is walking? And if he should think that, he will be deceived: he will decide that anyone who walks a longer or shorter distance that I have walked, is not walking. And what I have said about this one word applies to all the things which I had agreed can be shown without a sign, save those two which we have excepted.[49]

30. *Aug.* Very well, I accept that. But does it not seem to you that speaking is one thing, and teaching another?

Ad. It certainly seems so. For if they were the same, no one would teach except by speaking; but since we also teach many things by means of other signs besides words, who can doubt that there is a difference?

Aug. Well, then, are teaching and signifying the same? Or is there some difference?

Ad. I think they are the same.

Aug. Is he not right who says that we signify in order to teach?

Ad. Absolutely right.

Aug. What if another should say that we teach in order to give signs? Would it not be easy to refute him by the norm we established before?

Ad. Yes.

Aug. Wherefore, if we give signs in order to teach, but do not teach in order to give signs, teaching and signifying are two different things.

Ad. You are right, and I was wrong in answering that both are the same.

12 9

Aug. Now answer this: does he who teaches what teaching is, do so by giving signs or in some other way?

Ad. I do not see how he can do it otherwise.

Aug. Therefore, it is incorrect to say what you said a while ago, that in the case of the question what teaching is, the reality in question can be taught without signs. For we see that not even this can be done without giving signs, since you have granted that signifying is one thing, and teaching another. Now, if they are different, as they appear to be, and the latter cannot be manifested except by the former, then certainly it is not manifested by itself, as you thought. Consequently, we have as yet found nothing which can be manifested by itself, except speech, which also signifies itself along with other things. Still, since speech itself is also a sign, it is not yet entirely clear that anything can be taught without signs.

Ad. I have no reason for not agreeing.

31. *Aug.* It has been settled, then, that there is no teaching without signs, and that knowledge itself ought to mean more to us than the signs by means of which we know —though not all things which are signified can be superior to their signs.

Ad. So it seems.

Aug. Can you, I ask you, retrace the long circuitous route we came to find this slight result? Mind you, since we began fencing with words, and this has occupied us this entire time, we have labored to discover these three points: whether it is impossible to teach anything without signs; whether certain signs are to be preferred to the things they signify; and whether the knowledge of realities is better than the signs. But there is a fourth, and this I would like you to inform me about briefly: whether you think our conclusions to be such as to put them beyond any doubt on your part.

Ad. I should certainly hope that by such winding and tortuous roads we have arrived at some certainties. But somehow or other this question of yours disturbs me and keeps me from saying yes. For I think you would not ask me this, unless you had some objection to make; and the very complexity of these matters does not permit me to see through the entire problem and to answer with assurance. I am afraid that where so much is involved, something might escape me and my mind not prove keen enough to penetrate it.

Aug. I am glad to see your hesitation; for it betokens a cautious attitude of mind, and that is the greatest safeguard of tranquillity. Obviously, it is extremely difficult not to be perturbed when those things which we considered easily and readily proved are made to totter by contrary arguments, and, as it were, are twisted from our hands. The lesson is, just as it is right to yield to arguments that have been thoroughly investigated and weighed, so is it hazardous to consider as known what is not known. Since things which we presume are going to stand firmly and endure, are frequently undermined, there is the danger of our falling into such a great dislike or distrust of reason that we might decide not to place confidence even in evident truth.[50]

32. Anyway, let us now quicken our pace and reconsider whether you were right in doubting about these things. Suppose, for example, someone who is unfamiliar with the art of snaring birds,[51] which is done with reeds and birdlime, were to meet a fowler equipped with his instruments, though not actually fowling but just walking along. On seeing him, he hurries to catch up with him and, as is natural, reflects and asks himself in his astonishment what the man's equipment means. Suppose that the fowler, when he sees the

other man's attention riveted on himself, wishing to show off, disengages the reeds and with his rod and his hawk intercepts, subdues, and captures some little bird he happens to observe close by: would he not, I ask you, teach that spectator of his what he wanted to know, not by signifying, but by means of the reality itself?

Ad. I am afraid we have here a repetition of what I said of the man who asks what walking is: again I fail to see that the whole art of fowling has been manifested in this case.

Aug. It is easy to relieve you of that misgiving. Let me add that we suppose him to be intelligent enough to understand all the details of the art from what he sees. It is sufficient for our point that it is possible to teach at least some men some matters, though not all, without signs.

Ad. To that I can also add this: if he is really intelligent, he will grasp all there is to walking, when walking is demonstrated by a few steps.

Aug. So far as I am concerned, you may add that; and I not only do not object, but I am partial to it. You see that actually both of us have come to the conclusion that some people can be taught certain things without signs and that it is false that, as we thought a little while ago, absolutely nothing can be manifested without signs. Indeed, these examples suggest not one or the other, but thousands of things which are manifested by themselves, without any sign being given. Why, then, I ask you, should we doubt this? For, not to mention the countless performances of men in all the theatres who give exhibitions of things directly as they are without signs, does not God, and does not nature exhibit and manifest directly to the gaze of all, this sun and the light that bathes and clothes all things present, the moon

and the other stars, the earth and the seas, and all the countless things that are begotten in them?[52]

33. Now, if we consider the matter more diligently, perhaps you will find that there is nothing that is learned by
signs proper to it. For when a sign is presented to me, if
it finds me ignorant of the reality of which it is a sign, it
cannot teach me anything; but if it finds me knowing the
reality, what do I learn by means of the sign? Thus, when
I read: *And their saraballae were not altered*,[53] the word
saraballae does not manifest to me the reality which it signifies. If it is head-coverings of some sort that are called by
this name, did I upon hearing this learn either what a head
is or what coverings are? These I had known before; and
my knowledge of them was gained not when they were
called such by others, but when they were seen by myself.
The first time the two syllables *cap-ut* ["head"] struck my
ears, I was just as ignorant of what they signified as when I
first heard or read *saraballae*. But when "head" was repeatedly expressed, noting and observing when it was used,
I discovered that it was the word for a thing which was already most familiar to me from sight. Before I made that
discovery, this word was a mere sound to me; but I learned
it was a sign, when I found of what thing it is the sign; and
I had learned that reality, as I said, not by any signifying,
but by seeing it. Therefore, it is a case of the sign being
learned from the thing cognized rather than that the thing
is learned from a given sign.[54]

34. That you may understand this more clearly, suppose
that we now hear the word "head" spoken for the first time,
and, not knowing whether it is only a vocal sound or whether
it also signifies something, we ask what "head" is. (Remember, we wish to acquire knowledge not of the reality

which is signified, but of the sign itself, which knowledge we of course lack as long as we do not know of what it is the sign.) If, then, when we put the question, the reality itself is pointed out to us, we learn the sign which we had only heard and not yet understood, by seeing this reality. But since there are two elements in that sign—the sound and the signification—we certainly perceive the sound not by means of the sign, but by the simple fact that the sound strikes the ear. We learn the signification, however, by seeing the reality which is signified. For that pointing of the finger cannot signify anything else than what the finger points out; and it indicates not the sign, but the member which is called "head." Therefore, by means of the pointing I cannot learn either the reality—since I already knew it—or the sign, for the finger was not pointed at that.

But I am not stressing the pointing of the finger; because it seems to me that it is only a sign of the indication itself, rather than of any realities indicated. It is just like the adverb "look!" [ecce]. In fact, we are accustomed to point the finger even when we use this adverb, lest one of them would not be a sufficient sign of the indication. What I am above all striving to convince you of, if I can, is that we do not learn anything by means of the signs called words. For, as I have said, we learn the meaning of the word—that is, the signification that is hidden in the sound—only after the reality itself which is signified has been recognized, rather than perceive that reality by means of such signification.

35. And what I have said regarding "head," I might also say of "coverings" and countless other things. But even though I already know what these are, I still do not know what those *saraballae* are. If someone should signify them

to me by making gestures or if he should draw them for me
or show me something similar to them, I shall not say that
he would not be teaching me—which I could easily demonstrate if I cared to talk at a little greater length—but I do
say what is to the point, that it is not by means of words
that he would be teaching me. And if, chancing to see them
while I am present, he should bring them to my attention
by saying: "Here are *saraballae*," I shall learn the thing I
did not know, not by means of the words spoken, but by
seeing it; and this proved to be the means by which I grasped
and retained what the name itself signifies. Certainly, when
I learned the reality itself, I did not put my trust in the
words of another, but in my own eyes; though, perhaps, I
did put my trust in the words in order that I might direct
my attention, that is, in order that I might look for what
I should see.

CHAPTER 11

*We learn, not through words sounding in the ear,
but through truth that teaches internally.
Christ the Teacher.*

36. As we have seen them so far, the import of words—
to state the most that can be said for them—consists in this:
they serve merely to suggest that we look for realities. These
they do not exhibit to us for our knowledge. On the other
hand, a person teaches me something who presents to my
eyes or any other bodily sense or even to my mind itself
what I desire to know. By means of words, therefore, we
learn nothing but words; in fact, only the sound and noise
of words. For if things which are not signs cannot be
words, then, even though I have already heard a word, I do

not know it is a word until I know what it signifies. Consequently, with the knowledge of realities there also comes the knowledge of the words, whereas when words are heard, not even the words are learned. In fact, the words we do know we do not learn; and those we do not know we cannot but acknowledge that we learn them only on perceiving their meaning; and this occurs not by hearing the vocal sounds uttered, but by knowing the realities signified. It is indeed purest logic and most truly said that when words are uttered we either know what they signify, or we do not know. If we know, we recall[55] rather than learn; but if we do not know, we do not even recall, though perhaps we receive the impulse to inquire.

37. Now, should you say: granted that—unless we see them, we cannot establish what those head-coverings are whose name we recognize only as a sound, and we are in no better position regarding even the name, unless the objects themselves are recognized. Yet we do accept the story about those boys, how they triumphed over the king and the flames by their faith and religion, what praise they sang to God, what honors they received even from their enemy himself.[56] Have we learned these things otherwise than by means of words? I answer that we already knew everything that is signified by those words. For instance, what three boys are, what a furnace is, what fire is, what a king is, and finally, what it means to be unharmed by fire, and whatever else those words signify, I already knew. But Ananias, Azarias, and Misael are as unknown to me as the *saraballae;* and these names did not help me at all to know them, nor could they help me. Yet, that all the events which we read about in that account, actually happened at that time and in the manner described, is something that I admit I *believe*

rather than *know*.[57]   And here we have a difference of which those whom we believe were not unaware; for the Prophet says: *Unless you believe, you shall not understand.*[58]   He certainly could not have said that if he thought there is no difference between the two.   Wherefore, what I understand I also believe.   Again, everything I understand, I know; but I do not know all I believe.   But I am not for that reason unaware how useful it is to believe also many things which I do not know; and in this usefulness I also include the account of the three boys.   Hence, although the majority of things cannot possibly be known by me, yet I know how very useful it is to believe them.

38. Regarding, however, all those things which we understand, it is not a speaker who utters sounds exteriorly whom we consult, but it is truth that presides[59] within,[60] over the mind itself; though it may have been words that prompted us to make such consultation.   And He who is consulted, He who is said to *dwell in the inner man*,[61] He it is who teaches—Christ—that is, *the unchangeable Power of God and everlasting Wisdom.*[62]   This Wisdom every rational soul does, in fact, consult.[63]   But to each one only so much is manifested as he is capable of receiving because of his own good or bad will.[64]   And if one sometimes falls into error, that does not occur by reason of defect in the Truth consulted, any more than it is a defect of the light which is outside us that the eyes of the body are often deceived.[65]   And this is a light which we acknowledge that we consult in regard to visible things, that it may manifest them to us to the extent that we are able to perceive them.

CHAPTER 12

Internal light, internal truth.

39. Now, if regarding colors we consult light; and regarding the other sensible objects we consult the elements [66]
of this world constituting the bodies of which we have sense
experience, and the senses themselves which the mind uses
as interpreters to know such things;[67] and if, moreover, regarding those things which are objects of intelligence we
consult the truth within us through reasoning—then what
can be advanced as proof that words teach us anything beyond the mere sound which strikes the ears? For everything we perceive, we perceive either through a sense of the
body or by the mind. The former we call sensible, the latter,
intelligible; or, to speak in the manner of our own authors,[68]
we call the former carnal, and the latter spiritual. When
we are asked concerning the former, we answer, if the things
of which we have sense knowledge are present; as when we
are looking at a new moon we are asked what sort of a thing
it is or where it is. In this case if the one who puts the
question does not see the object, he believes words; and often
he does not believe them. But learn he does not at all,
unless he himself sees what is spoken about; and in that case
he learns not by means of spoken words, but by means of the
realities themselves and his senses. For the words have the
same sound for the one who sees the object as for the one
who does not see it. But when a question is asked not regarding things which we perceive while they are present,
but regarding things of which we had sense knowledge in
the past, then we express in speech, not the realities themselves, but the images impressed by them on the mind and

committed to memory.[69] How we can speak at all of these
as true when we see they are false,[70] I do not know—unless
it be because we report on them not as things we actually see
and perceive, but as things we have seen and perceived.
Thus we bear these images in the depths of memory as so
many attestations,[71] so to say, of things previously perceived
by the senses. Contemplating these in the mind, we have
the good conscience that we are not lying when we speak.
But even so, these attestations are such for us only. If one
who hears me has personally perceived these things and
become aware of them, he does not learn them from my
words, but recognizes them from the images that are stored
away within himself. If, however, he has had no sense
knowledge of them, he clearly believes rather than learns
by means of the words.

40. Now, when there is question of those things which
we perceive by the mind—that is, by means of the intellect
and by reason [72]—we obviously express in speech the things
which we behold immediately in that interior light of truth [73]
which effects enlightenment and happiness in the so-called
inner man. And at the same time if the one who hears me
likewise sees those things with an inner and undivided eye,
he knows the matter of which I speak by his own contemplation, not by means of my words. Hence, I do not teach
even such a one, although I speak what is true and he sees
what is true. For he is taught not by my words, but by the
realities themselves made manifest to him by God revealing
them to his inner self.[74] Thus, if he were asked, he could
also give answers regarding these things. What could be
more absurd than to think that he is taught by my speech,
when even before I spoke he could explain those same things,
if he were asked about them? [75]

As for the fact that, as often happens, one denies something when he is asked about it, but is brought around by further questions to affirm it, this happens by reason of the weakness of his vision, not permitting him to consult that light regarding the matter as a whole. He is prompted to consider the problem part by part as questions are put regarding those same parts that constitute the whole, which originally he was not able to see in its entirety. If in this case he is led on by the words of the questioner, still it is not that the words teach him, but they represent questions put to him in such a way as to correspond to his capacity for learning from his own inner self.

To illustrate: if I were to ask you whether it is true that nothing can be taught by means of words—the very topic we are discussing now—you would at first think the question absurd, because you could not see the problem in its entirety. Then I should have to question you in a way adapted to your capacity for hearing that Teacher within you. So I should say: "Those things which I stated and you granted as true, and of which you are certain and which you are sure you know—where did you learn them?" You would perhaps answer that I had taught them to you. Then I would rejoin: "Let us suppose I told you that I saw a man flying. Would my words give you the same certitude as if you heard that wise men are superior to fools?" You would, of course, answer in the negative and would tell me that you do not believe the former statement, or even if you did believe it, that you did not know it; whereas you knew the other statement to be absolutely certain. Certainly, the upshot of this would be that you would then realize that you had not learned anything from my words; neither in the case where you were not aware of the thing that I affirmed, nor in the case of that which you knew very well. For if you were

asked about each case, you would even swear that you were
unaware of the former and that you did know the latter. But
then you would actually be admitting the entire proposition
which you had denied, since you would now know clearly
and certainly what it implies: namely, that whatever we
say, the hearer either does not know whether it is true, or
knows it is false, or knows that it is true. In the first of
these three cases he either believes, or has an opinion, or is
in doubt; in the second, he opposes and rejects the statement;
in the third, he bears witness to the truth. In none of the
cases, therefore, does he learn. The obvious reason is that
the one who on hearing my words does not know the reality,
and the one who knows that what he has heard is false, and
the one who, if he were asked, could have answered precisely what was said, demonstrate that they have learned
nothing from my words.[76]

CHAPTER 13

*Words do not always have the power even to reveal
the mind of the speaker.*

41. Therefore, also in regard to the things which are
seen by the mind, it is of no avail for anyone who cannot
perceive them to hear the words of another who does perceive them, except in so far as it is useful to believe them,
so long as one is not acquainted with them. But anyone
who is able to perceive them is in his innermost a pupil of
truth and outside himself a judge of the speaker[77] or, rather,
of what he says. For often enough he has knowledge of
what is said even when the speaker lacks such knowledge.
For example, someone who is a follower of the Epicureans

and thinks the soul is mortal, sets forth the arguments for its immortality as expounded by wiser men. If one who is able to contemplate spiritual things hears him, he judges that the other is expressing the truth, while the speaker does not know whether the arguments are true; indeed he even thinks them utterly false. Is he, then, to be considered as teaching what he does not know? Yet he is using the very same words which one who does have the knowledge could also use.

42. Hence, not even this function is left to words, that they at least manifest the mind of the one who speaks them, since it is even uncertain whether he knows as true what he expresses. Take also the liars and deceivers: you can readily see that they employ words not only not to reveal their minds, but even to conceal them. I do not at all doubt, of course, that the words of those who tell the truth represent efforts and, in a way, promises, to manifest the mind of the speaker; and they would be sustained in this and find acceptance by all, if liars were not allowed to speak.

Of course, we have often experienced both in ourselves and in others, that words are uttered which do not correspond to the things thought about. This, I see, can happen in two ways: either a piece of diction that has been committed to memory and frequently repeated passes the mouth of one actually thinking of other things—as often happens to us when we are singing a hymn; or, contrary to our intention and by a slip of the tongue, some words will rush out in the place of others; obviously, in this case, too, what is heard does not represent the things that are in the mind. In fact, those who tell lies also think of what they express, so that even though we do not know whether they are expressing the truth, we nevertheless know that they have in mind what they are saying, if neither of the two things I spoke of applies to them. If anyone contends that these latter things occur only occasionally and that it is apparent when they occur, I make no objection; though they frequently do escape notice and they have often deceived me when I heard them.

43. But in addition to these there is another class, certainly very extensive, and the source of countless disagreements and disputes: when the one who speaks signifies exactly what he is thinking, but generally only to himself and certain others, while he does not signify the same thing to the one to whom he speaks and to a number of other persons. For example, let someone say in our hearing that man is surpassed in virtue [78] by certain brute animals. We resent that at once, and with great insistence we refute that statement as utterly false and harmful. Yet he may be using the term "virtue" to designate physical strength, and expressing by it what he has in mind; and he would not be lying, nor is he in error regarding the realities, nor is he reeling off words he has memorized, while he ponders something else in his mind; nor does he express by a slip of the tongue something he did not intend to say. But he merely calls the reality of which he is thinking, by another name than we do; and we should at once agree with him regarding that reality, if we could see his thought, which he was not able to manifest to us by the words he had already spoken in proposing his opinion.

They say that a definition can correct this type of error; so that, if in the present case the speaker should define what "virtue" means, it would be made clear, they say, that the dispute concerns not the reality, but the term used. Even granting that this is so, how many are there who can give good definitions? Even with regard to the method of defining, there has been much discussion; but it is not opportune to treat of that here, nor am I entirely satisfied with it.

44. I pass over the fact that there are many things we do not hear distinctly and that we enter long-drawn-out argumentations about them, as if we had heard them. Recently, for instance, when I had said that a certain Punic[79] word means "compassion," you said that you had heard from those who are more familiar with that language, that it means "kindness." But I objected to that, insisting that you forgot what you had been told; for I thought you had said not "kindness" but "fidelity," even though you were sitting right near me, and these two nouns are not at all deceptive to the ear by reason of similarity of sound. Yet, for a long time I thought you did not know what was said to you, whereas it was I who did not know what you had said. For if I had heard you distinctly, it would never have seemed absurd to me that "kindness" and "compassion" are expressed by the same word in the Punic language.

Such things happen very frequently; but, as I said, let us pass them by, lest I seem to raise a prejudice against words on account of the negligence of one who hears them, or even on account of human deafness. More disturbing are the cases which I enumerated before, where we are not able to know the thoughts of speakers, even though we speak the same language and the words are in Latin and most distinctly heard.

45. But listen to this—I now yield and concede that when words have been heard by one to whom they are familiar, he can know that the speaker has been thinking about the realities which they signify. But does he for that reason also learn whether what is said is true, which is the present point of inquiry?[80]

CHAPTER 14

*Christ teaches within the mind. Man's words are
external, and serve only to give reminders.*

Teachers do not claim, do they, that their own thoughts
are perceived and grasped by the pupils, but rather the
branches of learning that they think they transmit by speaking? For who would be so absurdly curious as to send his
child to school to learn what the teacher thinks? But when
they have explained, by means of words, all those subjects
which they profess to teach, and even the science of virtue
ard of wisdom, then those who are called pupils consider
within themselves whether what has been said is true. This
they do by gazing attentively at that interior truth, so far
as they are able.[81] Then it is that they learn; and when
within themselves they find that what has been said is true,
they give praise, not realizing that they are praising not so
much teachers as persons taught[82]—provided that the teachers also know what they are saying. But people deceive
themselves in calling persons "teachers" who are not such
at all, merely because generally there is no interval between
the time of speaking and the time of knowing. And because they are quick to learn internally following the prompt-
ing of the one who speaks, they think they have learned
externally from the one who was only a prompter.[83]

46. But at some other time, God willing, we shall investi-
gate the entire problem of the utility of words,[84] which, if
considered properly, is not negligible. For the present, I
have reminded you that we must not attribute to words more
than is proper. Thus we should no longer merely believe,
but also begin to understand how truly it has been written
on divine authority that we should not call anyone on earth

a teacher, since *there is One in heaven who is the teacher of all.*[85] What "in heaven" means He Himself will teach us, who has also counselled us through the instrumentality of human beings—by means of signs, and externally—to turn to Him internally and be instructed. He will teach us, to know and love whom is happiness of life,[86] and this is what all proclaim they are seeking,[87] though there are but few who may rejoice in having really found it.[88]

And now I would like you to tell me what you think of this entire disquisition of mine. Indeed, if you have come to realize that what has been said is true, then if you had been asked about the several propositions, you would have stated that you knew them. You see, then, from whom you have learned these things.[89] No, it is not from me, for you would have given me all the answers as I questioned you. But if you have not ascertained that what has been said is true, neither have I taught you, nor has He. Not I, because I am unable to teach in any case; not He, because you are still unable to learn.

Ad. As for me, I have learned, thanks to being reminded by your words, that words do no more than prompt man to learn, and that what appears to be, to a considerable extent, the thought of the speaker expressing himself, really amounts to extremely little. Moreover, as to whether what is said is true, He alone teaches who when He spoke externally reminded us that He dwells within us. I shall now, with His help, love Him the more ardently the more I progress in learning.

Meanwhile, I am grateful for this disquisition delivered by you without interruption, especially for this reason, that it has anticipated and refuted every objection I was prepared to make. Not one misgiving of mine have you ignored; and there is nothing regarding which that hidden Oracle[90] did not give me the same answer as was stated in your words.

NOTES

THE GREATNESS OF THE SOUL

INTRODUCTION

[1] *De ord.* 2. 18. 47: 'The study of philosophy . . . treats of two problems: one regarding the soul, and the other regarding God. The goal of the first is to know ourselves; the goal of the second is to know our origin. The former is more pleasing to us; the latter, more valuable. The former makes us fit for a happy life; the latter gives us happiness. The first is for those beginning to learn, and the other for those who are well-instructed.' The well-known words of the *Soliloquia* (1. 2. 7) mention the same realities as completing the scope of Augustine's personal interest: *Augustine*—'I desire to know God and my soul.' *Reason*—'Nothing else?' *Augustine*—'Nothing at all.' In the present treatise, *De quant. an.* 14. 24, he speaks of the knowledge of self and of God as being equivalent to 'knowledge of truth.'

[2] *Conf.* 5. 10. 19: 'Et quoniam cum de Deo meo cogitare vellem, cogitare nisi moles corporum non noveram—neque enim videbatur mihi esse quicquam, quod tale corporeale non esset—ea maxima et prope sola causa erat inevitabilis erroris mei.' Cf. *ibid.* 3. 7. 12; 4. 2. 3; 4. 16. 31; etc.

[3] *Ibid.* 5. 10. 20. This materialistic solution appealed to him, not for its theoretical merits, but because it was apparently the simplest answer to a problem that tortured him; besides, it was reassuring to him, in his turbulent youth, to believe that the immorality of which he was conscious was caused by something outside himself. There were, however, other factors that influenced him to accept the heresy. The adherents of the sect claimed that they were Christians, and that their founder, being an incarnation of the Paraclete, was another Christ; and from his tenderest years, Augustine had a deep devotion to Christ, at least as a man. Again, he nursed an innate desire to *understand* everything, so that faith in Catholic mysteries repelled him, whereas the rationalistic Manichaeans claimed that all truth could be seen, not merely believed. Augustine was never completely convinced of the truth of Manichaeism (*Conf.* 8. 7. 17), although he remained an adherent for about nine years.

[4] Cf. *Conf.* 5. 14. 25.

[5] The Saint acknowledges this indebtedness in the preface to his book *De beata vita* (1. 4) which he addresses to Theodorus. In the

189

Retractationes (1.2.2) he expresses regret at having attributed to Theodorus more than was proper (*plus tribui quam deberem*). It is not clear whether he wishes to retract the acknowledgment of the influence of the Platonist on his conception of the immaterial, or merely the fulsomeness of praise he had bestowed on his benefactor. As for the influence of St. Ambrose in making him understand that the teaching 'man is made in the *image* of God' does not mean that either God or the human soul is material, Augustine pays further tribute to it in *Conf.* 6. 3. 4.

⁶ See *De civ. Dei* 8. 5 f. In the much-quoted passage of *Conf.* 7. 9. 13-15, Augustine claimed to find in the 'Platonists' specifically Christian teachings such as the divinity and eternity of the Word (Λόγος), His equality with the Father, and His supernatural influence on the souls of men. He misses as omitted in these writings only the truths of the Incarnation and Passion of Christ. But, whether Marius Victorinus, the celebrated African rhetorician who translated the works of Plotinus and other Platonists, had interpreted them according to Christian norms, or whether Augustine himself read into the works a Christian interpretation, the fact is that neither Plotinus in his *Enneads* nor any of the other Neoplatonic writers were so close to Christian truth as the *Confessions* would indicate. See A. C. Pegis, "The Mind of St. Augustine," *Med. Stud.* 6 (1944) 24. On the influence of Marius Victorinus upon Augustine, see C. Gore in *Dict. of Chr. Biogr.* 4. 1129-38. But Gore goes too far—cf. F. Ueberweg—M. Baumgartner, *Grundriss der Geschichte der Philosophie* 2: *Die mittlere oder die patristische und scholastische Zeit* (10th ed., Berlin 1915) 148.

⁷ Cf. *Retract.* 1.8.1. Augustine had received baptism in Milan late in April, 387. With his mother and a group of friends he left Milan, probably early in the summer of that year, to return to Africa. When Monnica died en route at Ostia, the return to Africa was postponed and Augustine stayed at Rome till August of the following year. Cf. S. M. Zarb, *Chronologia operum S. Augustini* (Rome 1934) 30 f.

⁸ Cf. *Conf.* 9. 8. 17.

⁹ *Ibid.* 9. 12. 31.

¹⁰ Cf. *Retract.* 1. 9. 1.

¹¹ Cf. Possidius, *Vita Aur. August.* 5.

¹² This correspondence, dating from the years 414-415, is given by A. Goldbacher, S. *Aurelii Augustini Hipponiensis Episcopi Epistulae*, Pars 3, CSEL 44. The letters of Evodius to Augustine are:

158 (pp. 488-97), 160 (503-6), 161 (507-511), 163 (520 f.). Augustine's answers to the questions are contained in letters 159 (497-502), 162 (511-20), 164 (521-41), 169 (611-22). In *Epist.* 162. 2 (513), Augustine gently reproves his friend for asking so many questions, and reminds him that he will find the answers to some of them in the works on which Evodius himself had collaborated, *De quantitate animae* and *De libero arbitrio*. For a sketch of the life of Evodius (d. Oct. 16, 424), cf. P. Godet, 'Evodius,' *DTC* 5. 2 (1923) 1731.—A short work ascribed to Augustine, the *De fide contra Manichaeos* (ML 42. 1139-54), was probably written by Evodius: cf. O. Bardenhewer, *Geschichte der altkirchlichen Literatur* 4 (Freiburg i. Br. 1924) 466 f.

13 Cf. *Retract.* 1. 8. 1.

14 See text, 3. 4.

15 See text, 21. 35 - 22. 40; also 31. 63 and n. 80.

16 See text, 7. 11 - 14. 24.   On Augustine's enthusiasm for numbers and geometrical illustrations, see especially A. Schmitt, "Mathematik und Zahlenmystik," in M. Grabmann—J. Mausbach, *Aurelius Augustinus: Festschrift der Görres-Gesellschaft zum 1500. Todestage des hl. Augustinus* (Cologne 1930) 353-66.

17 Cf. C. Butler, *Western Mysticism* (New York 1924) 23-88, esp. 37, 59 f., 63, 68 f.; also P. Pourrat, *Christian Spirituality* (trans. by W. H. Mitchell and S. P. Jacques, London 1922) 209-217.

18 *De mor. Eccl. Cath.* 1. 2. 3: 'Where, then, shall I begin? With authority or with reason? In the natural order, when we learn anything, authority precedes reason.' Augustine had expressed himself to somewhat the same effect in the first work he published after his conversion (*Cont. Acad.* 3. 20. 43): 'No one doubts that we are incited to acquire knowledge by a twofold influence, that of authority and that of reason. As for me, I am firmly resolved never to deviate in the least from the authority of Christ; for I find no stronger one. But as to what is to be attained by profound reasoning—for I am so constituted that I impatiently desire to apprehend truth not by belief alone but also by understanding—I am confident that I shall meanwhile find among the Platonists what is not in opposition to our sacred writings.' In accordance with the same attitude, his reading —at the age of nineteen—of Cicero's *Hortensius* with its exhortation to philosophy, thrilled him with religious enthusiasm and made him ardently long for imperishable wisdom, yet it sorely disappointed him because 'the name of Christ did not appear in it' (*Conf.* 3. 4. 8). He was attracted to the philosophy of the Platonists not merely be-

cause 'they are nearer to the truth than the others' (*De civ. Dei* 11. 5), but also, and, we might even say, especially, because 'no others have approached more closely to us then they have' (*ibid.* 8. 4), so that 'by changing a few words and propositions, they might be made Christian' (*De vera rel.* 4. 7).

[19] *Serm.* 150. 3. 4: 'It has been the common aim of all philosophers *to attain happiness of life* by studying, making enquiries, engaging in discussions, and by their very manner of living. This has been the sole purpose of pursuing philosophy. And I think that even this purpose the philosophers have in common with ourselves. For if I should ask you why you believe in Christ, and why you have become Christians, every man among you will truthfully answer: "To attain a happy life." The desire of a happy life, then, is common to philosophers and to Christians.'

[20] Cf. *Cont. Acad.* 3. 20. 43; also *De civ. Dei* 8. 4 and 11. 5.

[21] This thesis, first suggested by G. Boissier, in "La conversion de saint Augustin," *Revue des deux mondes* 85 (1888) 43-69, and accepted and variously developed by many other French and German Patristic scholars, received its classic formulation and most detailed defense in the work of P. Alfaric, *L'évolution intellectuelle de saint Augustin. I. Du manichéisme au néoplatonisme* (Paris 1918). For a good history of the problem, cf. C. Boyer, *Christianisme et néoplatonisme dans la formation de saint Augustin* (Paris 1920) 2-16. A full and useful summary of the literature for and against the thesis is given by Sr. M. P. Garvey, *Saint Augustine: Christian or Neo-Platonist?* (Milwaukee 1939) 3-38.

[22] Throughout the whole discussion of sensation in the *De quantitate animae* (23. 41 - 30. 61) it becomes clear that Augustine considers the soul alone as the principle from which the act of sensation proceeds. See below, n. 73 to the text, where the identical view of Plotinus is cited.

[23] The seven levels of the soul that Augustine describes in this book (33. 70 - 36. 69) correspond to activities of the soul delineated by Plotinus in various parts of the *Enneads*. See Garvey, *op. cit.* 150, 152 f.

[24] Augustine can be said to 'exaggerate' the superiority of the spiritual human soul over material things, insofar as he could never realize clearly that the soul is united to the human body to constitute one entity, and that the body also is an intrinsic co-principle in the act of sensation; cf. nn. 73, 75, 115, and 123 to the text.

[25] See n. 2 on text 1. 2.

[26] See below, n. 111 on the text.

[27] Porphyry, his biographer, says of him (*Plotini Vita* 1): 'Plotinus, the philosopher, our contemporary, seemed ashamed of being in the body. So deeply rooted was this feeling that he could never be induced to tell of his ancestry, his parentage, or his birthplace. He showed, too, an unconquerable reluctance to sit to a painter or a sculptor, and when Amelius persisted in urging him to allow a portrait being made, he asked him: "Is it not enough to carry about this image, in which nature has enclosed me? Do you really think I must also consent to leave, as a desirable spectacle to posterity, an image of the image?"' (trans. by S. MacKenna, in *Plotinus: Enneads* [London 1921] 1.9).

[28] See text 33.76 and 36.81.

[29] See text 36.81 and n. 123.

[30] See text 33.76 and 34.77.

[31] See text 34.80. Plotinus conceives of the soul attaining to union with the Absolute by its own unaided powers; cf. *Enn.* 1.6.9.

[32] See text 33.73 and n. 94.

TEXT

[1] *Quod supra nos, quid ad nos?* This is a saying ascribed to Socrates (cf. Xenophon, *Mem.* 1.1.11, 4.7.6): ʽΑ ὑπὲρ ἡμᾶς τί πρὸς ἡμᾶς; the formula also occurs in Minucius Felix, *Oct.* 13.1; Lactantius, *Inst. div.* 3.20.10; etc.: cf. A. Otto, *Die Sprichwörter und sprichwörtlichen Redensarten der Römer* (Leipzig 1890) 335.

[2] *Propriam quamdam habitationem animae ac patriam Deum ipsum credo esse a quo creata est.* The reference to *patria* is reminiscent of Plotinus (*Enneads* 1.6.8): 'The fatherland, for us, is where we came from and where our Father is.' It is especially significant, however, that Augustine, now that he is a Catholic, thus early and clearly acknowledges the total dependence of the human soul upon the creative act of God. This is a distinct advance over the view he held at, and after, the age of twenty, when he considered that God was 'a luminous and tremendous body and that man was a fragment of that body' (*Conf.* 4.16.31). It is also definitely at variance with the view of Plotinus that the human soul comes into being as an emanation from the Absolute—the 'One'—through the world-soul (*Enn.* 5.1.7). The acceptance of the notion of creation

definitely marks Augustine a Christian thinker, in essential disagreement with the Platonic philosophers. Cf. *De civ. Dei* 10. 31. See M. C. D'Arcy, 'The Philosophy of St. Augustine,' in *A monument to St. Augustine* (London 1930) 186 f.

Regarding the time and precise nature of the creation of the human soul, however, he has given no definite conclusion. He treats lengthily and repeatedly of two distinct questions: (1) the origin of the *first* human soul, and (2) the origin of the souls of the descendants of Adam and Eve.

The first problem received extended treatment in his great work *De Genesi ad litteram*, which was begun in the year 401 and finished in 414 or 415. Although he shows no hesitancy in rejecting the views that the human soul is a part of God, or formed from the souls of irrational animals, or from the accepted four bodily elements, or from a fifth distinct corporeal reality, the Saint finds it difficult to choose between direct creation without any material cause, and production of Adam's soul from some previously created spiritual substance which serves as the 'stuff' or material cause (*spiritualis materies*) in which the soul existed as in its *ratio seminalis* (*De Gen. ad litt.*, bk. 7). The last two views seem to him most compatible with Holy Scripture, but each has its advantages and disadvantages. He inclines toward the direct creation by God of the soul of the first man, and also, as more probable, the soul of the first woman. He remains undecided whether the first human soul was produced by God in the very beginning, together with the rest of the universe, or 'on the sixth day,' when it was united to a body, but he considers the former the more likely explanation. For, according to *Genesis*, all things were created together, and it seemed to Augustine that even human souls had to have some existence outside the Divine Mind from the beginning; and the 'spiritual stuff' would allow for this. However, he acknowledges (7. 22. 33) that it is hard to conceive such a thing and to understand what properties it would have.

As to the origin of the individual souls of descendants of Adam and Eve, Augustine found it a fascinating but perplexing problem. At least as early as the year 395, when he published *De libero arbitrio*, begun in the year 388, he knew of four different views: (1) that the individual human soul is propagated or generated by the soul of the parents; (2) that it is created by God and directly infused into the matter prepared by the parents; (3) that it is first created to exist separately before the body comes into being, and is put into the body by God; (4) that it first exists separately and is united to some body by its own choice. He is unable to come to a definite decision in the matter; cf. *De lib. arb.* 3. 21. 59-61. What concerns him most in that context, however, is how original sin is transmitted from Adam to all his progeny, and he thinks none of these four opinions definitely excludes that inheritance (*op. cit.* 3. 20. 55-58). His intention here is not so much to try to solve the problem of the origin of souls as to show that the goodness and justice of God can be safeguarded, no matter which of the four hypotheses be accepted. Later, in the tenth book of *De Gen. ad litt.*, he considers the first two of the four views as more compatible with Scripture. Since divine authority does not seem to favor either of the two more than the other, Augustine endeavors to come to a conclusion on a rational basis, but with little success. He inclines, however, toward the first view, later called 'spiritual traducianism,' or 'generationism,' since he thinks it accounts better for the transmission of original sin, without impairing the goodness and justice of God (see *Epist.* 166. 3. 6-5. 14). On the other hand, it does not readily account for the sinlessness of Christ; cf. *Epist.* 164. 7.

Although he labored over this problem recurrently through his whole lifetime, Augustine had to admit that the details of the origin of the human soul were to him unfathomable. In *Retract.* 1. 1. 3, he wrote: 'Quod attinet ad eius (animi) originem, qua fit ut sit in corpore, utrum de illo uno sit, qui primum creatus est, quando factus est homo in animam vivam; an similiter ita fiant singulis singuli, nec tunc sciebam, nec adhuc scio.' Cf. also *Opus imperf. cont. Julian.* 2. 178: '. . . *me nescire confiteor* . . .'; this was written at the very end of his life. See C. Boyer, "La théorie augustinienne des raisons séminales," in *Miscellanea Agostiniana* 2 (Rome 1931) 795-810; E. Gilson, *Introduction a l'étude de S. Augustin* (2nd ed. Paris 1943) 66-68; W. O'Connor, *The Concept of the Human Soul according to St. Augustine* (Cath. Univ. diss., Washington 1921) 67-77.

[8] Following the teaching of Aristotle, which was an adaptation of various earlier physical theories, it was commonly held that all matter was composed of different proportions and combinations of four primary *elements*—air, water, earth, and fire—having four fundamental qualities: hot, cold, dry, and moist. Interchanging these qualities could convert one element into another, but the elements themselves were considered irreducible to simpler bodies. It has been found, of course, that these four 'elements' are also composites, but the notion of basic and indivisible particles of matter has long survived in modern science. In the early nineteenth century it was

thought that the atoms of the so-called 'chemical elements' were the ultimate units of matter. Now, though they are still considered as indivisible by *chemical* means, they have an 'atomic structure' of their own and are *physically* divisible.

⁴ *Cum simplex quiddam et propriae substantiae videatur esse.* The purpose of the author in this context is merely to insist that the soul is not made up of bodily elements, and, therefore, that it is some sort of being distinct from anything corporeal. Hence, *substantiae* may be understood as denoting merely 'essence' or 'reality,' and not necessarily as implying that the soul is a complete nature, without any intrinsic relationship to the body. Similarly, in *De immortalitate animae* 2. 2, he says: 'Corpus nostrum nonnulla substantia est, et melius est esse substantiam quam nihil,' understanding *substantia* to mean 'an entity' or 'a positive reality.' Thus he could say later that 'whatever is not a substance is nothing at all'—*quod nulla substantia est, nihil omino est (Enarr. in Ps.* 68. 1. 5).

However, in the light of his definition of soul as *substantia quaedam rationis particeps, regendo corpori accommodata* (cf. text 13. 22 and n. 27, *infra*), the present expression also reflects vaguely his Platonic conception of the soul as a *complete* nature. Still, he is able to speak of it, two sentences before, as one of the elements composing man, and this is again stated in 33. 70: 'the soul by its presence gives life to this earth- and death-bound body.' It is evident, then, that all through the present work Augustine's lifelong inability to come to a clear doctrine on the nature of the union between the human soul and body makes itself felt. See below, n. 123.

⁵ *In mysteriis,* that is, the sacraments of baptism, confirmation, and eucharist, in which Augustine was instructed by Bishop Ambrose of Milan during Lent, 387, and which he received on the night of Easter Sunday. For *mysteria = sacramenta,* cf. Ambrose, *De mysteriis* 1. 2: 'Nunc de *mysteriis* dicere tempus admonet atque ipsam *sacramentorum* rationem edere.' Cf. *ibid.* 2. 6, in confirmation of what Augustine states in the present passage: '*Noli considerare corporum figuras,* sed mysteriorum gratiam.' The *De mysteriis* (cf. J. Quasten, *Monumenta eucharistica et liturgica vetustissima* [Bonn 1935] 113-39) and the *De sacramentis* (Quasten, *ibid.* 139-77) of Ambrose consist of instructions, probably taken down in shorthand and then edited, on the sacraments, such as Augustine and his friends had received at Milan—less than a year before the *De quantitate animae* was written.

⁶ Augustine's certitude on this central point, expressed so soon

and so definitely, shows that the purpose of his discussion is not to discover the truth for himself, but to settle it for Evodius and to show it as attainable by reason, no less than by faith. He had already come to accept this truth even before he became very familiar with the works of the Neoplatonists (see Introd. 3 ff. and n. 5 f.). Later he was even more emphatic in his declaration of the immateriality of the soul: 'That the soul is not corporeal, I state openly I not only believe, but know clearly and for certain' (De Gen. ad litt. 12. 33. 62).

⁷ Evodius is here expressing the attitude of the Stoics which Augustine himself had held some years earlier. See Conf. 4. 15. 24 and 5. 10. 19.

⁸ Augustine's word is altitudo, which can mean 'height,' or 'depth,' or even 'thickness' (as in the case of the thread, adduced by Evodius in 6. 10; cf. also the well-remembered example in Caesar's Bellum Gallicum [3. 13]: transtra ex pedalibus in altitudinem trabibus = 'crossbeams consisting of timbers a foot thick'). It obviously stands, therefore, in Augustine's present usage, for 'third dimension' in general. The ambiguity justifies the dubiousness of Evodius in the present context: 'Quam dicas altitudinem, non intelligo.' St. Augustine, in his answer, describes it as that which gives interior solidity to a body. As is evident from 12. 21, he considers length and width as being described on a horizontal plane, and altitudo as normally rising up from these.

⁹ In the natural order there is no body existing actually and concretely without the three dimensions, and that is all St. Augustine wants to establish here and in 3. 4, where he says: 'Non enim ullo modo aut longa, aut lata, aut quasi solida suspicanda est anima: corporea ista sunt, ut mihi videtur.' From these statements alone, I think, it cannot be argued that he held the view later espoused by Descartes (Principia philosophiae 2. 10 f.; Meditationes 2) that a body essentially consists of length, breadth, and thickness. That Augustine allows for an underlying 'substance,' or 'thing-in-itself,' is arguable, so far as the De quantitate animae is concerned. Elsewhere, however, he uses expressions that suggest, at least, that the essence of a body is extension. He defines body as 'naturam quamlibet longitudine, latitudine, altitudine, spatium loci occupantem' (De Gen. ad litt. 7. 21. 27); cf. also: De anima et eius origine 4. 21. 35 and Epist. 166. 2. 4. He states in Epist. 187. 6. 18: 'Nam spatia locorum tolle corporibus, nusquam erunt, et quia nusquam erunt, nec erunt. Tolle ipsa corpora qualitatibus corporum, non erit ubi sint, et ideo necesse est ut non sint.' These and similar passages

justify E. Gilson (*op. cit.* 59 n. 2) in pointing out 'le caractère déjà cartésien de cette définition du corps par l'étendue et le mouvement, ainsi que de la distinction entre l'âme et le corps qu'elle fonde . . .'

[10] Compare Monnica's words (*De beata vita* 3. 21): 'If reason compels this conclusion, I cannot deny it.'

[11] While it is perfectly true that an inanimate body cannot exercise memory, it is nevertheless likewise true that 'sensitive memory' or the power of reproducing and recognizing images of material things that have previously been known, is a function not of the soul alone, but of the composite of body and soul. In the present work (33. 71 f.) Augustine makes the distinction between sensitive memory, common to man and brute animals, and intellectual memory, which is proper to man; but because of his lack of a clear doctrine on the union between body and soul, he seems to ascribe even the former to the soul alone, as he also considers the soul alone to be the subject of external sense knowledge. In the present context, however, it is enough for his argument that memory requires the exercise of powers of the soul, and not merely of matter.

[12] The three dimensions, even considered separately from one another, are not incorporeal or immaterial in the sense of 'spiritual,' such as the human soul is. They pertain to quantity, which is a characteristic only of the material. But the author's point is that they can be considered by the intellect separately from matter, or 'abstractly.'

[13] This disregard for names, so long as the reality designated is properly understood, is often expressed by Augustine. See below, 11. 18, and also *De ordine* 2. 2. 4: 'If there were disagreement between us about words, it could easily be disregarded, so long as we see the reality itself as conceived in your mind'; and again, *Contra Cresconium* 1. 13. 16: 'When the reality itself is understood, we ought to be less concerned about what people have decided to call it.'

[14] There is here a slight trace of a feeling of superiority over those who are unable to speculate on the deeper meanings of the truths they believe. The same thing is suggested in *De ordine* 2. 5. 15: 'But if people are easy-going, or preoccupied with other affairs, or dull-witted, let them buttress themselves with faith, so that He who permits no one to perish who genuinely believes in Him through the mysteries, may by that bond draw them to Himself and free them from these dread entanglements of error' (see also *ibid.* 2. 9. 26; 2. 11. 30). This is even more evident in Augustine's other dialogue

with Evodius, *De libero arbitrio* 2.2.6: 'We must hold that these things can be perceived and grasped by people *of superior endowment (melioribus)* even while they live on this earth, and certainly by *all* who are good and holy, after this life.' However, in the present context he goes on to give complete approbation to reliance on authority as a safe procedure, and in *Soliloquia* 1.13.23 he indicates that the effort to understand what is believed also implies imperfection. Shortly after his ordination to the priesthood in 391 (cf. *Retract.* 1.14) Augustine wrote *De utilitate credendi*, in which he treats the question of the relative values of reason and belief, especially in matters of religion.

¹⁵ The Saint had already acknowledged that he himself had this desire: 'I am so constituted that I impatiently desire to apprehend truth, not by belief alone but also by understanding . . .' (*Cont. Acad.* 3.20.43).

¹⁶ This is reminiscent of Aristotle, *Nicomachean Ethics* 5.3: 'the just is the equal' (τὸ δίκαιον ἴσον). Aristotle goes on to illustrate and explain justice by illustrations from geometrical proportions. St. Augustine, treating of equality in mathematical figures, characteristically is reminded of moral notions.

¹⁷ *Et, quod in illa quae tribus lineis paribus clauditur, non inveniebamus, adest huic parilitas contrariorum: nam lineae linea; et angulus angulo est, ut cernis, contrarius.* McMahon translates: 'While we could not find this equality in the figure that is enclosed by three equal sides, yet this figure has an equality of opposites, for a side is opposite an angle and an angle opposite a side.' Besides involving a change of the meaning of the last part of the sentence (*nam lineae linea* . . .), this interpretation takes the *huic* to refer to *illa quae tribus lineis paribus clauditur*, whereas Augustine makes it refer to the words of the first sentence: *ea . . . quae quattuor lineis paribus, totidemque angulis paribus constet.*

¹⁸ *Ex diverso latere.*

¹⁹ *Quamvis latitudo sola sit*, that is, pure width, considered independently and wholly apart, e.g. from figures.

²⁰ 'Sign'—rendering Augustine's *signum*, which in turn is a mere translation of the Euclidean σημεῖον. This distinction of terms, *punctum* and *signum*, is not commonly preserved, the word 'point' being used, in mathematical as well as popular terminology, also for the termini of a line. The word 'dot' suggests itself as a possible rendering for *signum*, but it is scarcely current as a mathematical or geometrical term and is at best only slightly suggestive of what is

meant by σημεῖον—*signum*. For a convenient illustration of definitions of the present mathematical concept and others found in the
context under consideration, see the extracts from the *Elements*
(στοιχεῖα) of Euclid in Wilamowitz-Moellendorf's celebrated *Griech-
isches Lesebuch* 1: Text (3rd ed., Berlin 1906) 235 ff.

[21] See above, n. 13.

[22] See above, 4. 6, and n. 8.

[23] See above, n. 12.

[24] 'Soul': for one of the few times in this work, the author here
uses *animus* instead of *anima*. In his various writings he had difficulty in finding one word that adequately expresses all the functions
of the human soul (cf. *De Gen. ad litt.* 7. 21). In *De diversis
quaestionibus* 83, composed in the years 388-95, he writes (qu. 7):
*'Anima' aliquando ita dicitur, ut cum mente intelligatur; veluti
cum dicimus hominem ex anima et corpore constare; aliquando ita,
ut excepta mente dicatur. Sed cum excepta mente dicitur, ex iis
operibus intelligitur quae habemus cum bestiis communia. Bestiae
namque carent ratione, quae mentis semper est propria.* Hence, the
term *anima* is used generically to stand for both the principle of
rational life and the principle of vegetative and sensitive life in man.
In *De Trinitate*, written between 399 and 419, he uses the words
mens and *animus* as synonymous, and goes on to say (15. 1. 1): *Quo
nomine (animo) nonnulli auctores linguae latinae, id quod excellit in
homine, et non est in pecore, ab 'anima' quae inest et pecori, suo
quodam more distinguunt.* He indicates in the preceding sentence
that he uses *animus* or *mens* in that context only for what pertains
to the rational part of man. In *De Gen. ad litt.* 7. 21, he uses *spiritus
vitae* as synonymous with *anima*, while in *De natura et origine
animae* (or *De anima et eius origine*), written in the year 420 or
421, he says that *spiritus* refers to the higher functions of the soul,
and *anima* to the lower, although the latter also has a generic sense
which includes the meaning of *spiritus* (cf. *op. cit.* 4. 22. 36-23. 37).
Cf. E. Gilson, *op. cit.* 56 f., and W. O'Connor, *op. cit.* 38 f. So far
as the present work *De quantitate animae* is concerned, Augustine
uses the term *animus* only in 5. 8 and in chapters 13 and 14, where
he speaks especially of the soul's specifically rational functions; in
the rest of the work, and even in the outline of all the powers of the
soul (33. 70-76), he uses the word *anima* generically.

[25] This parallel between bodily sight and intellectual knowledge is
brought out again in 27.53, and it has frequently been mentioned
by Augustine elsewhere; for instance: '. . . understanding is to the

mind what seeing is to the sense-power' (*De ord.* 2.3.10). While the phrase he uses in the present context—'by some sort of remarkable affinity of realities' (*mira quadam rerum cognatione*)—suggests a Platonic viewpoint, the argument that since the objects of the knowledge or 'vision' of the soul or mind are immaterial, so must the soul be immaterial, is the same as that proposed by the Aristotelian St. Thomas Aquinas: *Summa theol.* I, 75, 5, c.

[26] He is referring to his statement that the soul 'seems to be something simple and to have an essence all its own' (above, 1.2; cf. also n. 4).

[27] *Nam mihi videtur esse substantia quaedam rationis particeps, regendo corpori accommodata.* This famous definition of the soul, especially in its last three words, reflects the Platonic view that the human soul is a complete entity, only accidentally united to the human body, somewhat as the rider to the horse or the sailor to the ship. Augustine is concerned primarily with showing the difference between the visible body and the invisible soul, and the superiority of the latter over the former. The Platonic conception helps him to achieve these ends. But it leads to a view of the nature of man which is untenable from a Christian standpoint, and which Augustine himself rejects; cf. below, n. 58. His inability to settle the problem of the nature of the union of spiritual soul and material body prevents him from giving an entirely satisfactory definition of the soul itself. Cf. Gilson, *op. cit.* 57 f., 62, 80, 115 ff. St. Thomas Aquinas considers the soul substantial, but insofar as it, together with matter, constitutes the complete and unified substance, man, he recognizes it as 'incomplete in the order of species,' although it is also complete or subsistent 'in the order of substance,' insofar as it can operate, and therefore exist, independently of the body (cf. *Summa theol.* I, qu. 75, arts. 1, 2, 4, 5; qu. 76, art. 1).

[28] See above, the last paragraph.

[29] See above, 4.6, and n. 9.

[30] Even the point, which is inextended, is not to be conceived as immaterial in the same sense that the human soul is immaterial; for it pertains to quantity, insofar as a point can be marked or even considered only in extended beings.

[31] St. Thomas Aquinas (*Summa theol.* I, 75, 2) goes further, arguing that the very fact that the human intellect is able to know the natures of *all bodies* proves that the intellect, and, therefore, the soul, must be immaterial. So efficacious does he consider this argument that he uses it alone in the *Summa theologiae*, the fruit of his maturity.

[32] Taken in itself, this sentence seems to indicate a direct and intuitive vision of the soul by itself. In the light of what follows, however, it may well be that the Saint is expressly concerned merely to show that the understanding of the nature of the soul (regardless of whether the knowledge is direct or indirect) is a function of intelligence, and, therefore, of the soul, not of the body, and that it requires more careful use of intelligence than most people are inclined or able to give. The 'few' are contrasted with the majority, for whom authority is prescribed as a safer and more acceptable guide; cf. above, 7. 12, and n. 14.

[33] *Tumor enim non absurde appellatur corporis magnitudo.* *Tumor,* lit. 'swelling,' is a favorite word with Augustine and other Fathers to designate 'pride,' 'conceit,' or 'bombast.'

[34] Reason is again described as the 'sight of the soul' in 27. 53.

[35] This 'greatness' of the soul, in accordance with the distinction drawn in 3. 4, is developed and illustrated in 33. 70-76.

[36] See Introd. 3 and n. 1.

[37] In some of the extant texts the following words are here inserted: 'Impudens dubitatio duobus modis fieri cognoscitur: dum aut homo qui ratione uti potest, in tantum hebes pigerque ad quaerendam veritatem efficitur, ut plus velit in tenebris vanitatis remanere, quam in eo quod a Creatore suo est conditus ad seipsum semel et Deum suum vera ratiocinatione inveniendum investigandumque laborare; aut tam improba contumacia ea quae ab aliis laborantibus studiose et pie quaerentibus et inventa et confecta sunt, inveniri et confici posse dubitare; neque aliam ob causam faciunt nisi quod a semetipsis inventa non sint; quod genus invidiae impudentissimum esse ratio probat.'

[38] Cf. *De immort. an.* 10. 17: 'Nothing could be more absurd than to say that what we see with our eyes exists, while what we see with our intelligence does not exist; it is simply foolish to doubt that the intelligence is incomparably superior to eyesight.'

[39] Horace, *Sat.* 2. 7. 86, speaking of the wise man:

Fortis, et in se ipso totus, teres atque rotundus.

The Stoics compared the perfect soul, that of the *sapiens*, to a sphere: cf. Marcus Aurelius Antoninus, *Med.* 8. 41; 11. 12.

[40] Vergil, *Aen.* 12. 687, describing a landslide:

Fertur in abruptum magno *mons improbus* actu.

[41] Vergil, *Georg.* 2. 460, to the farmers:

Fundit humo facilem victum *iustissima tellus*.

[42] See below, 33. 70-76.

[43] See above, 3. 4.

[44] This suggestion of observing the development of the communication of ideas under certain conditions of isolation is a reminder of the far more detailed 'controlled experiment' described in Arnobius, *Adv. nat.* 2. 20-23; cf. G. E. McCracken's translation: ACW 7 (1949) 133-7; also his observations, 317 n. 135.

[45] According to St. Augustine, although 'art' generally requires imitation (of which brute animals are also capable), it consists primarily and essentially in a quality or habit of reason, and hence is not found in irrational animals; cf. *De mus.* 1. 4. 6 and 6. 12. 35; also *De Gen. cont. Manich.* 1. 8. 13. In *De immort. an.* 4. 5, he points out that art is a unified collection of principles or directives (*rationum*) residing in the mind or soul (*animo*). In *De vera rel.* 30. 54 ff., he goes on to say that the common arts involve both a mental aspect—the memory of things experienced that have made an impression—and a physical aspect, the facility of activity in the body; and the former element involves principles which are eternal and immutable, and whose cause, ultimately, is God.

[46] Cf. above, 17. 30.

[47] The most learned scholar and most prolific writer of ancient Rome, M. Terentius Varro of Reate (116-27 B.C.). He is quoted often by St. Augustine and other early Christian writers. The present reference is not identifiable from any passage in his preserved works.

[48] *Anima . . . mihi omnes artes secum attulisse videatur; nec aliud quidquam esse id quod dicitur discere quam reminisci et recordari.* Augustine had given like emphasis to the same opinion shortly before (*Solil.* 2. 20. 35): 'Those who are well-versed in liberal studies . . . uncover in the process of learning things undoubtedly buried by forgetfulness within them, and in some way they disinter them.' This suggests the doctrine of Plato (in *Meno, Phaedo, Phaedrus*) that the human soul existed at a time previous to its present state of union with the body. It acquired knowledge in that former state and brings it back to mind in the present life. Knowledge, then, at least of universal principles, is *innate*, and what is called 'learning' is really only 'recalling.' (See Introduction to the *De Magistro*, 122 ff.). However Augustine's statements regarding 'remembrance' are to be interpreted, the fact is that he expressly disavowed, in later life, any Platonic view of the pre-existence of human souls. In *Retract.* 1. 1. 3, he excludes it as an interpretation of his expression ' *securior rediturus in coelum,*' used in his first work, *Cont. Acad.* 2. 9. 22; while he offers

a defense of his expression by adducing a similar one from Scripture (*Spiritus revertatur ad Deum*—Eccles. 12. 7), he insists that neither is to be taken as opposing the statement of St. Paul (Rom. 9. 11) that no one had done good or evil before birth.

Of the present passage he writes, *Retract.* 1. 8. 2: 'When I stated in that book that "in my view the soul has brought all the arts with it, and what is called 'learning' is nothing else than remembering and recalling," that is not to be taken as if approval is hereby given to the view that the soul has previously lived either here in another body, or elsewhere, whether in a body or independently of a body; and that the answers it gives to questions, since they were not learned here, were learned before in another life. For it can well be, as we have said before in the present work (*Retract.* 1. 4. 4), that it is able to do this because it is by nature intellectual, so that it is in communication with realities that are not only intelligible but also immutable. It is so constituted that when it turns toward those realities with which it is in contact, or when it turns toward itself, it is able to give true answers regarding those realities to the extent that it sees them. And it has not, of course, brought all the arts with it in the same state that it has them now; for with regard to the arts that require the use of the bodily senses, such as much of medicine, and all of astrology, the soul cannot express anything but what it has learned in this life. But what the intelligence grasps unaided, it can, for the reason I have given, recall to mind and answer about, when questions are properly put by itself or someone else.' In *De Trin.* 12. 15. 24 Augustine also makes a complete repudiation of the Platonic doctrine of pre-existence. For discussion of the subject, see especially J. Hessen, *Die Begründung der Erkenntnis nach dem hl. Augustinus* (Münster i. W. 1916) 55-62.

[49] Cf. above, 17. 29.

[50] Cf. above, 15. 26.

[51] Augustine here follows the ancient, erroneous teaching of the schools that bodies fall 'with velocities proportional to their weights.' Not until about the year 1590, when Galileo made his celebrated experiments from the tower of Pisa, was the error corrected.

[52] *Quis est qui . . . recte ac prudenter existimet,* rendered by Tourscher: 'Who is it that will *not* judge well and prudently'; and by McMahon: 'Who will *not* think it a sound and prudent inference to hold' (italics mine). Both indicate a conclusion quite the opposite of what St. Augustine obviously means to say.

[53] *Sensum puto esse non latere animan quod patitur corpus.* This

is a tentative formulation, which is to be rendered more precise later on, in 25. 48 and 30. 59; see below, n. 73.

[54] 'Sapere aude'—Horace, *Epist.* 1. 2. 40. The celebrated axiom is not inappositely quoted: in the original context the poet emphasizes that one can be *sapiens* only by one's own initiative. Cf. A. Kiessling-R. Heinze, *Q. Horatius Flaccus, Briefe* (Berlin 1914) 30.

[55] The ingenious but quite unsatisfactory account of sight given here (23. 42-44), according to which sight 'darts forth through the eyes' so that the sensation takes place outside the human body, arises from the Saint's unwillingness to consider the body as co-principle with the soul, of the act of sensation. See below, n. 73. In *De Trin.* 11. 2. 5, he discusses the form (*species*) of the object of sight as impressed upon the body, and being in the soul through the body: '. . . The image of the body impressed on the sense . . . belongs to the nature of the living subject . . . insofar as it is produced in the body, and through the body, in the soul; for it is produced in the sense, which does not exist either without the body or without the soul.' Thus, in this later work he admits some sort of action of the object of sight upon the organ of sight; even so, it seems that he still, though less emphatically, considers the soul as the single agent actually exercising the power of sight.

[56] *Etenim videre sentire, et sentire pati esse iam supra consensimus.* See 23. 42 f. This assertion does not mean that sensation or sense perception consists solely of the reception of an action performed by some external object upon the sense organ, any more than the first clause means that sight is the only kind of sensation. All the author stresses is that sense knowledge requires the influence of an external reality that actually exists.

[57] Cf. 23. 41.

[58] Except for the insertion of the adjective 'mortal,' this definition, which is also given and explained in *De ordine* 2. 11. 31, is the traditional Aristotelian one. Elsewhere, however, St. Augustine gives definitions of man that reflect a Platonic conception and his own inability to conceive satisfactorily the union of body and soul. To quote the following formulation, most celebrated of all (*De mor. Eccl. Cath.* 1. 27. 52): 'Homo . . . ut homini apparet, anima rationalis est, mortali atque terreno utens corpore.' While this suggests that the soul is a complete being, only accidentally united to the body (cf. above, nn. 4 and 27), Augustine is concerned directly merely with what is noblest and most perfect in man. Both in accepting man as a composite of body and soul, which he does emphatically

elsewhere (cf. *De Trin.* 15. 7. 11; *Serm.* 150. 4. 5; *De nat. et orig. an.* 4. 2. 3; also 1. 2 of the present work), and in insisting that the soul is the higher and dominating principle in man, the Saint is influenced primarily by Catholic doctrine. The second truth he found philosophically defended by the Platonic writers, who were not particularly interested in maintaining the substantial unity of the two principles; hence, in borrowing their terminology and developing their concepts, he necessarily manifests a measure of philosophical inconsistency. See E. Gilson, *The Spirit of Medieval Philosophy* (tr. by A. H. Downes, New York 1936) 173 ff.; A. Pegis, "The Mind of St. Augustine," *Med. Stud.* 6 (1944) 37-41; I. Thomas, "The Definition of Man," *Dublin Rev.* 217 (1945) 1-10.

[59] *Fortasse enim verum est, omnis sensus passio corporis est animam non latens:* this is a slightly different wording from that of his original definition; see above, n. 53.

[60] *Per seipsam:* this insertion was suggested by Augustine near the end of 24. 46, but at the time not understood by Evodius.

[61] *Scientia:* it is evident from the context that Augustine uses this word to designate, first of all, knowledge by the intellect, as opposed to knowledge by sensation. But more than that, it is *certain*, for he states there is no *scientia* unless some reality is perceived and known by 'certain reason' (*firma ratione*). Furthermore, in *Cont. Acad.* 3. 11. 26, he writes: 'Sunt enim qui omnia ista quae corporis sensu accipit animus, *opinionem* posse gignere confitentur, *scientiam* vero negant, quam tamen volunt intelligentia contineri remotamque a sensibus in mente vivere. Et forte in eorum numero est sapiens ille quem quaerimus.' In *Conf.* 7. 17. 23, he makes further distinctions, describing his ascent from (1) sensitive knowledge of bodily things, to (2) the interior powers of the soul that reproduce sensible images, to (3) the reasoning faculty, proper to man 'to whose judgment is referred whatever is received from the bodily senses' (which power is still mutable), to (4) intelligence, which knows unchangeable realities, and ultimately, to THAT WHICH IS. In *De Trin.* 12. 15. 25 he distinguishes *scientia* from *sapientia*, considering the latter 'the intellectual knowledge of eternal realities' (corresponding to 4, above) and the former 'the rational knowledge of temporal things' (corresponding to 3).

[62] This statement is not proposed by Augustine as true; he later (30. 58) definitely labels it as false, though, in order to lead Evodius on to a correct understanding, he will meanwhile argue repeatedly as if it were true.

[63] Cf. Homer, *Odyssey* 17. 291-327.

[64] Quid tibi interesse videatur inter *rationem* et *ratiocinationem.*

[65] *Ut ratio sit quidam mentis aspectus, ratiocinatio autem rationis inquisitio, id est, aspectus illius, per ea quae aspicienda sunt, motio.* *Ratio*, then, is a basic power of knowing truth with certitude; it is a permanent faculty of the 'mind,' the superior part of the soul (cf. *De civ. Dei* 11. 2: '. . . mens cui ratio et intelligentia naturaliter inest'); being discursive (cf. *De ord.* 2. 11. 30), *ratio* is distinct from *intelligentia*, which is rather intuitive. *Ratiocinatio* is the exercise of *ratio*, searching, scrutinizing the objects to be known. The actual vision of the object, the actual possession of truth, as Augustine goes on to say, is *scientia*. He has already (14. 24) called reason the 'sight' (*aspectus*) of the soul; cf. also *Solil.* 1. 6. 12 f. See Gilson, *Introduction a l'étude de s. Augustin* 56 f., 157 f., and J. Geyser, 'Die erkenntnistheoretischen Anschauungen Augustins zu Beginn seiner schriftstellerischen Tätigkeit,' in M. Grabmann - J. Mausbach, *Aurelius Augustinus* (Cologne 1930) 80 ff.

[66] Cf. above, 26. 50, and n. 63.

[67] Obviously a reminiscence of a thought repeatedly expressed by St. Paul: Eph. 4. 22, 24 (*deponere* vos secundum pristinam conversationem *veterem* hominem—*induite novum hominem*); Col. 3. 9 f. (*expoliantes veterem hominem—induentes novum*).

[68] *Vellem hinc plura dicere, ac meipsum constringere, dum quasi tibi praecipio, ut nihil aliud agerem quam redderer mihi, cui me maxime debeo . . .* Of this sentence he writes in *Retract.* 1. 8. 3: 'In another place I state: "I would like to say more about this and tie myself down while I am, as it were, laying down the law to you, so that my one and only concern might be to render an account of myself *to myself*, to whom I am above all responsible." In that passage it would seem that I should rather have said: "render an account of myself *to God*, to whom I am above all responsible." Now, man must first render an account to himself, so that in that stage he may, as it were, advance a step and rise and be borne to God, as did that younger son who, *first returning to himself*, then said: *I will arise and will go to my father* (Luke 15. 17 f.). That is why I expressed myself in that way. Then I immediately added: "and thus to become . . . like a slave who is his master's friend." So, when I said: "to whom I am above all responsible," I was referring to human beings; I am, of course, responsible to myself more than to other human beings, although to God more than to myself.'

[69] Amicum mancipium domino: Horace, *Sat.* 2. 7. 2 f.

[70] Somewhat earlier Augustine had written in *De immort. an.* 13. 22: 'What is superior to the rational soul is God, as all agree.' On his view of the relation between the angels and the human soul, see below, n. 115.

[71] This is corrected a little further on, in 30. 58; it is asserted here, as before, to stimulate Evodius in testing the definition of sensation.

[72] See 26. 49 and 29. 56.

[73] *Sensus est corporis passio per seipsam non latens animan.* . . . This is the final formula of the definition of sensation, which Augustine had introduced in incomplete form in 23. 41, and later, 24. 46 and 25. 48, completed with the phrase *per seipsam*, and which he has continued to discuss through all these pages. In this interesting and famous, but scarcely acceptable definition, sensation is viewed as an act of the soul alone, occasioned by a physical effect (*passio*) on the body, produced by the action of an external material thing.

At the basis of this conception of sensation are the principles: (1) that the human soul is never inferior to the body (*De mus.* 6. 5. 8) and (2) that all subject matter is inferior to that which acts upon it (. . . *omnis materia fabricatore deterior* [*ibid.*]). Hence, it follows that the soul cannot receive anything from the body, or be acted upon by it. It is the soul alone that acts, and it notices the physical effects that occur in the body. After a long discussion of the process in *De mus.* 6. 5. 8-10, Augustine gives this summary (10): 'To put it briefly, it seems to me that when the soul exercises sensation in the body (*cum sentit in corpore*), it is not acted upon by the body (*non ab illo aliquid pati*), but it pays special attention to the actions undergone by the body (*in eius passionibus attentius agere*); and these actions (*actiones*) may readily enter the soul's awareness (*non eam latere*) according as they appeal to it, or they may not do so very readily, if such appeal is wanting. And this is all there is to what is called sensation.' For a similar description, see also *De Gen. ad litt.* 7. 19. 25-20. 26.

The external action of material objects on the human body, therefore, does not constitute sensation, nor even directly produce it. But, while the body does not act on the soul, the soul does act on the body. If the soul fails to notice what occurs in the body, there is no act of sensation. If, however, the soul becomes aware of an effect produced in the body, that very act of attention is the act of sensation. Thus it is the soul alone that performs the precise operation of sensitive cognition, though it requires as a *sine-qua-non* that the body be acted upon by an external agent, by an influence of light or sound or savor, and the like. The soul uses the body as a sort of messenger or instrument whereby it realizes knowledge within itself, of external material realities (cf. above, 33. 41: *sensus quo anima per corpus utitur*; also *De Gen. ad litt.* 12. 24. 51: 'neque enim corpus sentit, sed anima per corpus, *quo velut nuntio utitur* ad formandum in seipsa quod extrinsecus nuntiatur'). For the impression which objects make on the body is either conformable or not conformable to the actions of the soul, and, therefore, in varying degrees of intensity, attracts the attention of the soul (cf. *De mus.* 6. 5. 9 f.). In *De Trin.* 11. 1.1-2. 5, Augustine speaks of a 'form' impressed on the body, but it is, even in this later description, only the body that is passive; the soul actively perceives the effect and is the sole agent of the cognitive act.

This account of sensation reflects Augustine's inability to formulate a satisfactory theory of the union of body and soul. In his view, the soul exists conjointly with the body and dwells within it, but he never arrived at a clear and consistent explanation of the unity of man (cf. above, nn. 27 and 58, and below, n. 123). The doctrine on sensation also reflects an emphatic and rather extreme spiritualism that is the antithesis of the materialism he held as a Manichaean—a quite typical reaction in an enthusiastic convert.

The negative formula *non latens animam* of the definition of sensation indicates that the soul is conceived as always being aware of the presence of the body and always vigilant and alert to what transpires in it (cf. E. Gilson, *Introduction a l'étude de saint Augustin* 84). It also suggests a lack in the knowledge thus accounted for, of the complete certitude that is possible in the highest intellectual knowledge—'non est expectanda sinceritas veritatis a sensibus corporis' (*De div. quaest.* 83, qu. 9).

Augustine's teaching unquestionably shows the influence of Plotinus, who holds (*Enn.* 4. 7. 8): 'Sensation is the perception of material objects by the soul using the body.' The *non latere* of Augustine quite certainly derives from the μὴ λαθεῖν of Plotinus (*op. cit.* 4. 4. 19). Plotinus had also described the sense as a 'messenger' of the soul (*op. cit.* 5. 3. 3; see W. Ott, "Des hl. Augustinus Lehre über die Sinneserkenntnis," *Philosophisches Jahrb.* 13 [1900] 138).

St. Thomas Aquinas is quite certainly referring to this view when he writes (*Quaest. disp. de ver.* 10. 6): 'Others have said that the soul . . . does not receive knowledge from sensible objects in such a way that the likenesses of things reach the soul by some sort of action of the sensible objects; but the soul itself forms likenesses of

those objects within itself, when it is in the presence of those objects.'
He goes on to comment that 'this position does not seem entirely
reasonable,' for it implies that the soul must actually have those
likenesses within itself, without their being caused by the external
objects, and that would be equivalent to 'maintaining that the soul
naturally possesses the knowledge of all things. . . .'

Recently Augustine's theory has also received the fair criticism
that 'one of its chief defects lies in its essential subjectivity. There
is no natural guarantee that the representations which the soul makes
within itself of the extra-mental world do truly correspond with
physical events. Of course, in Augustinism, God is used as the
ultimate guarantee of the veracity of human knowledge' (V. Bourke,
Augustine's Quest of Wisdom [Milwaukee 1945] 112). We can
further agree with the same author that 'this active theory of sensation is one of the weakest elements in the philosophy of St. Augustine' (*op. cit.* 237). For a convenient and very competent discussion
of Augustine's complete doctrine on sensitive knowledge, see Gilson,
Introduction . . . 73-87.

⁷⁴ Cf. above, 23. 43 f.

⁷⁵ Here is the import of the whole long discussion on sensation:
that the soul does not have to be extended spatially throughout the
parts of the body in order to perceive sensible objects. The reason
given here is that the eyes see, and hence are acted upon, in a place
where they are not spatially present (cf. 23. 42-44, and n. 55); but
it is due to the soul that the eyes see. Hence the soul *a fortiori* is
not present in a spatial way, but by a 'certain *vital attention*' (*Epist.*
166. 2. 4).

⁷⁶ W. Thimme, *Augustins erster Entwurf einer metaphysischen
Seelenlehre* (Göttingen 1908) 43 n. 1, suggests that the reference
might be to Plotinus, in the ambiguous exposition of *Enneades* 4. 3.

⁷⁷ *Pene serius quam credi potest, sed certe non serius quam deberem:* (Tourscher) 'so recently that it can be trusted, and I must
accept the fact'; (McMahon) 'so recently that it deserves credence.'
Augustine simply states that it is most strange he had not made the
observation long before, so strange that it makes him almost sus-
picious of the obvious he has observed only now.

⁷⁸ The boys referred to are, most probably, Licentius and Tryge-
tius, who were pupils of Augustine's; cf. *De beata vita* 1. 6. They took
part in the dialogues *Contra Academicos, De beata vita,* and *De
ordine.* They were both natives of Augustine's home town of Tagaste, and Licentius was the son of Augustine's patron and friend,

Romanianus. A rather stilted poem of 154 hexameters, composed by Licentius, has survived in certain manuscripts of Augustine's letters (under *Epist.* 26); cf. O. Bardenhewer, *Geschichte der altkirchlichen Literatur* 4 (Freiburg i. Br. 1924) 500.

[79] Alypius was a lifelong and very intimate friend of Augustine's. Being somewhat younger than Augustine, he became one of the latter's first pupils when he began his teaching career in Tagaste, the home town of both of them. When Augustine went on to Carthage, in 374, Alypius came under his influence again, although he did not at first attend the lectures of the young teacher, because of some disagreement between his father and Augustine. Although in his early adolescence he had given in to temptations of the flesh, he reformed himself much earlier than most of the youth of his time, and became distinguished for his virtue. His one serious failing was a passion for the gladiatorial contests in the Circus; and it was a chance illustration of Augustine's, during a lecture in Carthage, that converted him. He studied law in Rome, at the same time serving as assessor in the department of the treasury, and associated closely with Augustine there, finally following him to Milan. In *Conf.* 6. 7. 11-12. 21, Augustine relates the early career of his friend, gives enthusiastic testimony of his high character, and tells the interesting stories of his last pathetic lapse into bloodthirstiness at the Circensian games, and of his apprehension as a thief, because of his abstracted simplicity. Alypius followed Augustine into Manichaeism, and later shared the experience of Augustine's conversion in the garden at Milan (cf. *Conf.* 8. 8. 19-12. 30). Together they went into retirement for prayer and study at Cassiciacum, in 386; together they were instructed and baptized by St. Ambrose in 387 (*ibid.* 9. 6. 14); and together they returned to Africa in 388. Alypius joined Augustine's monastic groups at Tagaste and Hippo. He became bishop of Tagaste in 394 and eventually, primate of Numidia; and he was active with Augustine and the other bishops of Africa in the struggle against the Donatist heretics. He is not listed as a saint in the ancient catalogues, but in 1584 Pope Gregory XIII placed his name in the Roman Martyrology, taking the testimony of Augustine as sufficient evidence of his heroic virtue.

[80] Augustine could make a fair claim to having more than an ordinary knowledge of the physical theories current in his time. This is quite evident from the discussion about physical forces in the present work (see above, 21. 35-22. 40), and from his testimony that he had understood Aristotle's discussions of the categories before he

was twenty years old; cf. *Conf.* 4. 16. 28 ff. In *De ord.* 2. 16. 44, he insists that anyone who attempts to inquire into the nature of his own soul, let alone the nature of God, without understanding the nature of body, place, time, motion, and the like, is bound to fall into error, even though his intentions are of the highest.

[81] In *De immort. an.* 16. 25, Augustine states: 'The soul is simultaneously present, in its entirety, not only in the whole physical substance of the body, but in each single part of it.' In this he agrees with Plotinus, e.g. *Enn.* 4. 9. 1.

[82] The *De magistro* is concerned at length with the value of words; for the ambiguity arising from the use of words for themselves and for the things signified, which Augustine here illustrates with the word 'sun,' cf. *De mag.* 8. 22 ff.

[83] 'This language'—Augustine has *lingua Latina*.

[84] Lucifer, the planet Venus, the morning star—lit. 'the lightbringer' (so also in Greek: φωσφόρος): composed of *lux* (gen. *lucis*) = 'light,' and *-fer*, from *fero*= 'I bring.' In the composition the components appear as the dative (*luci*) and the imperative (*fer*), and they are so used by Augustine here and in the following.

[85] That is, 'Bring the book.'

[86] The reference is probably to Plotinus, who held that there is a 'world soul' which is indivisible, but which, in breathing life into bodies, is virtually multiplied into many individual souls, although it retains its fundamental unity (cf. *Enn.* 4. 1). However, the formula here given by Augustine—*animam per seipsam nullo modo, sed tamen per corpus posse partiri*—is practically the same as that of some of the Scholastics (notably Cajetan, Scotus, and Suarez) according to whom the souls, at least of inferior animals, are '*per se* inextended and indivisible, but *per accidens* (i.e., by reason of the matter), extended and divisible.' Other Scholastics, though, maintain that one or more new souls are 'educed from the potency of matter,' that is, produced anew whenever there is sufficient organization of the matter. Cf. F. Maquart, *Elementa philosophiae* 2 (Paris 1937) 222 ff.

[87] See above, 3. 4.

[88] The rather surprising doubt expressed here and in the following is due to the influence of Plotinus, who speaks of the 'world soul' (see above, n. 86) as being common to all men (*Enn.* 3. 5. 4), though he also admits distinct individual souls as proceeding from the world soul (*ibid.* 4. 9. 1). Augustine speaks somewhat vaguely to the same effect in *De immort. an.* 15. 24: 'Therefore, the body subsists by means of the soul, and the body exists by the very fact that it is

animated, whether in a universal way, as is the world, or in an individual way, as is every animal within the world.' He later, in *Retract.* 1. 5. 3, quoted this and gave his verdict: 'This was most thoughtlessly expressed.' Again, referring to the implications of *De mus.* 6. 14. 43, he wrote (*Retract.* 1. 11. 4) that he could neither disprove as false nor prove as true, the Platonic view that the world is an 'animal' with one soul; but he insists that if there is any such thing as a 'world soul,' it is not God but has been made by Him.

[89] Cf. the Introd. 7 f.

[90] Cf. above, n. 4. Plotinus (*Enn.* 4. 4. 18) also considers the soul the principle of life, as does Aristotle (*De an.* 2. 2 = 414 a): 'The soul is that fundamental principle by which we live and have sensation and intelligence.'

[91] The reference is to Manichaeism which Augustine himself had formerly espoused. He also refers to the same sentimental views in *Conf.* 3. 10. 18; also in *De haer. ad Quodvultdeum* 46 ('they charge the most innocent of all the arts—agriculture—with numerous homicides!').

[92] *Animadversione atque signis.* 'Memory' in this passage is considered as the storehouse of intelligible realities, which Augustine describes in *Conf.* 10. 14. 21 as *quasi venter animi.* See the Introd. to the *De Magistro* 123 f.

[93] The same achievements are ascribed to the soul by Plotinus, but he considers them signs of weakness and imperfection in the soul, insofar as the exercise of imagination distracts it from pure intellectual contemplation and brings it into contact with multiplicity, whereas the proper state of the soul is union with the 'One'; cf. *Enn.* 4. 4. 3 f. Augustine, however, here speaks of them enthusiastically as perfections.

[94] This praise of 'human society' is quite different from the utter aloofness and detachment that Plotinus counsels when he says (*Enn.* 3. 6. 5): 'The purification of the soul consists in leaving it to itself, and not permitting it to have any dealings with others.' This diversity of views is due to the fact that Augustine possessed, and Plotinus lacked (at least as part of his philosophy), the Christian concept of human charity based on the love of God.

[95] 'Goodness'—Augustine's word is *iustitia*, which is evidently used in the more general sense of 'rightness' or 'goodness.'

[96] This does not mean that God could not create a better material universe or better objects within the present universe; for this would be to limit the power and freedom of God. But if any single thing

were improved, the *order* of the whole universe would be upset; hence, considering the degree of glory God intended this universe to manifest, and the order of parts He has established, it can be said that the universe could not be any better than it is. For this explanation as also adopted by St. Thomas Aquinas, see A. Rozwadowski, "De optimismo universali secundum S. Thomam," *Gregorianum* 17 (1936) 254-64.

[97] Augustine could speak from personal experience; he himself had approached the vision and understanding of God and had then been repulsed because of his own state of spiritual unpreparedness. 'When first I knew Thee, Thou didst raise me up that I might see there was something for me to see, though I was not yet fit to see it. And Thou didst repel the weakness of my sight, darting Thy beams upon me vehemently, and I trembled with love and dread, and I found myself to be far from Thee in a region of no resemblance to Thee...' (*Conf.* 7. 10.16). Again, in the magnificent passage of *Conf.* 7. 17. 23, he describes himself as having been 'drawn to Thee by Thy beauty, but at once torn away from Thee by my own weight . . . and this weight was carnal custom'; and at length he was elevated to the point where 'in the flash of a trembling glance, I arrived at THAT WHICH IS . . . but I was unable to hold my gaze. . . .'

[98] Ps. 50. 12.

[99] A similar thought is expressed in *Enarr. in Ps.* 41. 9: '(The soul) arrives at the house of God by withdrawing itself from all noise of flesh and blood.' Plotinus also emphatically stresses the need of eliminating material things from our thoughts to enable us to contemplate the truth; cf. *Enn.* 5. 1. 2.

[100] These words are reminiscent of Plotinus (*Enn.* 1. 6. 7): 'Whoever beholds the Good—with what loves does he burn, with what ardor is he inflamed, how passionately he desires to become one with it, how marvelously does he experience a mingling of delight and of awe!'

[101] These 'great and peerless souls' who have attained to the vision of God probably include St. Paul (cf. 2 Cor. 12. 2-5) and, possibly, Plotinus, of whom Porphyry, *Vita Plotini* 23, attests that he enjoyed mystic contemplation in the highest degree, and who himself gives indications of ecstasy (*Enn.* 1. 6. 7; 6. 7. 34). If it seems strange to see a pagan, more or less pantheistic, bracketed with Christian saints and mystics, it must be remembered that Augustine considered the 'Platonists' to have nothing that is in opposition to the Sacred Scriptures (*Cont. Acad.* 3. 20. 43) and that he had already called

them *magni homines et pene divini* (*De ord.* 2. 10. 28). Cf. C.
Butler, *Western Mysticism* (New York 1924) 344.

[102] Dom Cuthbert Butler, *op. cit.* 209, considers this clear testimony that in Augustine's opinion mystical contemplation is attainable by all who faithfully strive for it and prepare for it. This view
is brought out quite explicitly in *Epist.* 120. 1. 4: 'If we are faithful,
we shall arrive at the path of faith; and if we do not stray from that,
we shall without doubt come not merely to so great an understanding
of incorporeal and unchangeable realities as cannot in this life be
grasped by all, but even to the height of contemplation which the
Apostle calls "face to face" (I Cor. 13. 12). For some of the least
ones, who nevertheless perseveringly walk in the path of faith,
arrive at that most blessed contemplation; while others, who have
true knowledge of what invisible, unchangeable, incorporeal nature
is, but refuse to keep on the path leading to that abode of happiness,
because it seems to them folly—for it is Christ crucified—are unable to
come to the sanctuary of peace itself, although their mind is already,
as at a distance, touched by the ray of its light.'

[103] These words, expressing the soul's appreciation of the supreme
fact that God is the Absolute Being, harmonize with what the
author himself experienced in his own mystical ecstasies: cf. *Conf.*
7. 17. 23 and 9. 10. 23-6.

[104] *Omnia sub sole vanitas vanitantium.*   There is reference, obviously, to Eccles. 1. 2 f., which is rendered in the Vulgate: '*Vanitas
vanitatum,' dixit Ecclesiastes, 'vanitas vanitatum et omnia vanitas.
Quid habet amplius homo de universo labore suo, quo laborat sub
sole?'*—'*Vanity of vanities,' said Ecclesiastes, 'vanity of vanities, and
all is vanity. What hath a man more of all his labor that he taketh
under the sun?*' Instead of *vanitatum* in the first sentence, Augustine
has *vanitantium* (supposing the deponent verb *vanitari*—'to act
vainly') and he goes on to explain it as *falsi vel fallentes vel utrique,*
clearly indicating persons. This text is cited thus more than once
in Augustine's early writings; e. g. in *De mor. Eccl. Cath.* 1. 21. 39.
Of this passage he states, *Retract.* 1. 7. 3: 'What I quoted from the
Book of Solomon, "*vanity of the vain*" said Ecclesiastes, I found in
many texts. But that is not in the Greek; the Greek has: *vanity of
vanities.* I saw that later, and I found that the Latin texts which
have *vanitatum,* not *vanitantium,* were more reliable. However,
what I said in connection with that misquotation bears its own evidence of truth.'

[105] 'The things that truly exist' (*ea quae vere sunt*) are unchange-

able realities. It is especially, though not exclusively, with regard to God that Augustine uses this expression. In *De immort. an.* 10. 17 he applies it to the human soul: 'Or ought we perhaps to believe, as some have thought, that life is some sort of organization of the body? But surely, they would never have thought this if by means of the same mind, withdrawn from familiarity with material things, and purified, they had been able to see those *things that truly exist* and remain unchangeable.' In *Conf.* 7. 11. 17 he applies it to God: 'And I examined all other things that are inferior to Thee, and I saw that they neither had complete being, nor were without any being at all. They have being, because they are from Thee; they lack being, because they are not what Thou art. For *that truly exists* which abides unchangeably. . . .'

¹⁰⁶ This title, with all that it implies, had been in use both in the East and the West long before the time of Augustine. It was especially popular in his native Africa (Tertullian, Cyprian, etc.). See J. C. Plumpe, *Mater Ecclesia: An Inquiry into the Concept of the Church as Mother in Early Christianity* (Stud. in Christ. Ant. 5, Washington 1943).

¹⁰⁷ I Cor. 3. 1 f.: *And I, brethren, could not speak to you as unto spiritual, but as unto carnal. As unto little ones in Christ. I gave you milk to drink, not meat; for you were not able as yet. But neither indeed are you now able, for you are yet carnal.*

¹⁰⁸ In *De Cathechizandis Rudibus* 25. 46 (trans. by J. P. Christopher, *ACW* 2. 77 f.), Augustine expresses a similar thought emphatically and picturesquely: 'Is it, then, too difficult a thing for God, who even in a moment brings together from their hiding places the cloudbanks and overcasts the sky in a twinkling of an eye, to restore that substance to your body as it was before, seeing that He was able to make it as before it was not?'

¹⁰⁹ Cf. *Conf.* 7. 19. 25, where Augustine acknowledges what difficulties he had in his youth, to accept the Incarnation.

¹¹⁰ In a letter written to Nebridius (*Epist.* 4. 2) about the same time as the *De quant. an.*, Augustine expresses a similar thought: 'When, after calling upon God for aid, I begin to be borne up to Him and to those things which are real in the truest sense, I am at times filled with such a vivid foretaste of things that abide, that I am surprised that I sometimes require any reasoning at all to convince myself of the existence of things which in my soul are as present to me as anyone is present to himself.'

¹¹¹ In saying that there is 'nothing closer to God' than the human

soul, he is ruling out any intermediary in divine illumination of the human mind, as he does also in *De mus.* 6. 1. 1, where he speaks of God presiding over human minds *nulla natura interposita.* In speaking enthusiastically of the proximity of the soul to God, however, he is also careful to insist upon the creature element in the human soul and its essential inferiority to God: 'The human soul is not what God is.' Augustine elsewhere (*De mor. Eccl. Cath.* 1. 11. 18) writes in a similar vein, but more distinctly: 'Striving toward God is the same as longing for happiness, and the attainment of God is happiness itself. Now, we tend toward God by loving Him; we attain Him, not by becoming what He Himself is, but by coming close to Him, by coming in contact with Him through an extraordinary use of our intellects, and by being internally enlightened and possessed by His Truth and His Holiness.' This is distinctly alien to the Plotinic notion of the soul's merging with God in ecstatic union so as to lose its identity and to become one thing with the Absolute. Plotinus (*Enn.* 6. 9. 10) says of the union between the soul and the 'One' that '(the soul) does not properly see it, nor is it distinguished from it as one who sees is distinguished from the object, nor are we to think of two beings. But the soul has been changed, and is no longer itself . . . but gives itself to the Absolute, and wholly becomes a part of it. It becomes one with it as centre coincides with centre. For here things that come together become one, and there are two realities only when they are separated.'

[112] The Saint is undoubtedly referring to the instructions he received in the Creed during the Lenten season of the year 387, when he was preparing for the reception of baptism.

[113] Cf. Rom. 11. 36: *For of Him and by Him and in Him are all things; to Him be glory for ever. Amen.*

[114] This inability of man to escape or avoid God, together with the difficulty of finding Him because of one's personal unworthiness, is inspiringly developed in *Conf.* 5. 2. 2.

[115] Being 'pure' spirits, not made for union with bodies, angels are essentially superior to men, and even to the human soul, in the hierarchy of being. St. Augustine considered them on entirely the same plane, entitatively, as spiritual human souls. Thus also in *De civ. Dei* 22. 1. 2, where he speaks of the angels as the crown of creation, he remarks that God has made nothing better than 'spirits to which He has given intelligence'—words applying, in his terminology, to human souls no less than to angels. It is possible that he was influenced by the words of our Lord: . . . *They are equal to*

the angels, and are the children of God . . . (Luke 20. 36; cf. Mark 12. 25), which, however, refer to the similarity between the angels and human beings (with risen bodies as well as souls) in heaven, and especially with regard to the exclusion of human marriage in that state. The fundamental reason for his error on this point is his consideration, at least implicitly, of the human soul as a *complete* being in itself, not essentially ordinated to union with matter. Cf. above, n. 4, and below, n. 123. In his *Enchiridion de fide, spe et caritate,* 16. 61 f., he speaks of human souls replacing the fallen angels in a way that seems to suggest that even late in his life he considered angels and human souls on the same level of entity. Cf. ACW 3. 63, and nn. 194 and 197.

[116] Matt. 4. 10; cf. Deut. 6. 13.

[117] Augustine knew from his own bitter experience that moral rectitude and purification were absolute prerequisites for the enjoyment of the delights of spiritual contemplation. See above, n. 97.

[118] *Ascendentibus igitur sursum versus, primus actus, docendi causa, dicatur animatio; secundus, sensus; tertius, ars; quartus, virtus; quintus, tranquillitas; sextus, ingressio; septimus, contemplatio.* For an interpretation of these seven 'levels' of the soul's activity in the light of Augustine's later threefold distinction of *esse, vivere, intelligere,* cf. J. Mausbach, 'Wesen und Stufung des Lebens nach dem hl. Augustinus,' in Grabmann-Mausbach, *Aurelius Augustinus* 184. See also E. Gilson, *Introduction a l'étude de s. Augustin* 159 f.

[119] *Possunt et hoc modo appellari: de corpore; per corpus; circa corpus; ad seipsam* (=animam, 'soul'); *in seipsa; ad Deum; apud Deum.*

[120] *Possunt et sic: pulchre de alio; pulchre per aliud; pulchre circa aliud; pulchre ad pulchrum; pulchre in pulchro; pulchre ad pulchritudinem; pulchre apud pulchritudinem.* This takes up and elaborates what was stated in 34. 78 *fin.*: 'For each one of these levels has a distinct excellence of its own.'

[121] This reconciliation of limitations and physical evils with the (relative) perfection of the whole universe by means of the *order* in the universe, is also adopted by St. Thomas Aquinas (*Summa theol.* 1, q. 25, art. 6 ad 3): 'The universe (supposing the present realities) cannot be better, because of the most fitting order given to these realities by God; for in that order the good of the universe consists. If any one thing were made better, the proportion of order would be destroyed; just as the tone of the harp would be destroyed, if one string were to be stretched tighter than it should be.'

[122] This thought is brought out more explicitly in the *De cate-chizandis rudibus* 18.30 (trans. by Christopher, ACW 1.59): 'Whatever man does, he finds God worthy of praise in His deeds; if he acts rightly, he finds Him worthy of praise for the justice of His rewards; if he sins, he finds Him worthy of praise for the justice of His punishments; if he confesses his sins and returns to an upright manner of life, he finds Him worthy of praise for the mercy of his forgiveness. Why, then, should God not have made man, even though He foreknew that he would sin, seeing that He was to crown him if he stood firm, make him conform to the divine order if he sinned, and help him if he repented, being Himself at all times and in all places glorious in goodness, justice, and mercy?'

[123] This question of the nature and purpose of the union between the human soul and body is one that St. Augustine never adequately answered. In the present text he is content to insist that the union must have a purpose because it fits somewhere into the order that God has established in the universe. Similarly, he says in *De mus.* 6.5.9: 'For my part, I think this body is animated by the soul only through the intention of its Maker.'

Although in the present work he has described the soul in a way that suggests that it is a complete and independent substance, and although he has in various works expressed a Platonic conception of man (cf. above, n. 58) which does not allow of an essential and intrinsic union of soul and body, in his later writings he did insist more emphatically on the unity of man. Thus, in the *De Trinitate* (written 400-416), he defines (15.7.11) man as 'a rational substance consisting of soul and body.' Between 413 and 426 he wrote *The City of God* and there (1.13) he explicitly states that human bodies are not mere ornaments or helps used in an extrinsic way, but they 'pertain to the very nature of man.' Further (10.29), 'we know by the testimony of our own nature that the body and the soul must be united to constitute a complete and perfect man.' Again, in the *De natura et origine animae*, written in 419, he says rather sharply (4.2.3): 'Anyone who wishes to separate the body from human nature is stupid.'

While, therefore, it can be said that his insistence on the unity of man was more emphatic in his later than his earlier works, this does not warrant the conclusion that in the course of time he abandoned the Platonic concept of the soul utterly and completely. For even in *De civitate Dei* he speaks (10.6) of the body being, by reason of its inferiority to the soul, subject to the soul as a servant or instrument (cf. also *ibid.* 9.9). On the other hand, even in the earlier works, along with his Platonic description of the soul, he had given definitions of man (see above, n. 58) that could be understood and explained only by granting a substantial union of soul and body. The explanation of the apparent inconsistencies seems to be that Augustine never proposed to solve the speculative problem of how the soul and body could constitute a unified nature, if the soul is a complete substantial being, using the body as an instrument. On that point he is content to say that the 'kind of union by which spirits are joined to bodies and become animals, is utterly marvelous and beyond the comprehension of man, although such a unit is what man himself is' (*De civ. Dei* 21.10). What does concern him throughout his entire life is the truth that in man the soul is the nobler and more important element, and that it is that part of man—indeed, of all physical nature—that is closest to God. See *De mor. Eccl. Cath.* 1.4.6-6.10. His interest, then, is predominantly practical and ascetical: to direct men to appreciate in themselves what most closely resembles God, so that they may be more closely united in thought and love to God.

Hence it is that Augustine does not encounter the difficulties that constituted one source of dispute between the 'Augustinian' theologians and philosophers, on the one hand, and the Aristotelian St. Thomas on the other, during the thirteenth century. However, his works do contain data and arguments for both sides of the controversy. He admits that the soul has a natural desire to be united with the body (*De Gen. ad litt.* 7.27) and that the soul is the link between the unchangeable Wisdom and Truth and the lowest living thing, the body (*De immort. an.* 15.24). Even so, because in the stream of the Platonic-Neoplatonic tradition, he stresses the superiority and independence of the soul, he does not recognize, as St. Thomas did, that its union with the body is also for the benefit of the soul. On this whole question, see E. Gilson, *op. cit.* 56-72; A Pegis, *op. cit.* 37-48.

[124] The Saint is possibly thinking of the result of original sin: the dying of the soul to heaven.

[125] In treating so briefly the questions Evodius had raised (1.1), Augustine characteristically emphasizes a practical and ascetical conclusion: that, whatever the solution of the speculative problems may be, and whatever God's purposes were in uniting the human soul to the body, and separating the two at death, the one and only way for us to fulfill those purposes is to conform our human actions to the will of God.

THE TEACHER

INTRODUCTION

[1] St. Thomas Aquinas composed his own *De magistro* (*Quaestiones disputatae de veritate,* qu. 11) mainly on the questions and objections raised by St. Augustine. For a comparison of the two works, see J. M. Colleran, *The Treatises 'De Magistro' of St. Augustine and St. Thomas* (diss. Pontif. Inst. 'Angelico': Rome 1945). St. Bonaventure, in his *Sermo* 'Unus est Magister vester, Christus' (*De humanae cognitionis ratione anecdota quaedam Seraphici Doctoris S. Bonaventurae et nonnullorum ipsius discipulorum:* Quarracchi 1883, pp. 73-86) shows a definite dependence on St. Augustine's dialogue. So does Matthew of Aquasparta, *Quaestio disputata prima* (*ibid.* pp. 87-108).

[2] The philosophical teachings are discussed by Colleran, *op. cit.,* 48-56, 65-83, 93-100, and, with rather idealistic implications, by A. Guzzo, in the introduction to his translation, *Aurelio Agostino, Il Maestro* (Florence 1927) 5-14. Regarding the pedagogical aspects of Augustine's treatise, see L. Allevi, 'I fondamenti della pedagogia nel *De Magistro* di Sant' Agostino e San Tommaso,' *Scuola Cattolica* 65 (1937) 545-61; M. Casotti, 'Il *De Magistro* di Sant' Agostino e il metodo intuitivo,' in *Sant' Agostino—pubblicazione commemorativa del 15 centenario della sua morte* (Milan 1931) 57-74; F. X. Eggersdorfer, *Der hl. Augustinus als Pädagoge und seine Bedeutung für die Geschichte der Bildung* (Freiburg i. Br. 1907). The implications for the study of language are touched upon by I. L. Glatstein, 'Semantics, too, has a Past,' *Quart. Jour. of Speech* 32 (1946) 48-51, and G. Leckie, in his preface to *Concerning the Teacher* (New York 1938) ix-xxxviii. See also W. Ott, *Über die Schrift des hl. Augustinus 'De Magistro'* (Hechingen 1898) and G. Valentini, 'Richerche intorno al De Magistro di S. Agostino,' *Sophia* 4 (1936) 83-9.

[3] See *Retract.* 1.12.36. The year 389 is definitely established by the Saint's own testimony in *Conf.* 9.6.14 that his son was 16 years old when he took part in the dialogue; for Adeodatus was baptized at the age of 15 (cf. *ibid.*) and it is known that he received the sacrament with his father at Easter, April 24, 388.

[4] *Conf.* 9.6.14. In *De beata vita* 1.6, the Saint also refers proudly

to his son: 'There was also in our company one who was the young-
est of all, but whose talent, unless love deceives me, shows great
promise, Adeodatus my son.'

⁵ This theory was very attractively advanced by C. Bindemann,
Der heilige Augustinus 2 (Berlin 1855) 94. Commenting on St.
Augustine's references to his son, J. Gibb and W. Montgomery
(*The Confessions of Augustine* [Cambridge 1908] 248) very appositely recall Eusebius's account (*Hist. Eccl.* 6.2) of Origen's
father who 'used reverently to kiss the breast of his son as he slept,
feeling that his high gifts were a manifestation of special Divine
favor.'

⁶ See text, 11.38.

⁷ Matt. 23.10.

⁸ See text, 12.39 f.

⁹ John 1.9.

¹⁰ In *De magistro* 11.38, Augustine indicates, and in 12.40 he
expressly states, that what is learned from the 'Inner Teacher,' is
also beheld in the 'inner light.' About the year 413 he wrote in the
form of a letter to Paulina his little treatise *De videndo Deo,* in
which he speaks of the internal light, by means of which we see
and judge many things (*Epist.* 147.17.41-4). That the Inner
Teacher is the same as the inner light becomes clear especially in
his *De gratia Novi Testamenti* (*Epist.* 140.37.85): 'By the very
fact that with inerrant judgment we give approval to someone who
properly counsels us externally, to what else do we bear witness than
that we have as our teacher an internal light?'

¹¹ In his very first Christian publication, *Contra Academicos,*
which was written in 386, Augustine says (3.6.13) to Alypius:
'With succinctness as well as reverence you have stated that only
some Deity is able to show man what truth is.' Again, in *De b. vita*
4.35, written in the same year, he speaks of God as an internal light,
the source of all truth. Perhaps the clearest and fullest anticipation
of the message of the *De magistro* is found in *Solil.* 1.8.15: 'The
earth is visible and so is light. But the earth cannot be seen unless
it is illumined by light. In the same way, then, we must hold that
those things taught in the sciences which anyone understands and
concedes without any hesitation to be absolutely true, cannot be
understood unless they are illumined by a second sun, as it were—
a sun properly their own. Hence, just as we can distinguish three
aspects in the sun we see—that it exists, that it shines, and that it
illumines—so there are three aspects in that most hidden God whom

you purpose to understand: that He exists, that He is known, and that He enables all other things to be known.' This was written two years prior to the *De magistro*.

[12] *Epist.* 144. 1: 'Through His representatives (God) gives us counsel by external signs of reality; but He Himself teaches us internally by means of the realities themselves.' *In Ioan. Evang. tract.* 15. 19: 'In our soul there is a something which is called "intellect." This very power of the soul which is termed "intellect" and "mind" is illuminated by a higher light. Now that higher light by which the human mind is illuminated, is God.' See also *ibid.* 20. 3, 26.7; *Serm.* 23. 1. 1-2. 2; 298. 5. 3; *Epist.* 166. 4. 9.

[13] *Conf.* 7. 9. 13. See also *De civ. Dei* 8. 7, where, extolling the 'Platonic philosophers' for having a doctrine on knowledge superior to the teachings of the Epicureans and Stoics, he says that the Platonists 'have affirmed the light of our understanding, by which we learn all things, to be God Himself by whom all things were made.' Augustine sees more of a similarity to Christian teaching in the Neoplatonic philosophy than can reasonably be verified; see the Introd. to *The Greatness of the Soul*, n. 6.

[14] Cf. *De civ. Dei* 8. 12.

[15] Plato, *Rep.* 6. 18 (508 c-e).

[16] Cf. *Cont. Acad.* 3. 18. 41. In *Retract.* 1. 1. 4, he disapproves as too lavish the praise given in his first published work to Plato and the Platonists.

[17] Plotinus, *Enn.* 3. 8. 8; 5. 4. 1; 6. 8. 9.

[18] *Enn.* 2. 9. 1; 6. 8. 9.

[19] *Enn.* 3. 8. 9.

[20] *Enn.* 5. 1. 6.

[21] *Enn.* 3. 8. 8; 5. 3. 15 f.

[22] *Enn.* 5. 7. 1 ff.

[23] *Enn.* 3. 8. 3.

[24] *Enn.* 5. 3. 17; 6. 9. 11. A convenient and competent summary of the entire philosophy of Plotinus is given by F. Copleston, *A History of Philosophy* (Westminster, Md. 1945) 1. 464-72.

[25] In *De b. vita* 4. 34, after arguing that happiness consists in wisdom, he goes on to say that the highest wisdom is the Wisdom of God, the Divine Son of God. See also *De civ. Dei* 10. 2.

[26] Cf. *De mag.* 11. 38 and n. 64; Plotinus, *Enn.* 4. 7. 10.

[27] See, among many testimonies, *De b. vita* 4. 35; *Serm.* 4. 5. 6-6. 7; 68. 5. 9; *Enarr. in Ps.* 42. 4.

[28] Cf. *De Gen. ad litt.* 4. 28. 45.

[29] Cf. E. Gilson, *Introd. a l'étude de saint Augustin* (2nd ed. Paris 1943) 106.

[30] Cf. N. Malebranche, *De la recherche de la vérité* (Paris 1837) t. 1, p. xx.

[31] Cf. E. Portalié, ' Augustin,' *DTC* 1. 2 (1903) 2336.

[32] Cf. Gilson, *op. cit.* 118 ff.

[33] Cf. C. Boyer, *L'idée de vérité dans la philosophie de saint Augustin* (Paris 1921) 156-220, and *Essais sur la doctrine de saint Augustin* (Paris 1932) 166-83; T. Zigliara, *Della luce intellettuale e dell' ontologismo secondo la dottrina dei Santi Agostino, Bonaventura e Tommaso d'Aquino* (Rome 1874) 1. 388 ff. These authors maintain that their interpretation is that of St. Thomas himself. It is true that St. Thomas seems to take for granted that the 'light of the soul,' that is, the created 'light,' is the agent-intellect. But he does not state that this is what Augustine had meant by his metaphor. He is not concerned with the interpretation of Augustine's texts, but with the exposition of what he considers the truth, and he accommodates the expressions of Augustine to his own meaning. See Colleran, *op. cit.* 65-92.

[34] *De Trin.* 12. 15. 24. Regarding the different interpretations of this famous and disputed text, see Gilson, *op. cit.* 107 n. 1.

[35] See Colleran, *op. cit.* 67-70.

[36] See *De mag.* 11. 40; 13. 45.

[37] See Plato, *Theaet.* 6 f. (149a-151d).

[38] See Plato, *Phaedo* 18-22 (72e-77a); *Meno* 20 (85c-86c).

[39] Expressions that seem to imply pre-existence are used in *De qu. an.* 20. 34 (see n. 48) and *Solil.* 2. 20. 35. Boyer, *L'idée de vérité,* 188, Gilson, *op. cit.* 94, and J. Hessen, *Die Begründung der Erkenntnis nach dem hl. Augustinus* (Beitr. z. Gesch. d. Philos. u. Theol. d. Mittelalters 19. 2, Münster i. W. 1916) 55-62, maintain that Augustine, in his early years, at least inclined toward pre-existence. However, in *Solil.* 1. 8. 15, he teaches 'illumination,' which would render pre-existence unnecessary.

[40] See above, citations in n. 48, *The Greatness of the Soul.* In *De Trin.* 12. 15. 24, Augustine explicitly and emphatically rejects Plato's argument that the answers of the uninstructed on geometrical problems prove that the knowledge was acquired in a previous existence. He retorts that since there are so few geometricians in the present life, we can hardly expect that all were geometricians before, and yet all can give the same answers now. Then he goes on to offer his own explanation of the inner, incorporeal light; see above, n. 34.

[41] *Conf.* 10. 14. 21.

⁴² Cf. *ibid.* 10. 8. 12-10. 26. 37.   On Augustine's conception of 'memory,' see E. Gilson, *op. cit.* 134-9, and G. Söhngen, "Der Aufbau der augustinischen Gedächtnislehre," in M. Grabmann-J. Mausbach, *Aurelius Augustinus: Festschrift der Görres-Gesellschaft zum 1500. Todestage des heiligen Augustinus* (Cologne 1930) 367-94.
⁴³ Cf. *De Trin.* 14. 6. 8.
⁴⁴ *Ibid.* 14. 11. 14. *Epist.* 7. 1 f.: 'Videndum est, non nos semper praetereuntium meminisse, sed plerumque manentium.' This letter to Nebridius was written in 389, the same year as the *De mag.*
⁴⁵ Cf. Gilson, *op. cit.* 135 n. 2.
⁴⁶ Cf. *De b. vita* 1. 1.

TEXT

¹ 'Teach' (*docere*) is used in this treatise in the general sense of 'make known," or 'communicate knowledge,' and in this introductory paragraph it is posited that the apparent and intended function of words is to cause knowledge in the hearer. The assertion in the later part of this work (10. 33-14. 45), that words do not serve to teach, assumes Augustine's thesis that the vocal sounds themselves are not the reason for the truth of the knowledge attained.

² See text 11. 36 and 14. 45, where the Saint maintains that teaching by words is merely a 'reminding' or directing of the attention of the learner to truth that can be attained by reflection upon an inner source of truth, or upon realities of which he has already had sense experience.   In this introductory chapter he provisionally grants a distinction between (1) teaching, or imparting new knowledge, and (2) reminding, or bringing back to attention what had been previously known; and he includes both in the purpose of speech.

³ *In clausis cubiculis*—cf. Matt. 6. 6: *But when thou shalt pray, enter into thy chamber, and having shut the door, pray to thy Father in secret; and thy Father who seeth in secret, will repay thee.* On this text Augustine comments, in *De sermone Domini in monte* 2. 3. 11 (trans. by J. J. Jepson, ACW 5. 101): 'What are these "chambers" but the hearts themselves which are also signified in the Psalm (4. 5) when it is said: *The things you say in your hearts, also be sorry for them upon your beds.* . . . It is not enough merely to go into the chamber, leaving the door open to the importunate: in through the

door plunge without shame the things that are outside and they make for the privacy of ourselves. The things without, we have said, are all the transitory and visible things which through the open door, that is, our fleshly senses, noise in upon us while we pray, with a whirl of idle fancies. Therefore the door must be closed—we must resist our carnal senses so that the prayer of our spirit may be directed to the Father; and this arises from the depths of our heart when we *pray to the Father in secret.*'

⁴ 1 Cor. 3. 16.

⁵ This is apparently a summarized quotation from Eph. 3. 14-17.

⁶ Ps. 4. 5 f.: *Dicite in cordibus vestris, et in cubilibus vestris compungimini; sacrificate sacrificium iustitiae, et sperate in Domino.* The Gallican text, incorporated in the Vulgate, reads somewhat differently: *Quae dicitis in cordibus vestris, in cubilibus . . .* The new Latin version approved by Pope Pius XII in 1945 gives: *Recogitate in cordibus vestris, in cubilibus vestris, et obmutescite. Sacrificate sacrificia iusta, et sperate in Domino.*

⁷ Cf. Matt. 6. 9-13, the words of the Our Father, introduced by our Lord with *Thus, therefore, shall you pray.*

⁸ See St. Augustine's further remarks on this subject in *De serm. Dom. in monte* 2. 3. 14-4. 16 (ACW 5. 103-6).

⁹ In his work *De doctrina Christiana* 2. 1. 1, Augustine gives his definition of 'sign': 'a thing that, besides the form (*speciem*) which it impresses on the senses, by itself produces something else in one's thought'; for example, when we see a footprint, we at once think of the animal which trod there, when we see smoke, we think of fire, etc. *Signa* are distinguished (*ibid.* 1. 2. 2) from *res*, which are not normally used to represent other things; for example, trees, stones, and the like. Such realities, however, may by way of exception be used as signs, like the tree cast into the waters (Exod. 15. 25). The principal signs, Augustine points out (*op. cit.* 1. 2. 2), are words, whose whole function is to be signs.

¹⁰ Vergil, *Aen.* 2. 659:

Si nihil ex tanta superis placet urbe relinqui.

The translation is not quite adequate, as it had to be compressed into eight words, corresponding to the Latin. The first three words, 'If nothing from,' correspond to the first three Latin words discussed in the following—*Si nihil ex.*

¹¹ See below, 8. 22-24, where Augustine discusses the apparent contradiction and resultant confusion that arise from the use of a word, in the same context, to designate itself as a sign, and also the reality (or absence of reality) the word signifies.

¹² In *De doct. Chr.* 2. 3. 4, the author calls the meaningful gestures, ogles, and motions of the pantomimists 'visible words, so to say' (*quasi verba visibilia*). He also points out (*ibid.* 2. 25. 38) that only the experienced spectators can fully and easily understand the pantomimes, unless a commentator gives an explanation accompanying the entertainment. For the Saint's moral judgments and pastoral warnings regarding these and other popular diversions, see *Enarr. in Ps.* 39. 8 f. and 102. 13.

¹³ The opinion Adeodatus expresses here (and in the summary, 7. 19) is to be revised later in 10. 29, again in 10. 30, and finally in 10. 32. See below, n. 52.

¹⁴ Augustine points out, in *De doct. Chr.* 2. 3. 4, that besides the word-signs that are directed to the hearing, and the gestures and actions directed to sight, there are some few signs pertaining to the other senses; e.g., the fragrance of the ointment poured on our Lord's feet (John 12. 3) was a sign directed to the sense of smell, and the sacrament of the Lord's Body and Blood is a sign directed to the sense of taste.

¹⁵ The word used is *nomen*, which means both 'name' and 'noun,' and is used with both meanings in what follows.

¹⁶ *Placetne appellemus significabilia ea quae signis significari possunt* . . . He is asking for agreement on the use of the term *significabilia* because he is using it as a noun ('signifiables'), and also because he is giving it a special meaning, restricting it to the things that are signified without themselves being signs of something else.

¹⁷ The reason for this implied defense of the word is that Adeodatus is using *audibilia* as a noun—'audibles'—as his father had previously done with *significabilia*.

¹⁸ *Bona verba, quaeso:* Terence, *Andria* 1. 2. 33. The words are spoken ironically by the slave Davos to his master Simo, when the latter is angrily threatening him with heavy penalties.

¹⁹ There is no perfect English equivalent for the Latin *verbum* which has the generic meaning 'word,' and the more restricted one 'verb.' In trying to show that *verbum*, meaning 'word,' is a generic notion, embracing 'noun' as one of its species, Augustine allows for the difficulty that *verbum*, meaning 'verb,' may also be considered as a co-ordinate species, along with 'noun.' It may also be observed that he speaks of the verb being 'declined' (*ea quae per tempora declinantur*), which was the word used for both forms of inflection, declension and conjugation; cf. Quintilian, *Inst. orat.* 1. 4. 22: '*Nomina declinare et verba* in primis pueri sciant.'

[20] *Dicimus item signa militaria, quae iam proprie signa nominantur, quo verba non pertinent.* A. Guzzo, *Aurelio Agostino: Il maestro* (Florence 1927) 41 and nn. 4 and 5, interprets this sentence as meaning that the word *signa* originally and literally designated military standards or insignia, and that words are called 'signs' only in a transferred sense. He translates: 'Diciamo egualmente "segni militari," che sono segni in senso proprio: *il che non potrebbe dirsi delle parole*' (italics mine). This does not seem to be Augustine's meaning, for he goes on, in the next sentence, to consider 'sign' as a genus, of which both 'word' and 'insignia' are species, and this would not be proper, if the term 'sign' were not applied univocally to the two.

[21] Cum dicimus *si, vel, nam, namque, nisi, ergo, quoniam,* et similia.

[22] *Scis, igitur, tam nomen verbo, quam etiam verbum nomine significari.* G. Leckie, *Concerning the Teacher* (New York 1938) 18, translates: 'Then you know that *noun* is signified by means of a word, and *word* by means of a noun.' So also F. Tourscher, *The Philosophy of Teaching* (Villanova 1924) 31. But 'a word' could mean only the word 'noun,' and 'a noun' could refer only to the noun 'word'; and it seems from the context that Augustine is saying more than that, namely that 'noun' and 'word' are reciprocal. Yet, by making 'noun' and 'word' reciprocal in meaning Augustine seems to be lapsing into sophistry. For he argues that since 'word' is a noun, and 'noun' is a word, each one signifies the other. That conclusion would follow, however, only if 'word' as such, or every word (not merely the noun or name 'word') were a noun, which is not true. Obviously, as Adeodatus goes on to suggest, 'word' has greater extension and is more generic in meaning than 'noun.'

[23] It may be that Augustine is right in linking *nomen* with *noscere*. Among modern etymologists, Ernout-Meillet, *Dictionnaire étymologique de la langue latine* (2nd ed. Paris 1939) s.v., approve the relationship; it is denied by Walde, *Lateinisches etymologisches Wörterbuch* (Heidelberg 1910) s.v. Augustine's derivation of *verbum* from *verberare* (cf. also Isidore, *Etym.* 1.9.1: *verbum dictum eo quod verberato aere sonat* = 'because of the sound made by the air being struck') is less fortunate. The word has an Indo-European root: *wer-, cf. the Greek digammated stem ϝερ- in ἐρέω (ἐρῶ) = 'I shall say.' See especially C. D. Buck, *Comparative Grammar of Greek and Latin* (Chicago 1933) 122, 138.

[24] *Pronomen est pars orationis, quae pro ipso posita nomine, minus*

quidem plene, idem tamen significat. This definition survives in a spurious fourth-century grammatical work which some scholars attributed to the first-century grammarian M. Valerius Probus: *Instituta artium* 131.1 f. Keil.

[25] *Non erat in Christo est et non, sed est in illo erat:* 2 Cor. 1.19. The Vulgate reads: Dei enim Filius Iesus Christus . . . non fuit EST et NON, sed EST in illo fuit. The meaning of the original Greek words Ναὶ καὶ οὔ is 'yea and nay' or 'yes and no.' It has seemed best to preserve 'is' in the text, because Augustine goes on to speak of it as a verb, arguing also that it can have the force of a noun.

[26] See 2 Cor. 11.6.

[27] He has enumerated seven: a pronoun, *quis* = τίς = 'who?'; a verb, *volo* = θέλω = 'I wish' (not 'I fly' — Leckie); an adverb, *bene* = καλῶς = 'well'; a participial noun, *scriptum* = τὸ γεγραμμένον = 'writing'; a conjunction, *et* = καί = 'and'; a preposition, *ab* = ἀπό = 'from'; an exclamation, *heu* = οἴ = 'alas.'

[28] The only occurrences of *coram* in the *Verrine Orations* are in *act.* 2.2.101 and 104 (the latter a repetition of the former). Here Cicero discusses the illegal action of Verres in trying and sentencing a prominent Sicilian *in absentia.* When this abuse of his praetorship brought him into difficulties, Verres forged the records of the trial, making them to read that the accused had been tried while present; as Cicero says—*tollit ex tabulis id quod erat, et facit coram esse delatum.*

[29] Cicero, *Tusc.* 1.7.14: 'Omne pronuntiatum—sic enim mihi in praesentia occurrit ut appellarem ἀξίωμα . . . est . . . quod est verum aut falsum'—'Every proposition—that is the way it occurs to me, at present, to translate ἀξίωμα . . . is . . . an assertion that is true or false.' In the present text Augustine writes: *sententiam quae affirmari negarique potest.* It has seemed preferable to render 'a sentence which may be said to be true or false,' rather than 'a sentence which may be affirmative or negative,' because the reference to Cicero indicates that he wishes to express the same meaning as the Roman orator. In either case, he is concerned with differentiating the proposition (a sign of judgment) from other types of grammatical sentences, such as questions and exclamations.

[30] *Vocabula.*

[31] On the parts of speech—*partes orationis*—and their number, see Quintilian, *Inst. or.* 1.4.18-21.

[32] *Vilia ludicra.* There is reference especially to the play on the word 'nothing' in 2.4, above.

[33] 'Truth' is one of Augustine's favorite designations of God.

[34] It is quite impossible to convey in English Augustine's play on words: 'Dabis igitur veniam, si *praeludo* tecum, non *ludendi* gratia.'

[35] Happiness, for St. Augustine, consists in the possession of God; see below, 14. 46, and *De b. vita* 2.11. Consistent with our Lord's words, *This is eternal life, that they may know Thee* (John 17. 3), he always includes knowledge in his notion of the happy life; cf., e. g., *De div. quaest.* 83, 35. 2: 'To live happily, what else is that than to possess eternal knowledge?' To truly wise, to be a real 'philosopher,' one must have the wisdom that comes from God—the truth that abides eternally: cf. *De b. vita* 4. 34. He considers philosophy a port from which one enters the mainland of the region where life is happy: *ibid.* 1. 1. The exercise of reason on speculative questions such as the present one of *The Teacher*, is to Augustine, even at this early stage of his career, only a preparation for mystical contemplation, which is in turn but a prelude to the eternal knowledge of God in the beatific vision.

[36] Cf. *De doct. Chr.* 2. 31. 48, where the author gives, as an example of sophism, the ancient argument: 'What I am, you are not . . . but I am a man; therefore you are not a man,' and remarks that such captious speech is proscribed by Ecclus. 37. 23: *He that speaketh sophistically is hateful.*

[37] The Saint himself, in his discussions, is very careful to make distinctions before answering ambiguous questions. See, for example, above, *The Greatness of the Soul* 1. 2 and 3. 4, where he distinguishes the two-fold meanings of the questions of Evodius.

[38] For example, although it is merely the word 'lion,' not a lion, that comes out of the mouth, what is emitted when we say 'noun' or 'word' is itself a noun or word.

[39] The 'law of reason' is the tendency to think, when we hear a word, of the reality signified, even when we have had the intention of considering the word exclusively as a part of speech.

[40] On Augustine's definition of man, see above, *The Greatness of the Soul* 25. 47 and n. 58.

[41] See Rom. 16.18: *Huiuscemodi enim Christo Domino nostro non serviunt, sed suo ventri.*

[42] 'We eat to live, not conversely' is an aphorism familiar to the ancients. Thus, *Auctor ad Herennium* 4. 28. 39: 'Esse oportet ut vivas, non vivere ut edas.' See also Quintilian, *Inst. orat.* 9. 3. 85. See also A. Gellius 19. 2. 7, who ascribes the same maxim to Socrates.

For other examples, cf. A. Otto, *Die Sprichwörter und sprichwört-lichen Redensarten der Römer* (Leipzig 1890) 123.

[43] Namely, that what exists to serve another is inferior to it.

[44] Rendering *docere—doctrina* with ' teaching '—' instruction.'

[45] *Sed stupet hic vitio . . .*: Persius, *Sat.* 3. 32.

[46] Here Adeodatus, and in his reply Augustine, refer to the follow-ing verses (35-8) in the same satire:

> Magne pater divum, saevos punire tyrannos
> Haud alia ratione velis, cum dira libido
> Moverit ingenium ferventi tincta veneno
> Virtutem videant intabescantque relicta.

[47] ' The best instruction of all ' (*Optima omnium disciplina*) is moral science, which provides an understanding of both virtues and vices. In *De immort. an.* 1. 1, the Saint defines *disciplina* as *quarum-cumque rerum scientia*—' the (certain) knowledge of things of all kinds,' referring especially to the ' liberal arts,' which he enumerates in *Retract.* 1. 6. Since he points out that the word *disciplina* is derived from *discere* (*De lib. arbit.* 1. 1. 2), he takes it to mean knowledge that is learned, or acquired by instruction; and he argues at length (*ibid.*) that it is always something good. In the present passage, Adeodatus, realizing that moral philosophy imparts knowledge of vices, without in any way demeaning the person who studies it, cor-rects his former insinuation in his question that knowledge of vice is inferior to the noun ' vice.'

[48] See above, 3. 6.

[49] Speaking and teaching.

[50] This observation is reminiscent of Plato, who, in *Phaedo* 39 (89d - 90c) represents Socrates as warning his hearers not to become ' misologists' or haters of argument (analogous to ' misanthropists' or haters of men). The sage points out, as Augustine does here, that it is hazardous to accept arguments as valid without carefully scruti-nizing and criticizing them, for if they are afterwards proved flimsy, one may lapse into skepticism. Augustine, having personally suc-cumbed to skepticism (cf. *Conf.* 5. 14. 25), devoted his first Chris-tian work, *Contra Academicos*, to its refutation.

[51] On the ancient art of fowling, see A. J. Butler, *Sport in Classic Times* (London 1930) 179-98.

[52] On this question, whether the meaning of words or the reality signified by words can be manifested without the use of signs, the dialogue has produced several fluctuations of opinion, which it seems well to summarize here:

a) In 3.6 (and the summary, 7.19), it is maintained that the meaning of words denoting some action can be manifested by simply performing the action, without words, provided one is not engaged in performing that action at the time the question is put. Speech is an exception, since to explain or even to illustrate what speech is, one has to speak—and, therefore, to give signs.

b) In 10.29, Adeodatus holds that nothing can be made manifest by the mere performance of an action designated by a word, except perhaps speaking, and possibly teaching too—quite the opposite of what he had agreed to earlier.

c) In 10.30, Augustine shows that the meaning of teaching cannot be manifested by itself or directly, without signs, although the meaning of speech can be manifested by speech itself; yet, since speech consists of signs, it is not to be admitted as an exception to the rule that nothing can be manifested without signs.

d) Finally, in 10.32, Augustine decides that a more intelligent observer can understand the meaning of certain actions, the essence of some natural phenomena, and, therefore, the meaning of words he has heard, by observation of the realities themselves, without any verbal explanations.

The upshot seems to be that in exceptional cases the essence of some reality can be understood from an example or individual case, but that generally words or some equivalent signs are necessary to make clear what a thing is essentially, or what a term means.

As to whether the meaning of 'speaking' can be manifested merely by giving an example—a question on which Adeodatus gives contradictory answers (a and b above) in different statements—the observation may be made that the difference between speaking and other actions is not so marked as is implied by both disputants. If someone asks what 'speaking' means, and I proceed to speak of things other than speech, I am indeed exercising an act of speech, or giving an example of it, but not a *sign* of what speech is. If I express in words what 'speaking' means—that is, if I give a verbal definition of it—it is parallel to expressing in words what 'walking' or any other word means.

[53] Dan. 3.94. Regarding both the form and the meaning of *saraballae*, a word foreign to both Latin and Greek, there is no little confusion. Some of the other forms that occur are: *sarabal(l)a, -orum, sarabara, -ae, -orum,* σαράπαραι. Cf. A. Hug, 'Saraballa, -orum,' Pauly-Wissowa-Kroll, *RE* 2.R. 1 (1920) 2386. Some MSS of the

De Magistro also have *sarabarae (-arum)*. St. Jerome, in the Vulgate, gives: . . . *et sarabala eorum non fuissent immutata*. Regarding the meaning of the word as given by St. Augustine, the Maurists adopted the reading, here followed, *quaedam capitum tegmina;* but some MSS have: *quaedam pedum tegmina*, that is, 'footwear of some sort.' In addition, in various versions of the Book of Daniel and elsewhere, the word is rendered 'trousers,' 'coverings for the limbs,' 'garments,' and even 'coat.' The Douay version reads: *nor their garments altered*. In any case, the meaning accepted makes no essential difference in Augustine's argument; but he made a very fortunate choice when he sought an obscure word to illustrate his point.

[54] St. Thomas in his *De magistro* (*Quaest. disp. de ver.* qu. 11, a. 1, ad 3) considers this objection of Augustine's, namely, that the one to whom words or other signs are proposed either already knows the realities signified by the words (so that he does not learn them from the words), or he does not know them (in which case he cannot even understand the meaning of the word). He answers that the realities must previously be known in some respect, though they were previously unknown in other respects. For instance, to learn by means of words what man is, one must already have knowledge of animal, or substance, or at least of 'thing.' Similarly, when there is question of learning a proposition that is the conclusion of a reasoning process, the conclusion was previously unknown, but there must have been some knowledge of more general principles from which it flows. For a comparison of the teachings of the two Doctors regarding the power of language to convey thought, see Colleran, *The Treatises 'De Magistro' of St. Augustine and St. Thomas* 93-105.

[55] 'Recall' here means: consider the principles that remain habitually in the intellect, in order to understand the nature of realities. Concerning this conception of 'memory,' see Introd. 122 ff.

[56] The reference is, of course, to various details of the account of the three youths in the fiery furnace: Daniel Ch. 3, where (in the Septuagint vv. 21 and 94, Vulgate v. 21) the word or variant of the word, *saraballae*, occurs.

[57] *Haec autem omnia . . . credere me potius quam scire fateor.* *Scire* is used here, as the context indicates, to mean not merely 'to know' in a general way—for the author has just admitted that we have some knowledge of the things concerned—but 'to know directly' or 'to perceive,' that is, to have direct sense experience of sensible things, or to have intuitive understanding of realities proportionate to the intellect alone. See *De Trin.* 12. 12-13. 20, where the Saint

later gave a more detailed and more developed analysis of *scientia* as contrasted with *sapientia;* also cf. above, *The Greatness of the Soul,* 26. 49 and n. 61.

Credere is defined (*De praedest. sanct.* 2. 5) as *cum assensione cogitare.* There may be thought without belief, for some may think precisely to avoid giving assent (*ibid*). In the present passage, Augustine goes on to say that belief is a general act of knowledge that includes 'understanding' (*Quod ergo intelligo, id etiam credo; at non omne quod credo, etiam intelligo*), whereas 'knowing' is coextensive with 'understanding' (*Omne autem quod intelligo, scio: non omne quod credo, scio*). His teaching on the relation between *scire* and *credere* is also brought out succinctly in *De civ. Dei* 11. 3: 'Si ea sciri possunt testibus nobis, quae remota non sunt a sensibus nostris, sive interioribus sive etiam exterioribus, . . . profecto ea quae remota sunt a sensibus nostris, quoniam nostro testimonio scire non possumus, de his alios testes requirimus, eisque credimus, a quorum sensibus remota esse vel fuisse non credimus. Sicut ergo de visibilibus, quae non vidimus, eis credimus qui viderunt, atque ita de ceteris quae ad suum quemque sensum corporis pertinent: ita de his quae animo ac mente sentiuntur . . ., hoc est de invisibilibus quae a nostro sensu interiore remota sunt, iis nos oportet credere, qui haec in illo incorporeo lumine disposita didiccrunt; vel manentia contuentur.'

[58] *Nisi credideritis, non intelligetis:* Isa. 7. 9. The Vulgate reads: *Si non credideritis, non permanebitis.* The text is also appealed to by Augustine in *De lib. arb.* 1. 2. 4 and 2. 2. 6.

[59] St. Augustine frequently uses the verb *praesidere* regarding God or truth. Thus, in another early work, *De mus.* 6. 1. 1, he speaks of men 'adhering, by love of unchangeable truth, to the one God and Lord of all things who *presides over* human minds, without the intervention of any nature.' In *Conf.* 10. 26. 37 he addresses God: 'Everywhere, O Truth, Thou dost *preside over* all who consult Thee, and at the same time givest answers to all who consult Thee on different subjects.' In *De div. quaest.* 83, qu. 79. 1, it is the soul over which God is said to preside for its own utility and health.

[60] Cf. *De vera rel.* 39. 72: 'Do not go outside, but go back into yourself. Truth dwells within man.'

[61] Eph. 3. 14-17: *For this cause I bow my knees to the Father of our Lord Jesus Christ, . . . that He would grant you, according to the riches of His glory, to be strengthened by His Spirit with might unto the inward man; that Christ may dwell by faith in your hearts.* The

Apostle is obviously concerned with the *supernatural* presence of Christ through grace, whereas St. Augustine is applying his words to the natural order. It is true, of course, that God is present in all His creatures, and therefore the Eternal Word, the Second Person of the Blessed Trinity, is 'within man.' That is all Augustine wishes to insist upon.

[62] 1 Cor. 1.23 f.: *But we preach Christ crucified . . . Christ the Power of God and the Wisdom of God.* The Divine Person, the Word, is the Wisdom and Power of God (cf. John 1), and since God's Power and Wisdom are the efficient and exemplary causes of all created activity and all created knowledge, we can say that our ability to know is due to the Divine Word; cf. *De Gen. ad litt.* 4. 32. 49. True, when we speak of 'Christ,' we generally mean the Divine Person having a *human* as well as a divine nature, but St. Augustine is not referring to the former.

In *De vera rel.* 3. 3, he expresses the opinion that Plato himself, were he asked whether any human being could convince people, or at least persuade them to believe, what need there is of purifying heart and mind to understand eternal truth, would answer that no one could, unless the very Power and Wisdom of God should illumine him internally, equip him with grace, and fortify him with constancy.

[63] Regarding this entire paragraph, and especially the present sentence, see B. Jansen, "Zur Lehre des hl. Augustinus von dem Erkennen der Rationes aeternae," in M. Grabmann-J. Mausbach, *Aurelius Augustinus: Festschrift der Görres-Gesellschaft zum 1500. Todestage des heiligen Augustinus* (Cologne 1930) 125 f.

[64] Augustine frequently insists that the attainment of truth depends upon moral rectitude. In *De vera relig.* 3. 3, for example, he says that 'there is no greater impediment to the perception of truth than a life devoted to passion and to the false images of sensible things, which, being impressed on us by this sensible world through the body, give rise to various opinions and errors.' Speaking of the knowledge of the law of God (*De ord.* 2. 8. 25), he enumerates the virtues that are necessary for all, and especially the youth, to attain that knowledge: restraint of carnal excess, gluttony, jealousy, detraction, etc. When St. Monnica anticipated an opinion that he had learned from philosophical books, he ascribed her keenness to her being a 'soul devoted to God' (*De b. vita* 4. 27; see also 2.10, and *De ord.* 2. 1. 1). In *Solil.* 1. 1. 2 he addresses God 'who hast not willed that any but the pure should know the truth,' but he later

(*Retract.* 1. 4. 2) disapproved these words for the reasons that 'many who are not pure know many true things,' and that he did not define what he meant by 'truth' and 'know.'

⁶⁵ This analogy between corporeal sight and intellectual perception is very common in Augustine's works. In general, 'understanding is to the mind what seeing is to the sense faculty' (*De ord.* 2. 3. 10). Just as material objects are not visible without the help of external light, so universal and necessary truths are not intelligible without the help of an internal light; and as the sun is the source of material light, so God is the source of the light in the intellect: cf. *Solil.* 1. 6. 12. In the present passage he draws the further analogy that as a person can fail to see material objects despite the light of the sun, so one can fail to understand intelligible truth, even though the light of God shines within his mind.

⁶⁶ Regarding Augustine's notion of corporeal 'elements,' see above, *The Greatness of the Soul* 1. 2 and n. 3.

⁶⁷ On the Augustinian teaching regarding sensation, see above, *The Greatness of the Soul* 30. 59 and n. 73.

⁶⁸ 'Our own authors' are the inspired writers of the books of Holy Scripture. It is at least questionable, however, whether those writers mean 'sensible' by 'carnal,' or 'intelligible' by 'spiritual.' Such expressions as 'the carnal man' and 'the spiritual man' used in opposition to each other, generally designated 'man considered according to his nature (or even *fallen nature*)' in contradistinction to 'man considered according to his supernatural destiny, and hence endowed with grace.' However, since *caro* is also used in Scripture for 'flesh' or 'living body,' and *spiritus* for 'the rational principle in man,' there is foundation for the Saint's application of these terms. See M. Hagen, *Lexicon Biblicum* 1 (Paris 1905) *s.v.* 'caro'; 3 (1911) *s.vv.* 'spiritualis,' 'spiritus'; F. Prat, *The Theology of St. Paul* (tr. by J. Stoddard, New York 1927) 2. 401-7.

⁶⁹ See *Conf.* 10. 8. 13 for a detailed description of the sensible objects whose representations are stored in the sensitive memory.

⁷⁰ He speaks of these images as 'false,' because what they represent is not now actually existing in our presence; and he goes on to call them 'true,' in the sense that they represent what did so exist. More precisely, the images can be said to be neither true nor false, since they do not, of themselves, involve any affirmation or denial.

⁷¹ 'Attestations,' rendering *documenta.* In classical Latinity *documentum* generally meant 'proof,' 'example,' 'specimen'; cf. Varro, *De ling. lat.* 6. 7. 68: '*Documenta* exempla docendi causa dicuntur.'

Augustine's meaning is that the images are likenesses or replicas of objects previously known by the senses, and these replicas therefore bear witness to our assertions about those objects when we discuss them. He goes on to say that the attestations are internal, and hence are not of value to those to whom we speak.

⁷² *Cum vero de iis agitur quae* mente *conspicimus, id est* intellectu atque ratione. . . . *Mens*, in Augustine's usage, is the superior part of the rational soul (*animus*), whereby we know purely intelligible, not sensible things, and by which we ultimately attain to knowledge of God. Cf. *Enarr. in Ps.* 3. 3, *De Trin.* 9. 2. 2; also P. Gardeil, *La structure de l'âme et l'expérience mystique* (Paris 1927) 1. 50-130, 2. 281-312. In the present passage Augustine indicates that *intellectus* and *ratio* are the two powers or faculties of the *mens*; similarly, also, *De civ. Dei* 11. 2: 'mens, cui ratio et intelligentia naturaliter inest. . . .' *Intellectus* (sometimes also called *intelligentia*, though the latter word sometimes designates an *act* or *state* of the 'intellect') is superior to *ratio*; the former is intuitive, the latter, discursive. See above, *The Greatness of the Soul*, 27. 53 and n. 65. The assertion of the present text, that in the exercise of 'intellect,' there is required divine illumination, is made, with slightly different terminology, in *In Ioan. Evang. tr.* 15. 4. 19: 'Sic in anima nostra quiddam est quod intellectus vocatur. Hoc ipsum animae quod intellectus et mens dicitur, illuminatur luce superiore. Iam superior illa lux qua mens humana illuminatur, Deus est.'

⁷³ For the various interpretations of the 'interior light of truth,' see Introd. 120 ff. Although Augustine here states that 'we behold immediately in that interior light of truth' the objects of intelligence, it cannot be argued that he holds, as Malebranche later did, that we have direct vision of the attributes of God, and in them see all intelligible realities. For, as the context shows, he is concerned with the question, not of the formation of concepts, but of the *truth* of our knowledge, and, therefore, of the guarantee for the reliability of our judgments. He is insisting upon the *ontological* basis of truth: the fact that the human intellect is a participation of the intellect of God, and therefore exercises its knowledge with dependence on the power and veracity of God.

⁷⁴ In *Conf.* 11. 3. 5, Augustine later wrote that if Moses spoke to him in Latin, 'I would know what he was saying. But how would I know whether what he was saying was true? And if I knew this, too, would I be deriving my knowledge from him? Indeed, within me, within the dwelling of my thoughts, Truth, which is neither

Hebrew nor Greek nor Latin nor foreign, which knows no organs of speech and language, no sound of syllables, would say, "He is speaking the truth"; and I should forthwith say with certainty and confidence to that man of Thine, "You are speaking the truth."' Again, in an Easter homily of the year 416, *In Epist. Joan. ad Parth. tract.* 3. 13, he also stated and emphasized the same doctrine: 'The sound of our words strikes the ears, but the Teacher is within. Do not think that anyone learns anything from man. We can lend suggestion by the din of our voice; but if He is not within you to teach, our dinning is in vain. . . . External instructions offer helps and suggestions of a sort. But the One who instructs hearts exercises His teaching function [*cathedram habet*] in heaven. For that reason He Himself says in the Gospel (Matt. 23. 8 f.): *Do not call anyone on earth your teacher, for one is your teacher, Christ.* It is the inner teacher who teaches, Christ teaches—His inspiration teaches. Where His inspiration and His unction are not present, external words noise in vain.' As the contexts show, he is referring in these passages to the supernatural gift of grace and to understanding by supernatural faith, which are the direct results not of the preacher's words, but of God.

[75] Although Augustine has rejected Plato's pre-existence of the human soul, he remains profoundly impressed by the facts mentioned in the *Meno* whereby Plato seeks to establish his view. What he does retain with Plato is the conviction that the truth is not imposed on the mind from without, but is found within the mind itself. Plato has recourse to 'innate ideas' which were acquired in a previous existence; Augustine seeks the explanation in the 'interior teacher' and 'interior light.' Cf. R. Jolivet, "La doctrine augustinienne de l'illumination," in *Mélanges augustiniens = Rev. de philos. nouv. sér.* 1 (1930) 407-414, art. 3: 'Le Maître intérieur.'

[76] As St. Thomas Aquinas points out (*Quaest. disp. de ver.* qu. 11, a. 1 ad 17), the certitude that arises upon hearing such statements comes not indeed from the words themselves, but from the internal natural power of the intellect whereby we know first principles, with which we compare the propositions expressed. Since God is the cause of the intellectual powers, the Angelic Doctor goes on to explain, we can say that it is God who produces certitude in the mind, and not the words of the speaker. He adds (*ibid.* ad 18) that there is genuine learning of truth when one is brought around by questioning to express the truth himself, for what he would know before the questioning is the general principle involved, not the conclusion and exact application that is taught.

[77] *Intus est discipulus veritatis, foris iudex loquentis:* the force of *discipulus* (from *discere*), 'a learner,' is lost in the translation.

[78] *Virtute:* It is quite impossible to reproduce in a single English word the double meaning—of moral or physical excellence of one sort or another—attaching to the Latin word *virtus*. The English 'virtue' suggests none of the equivocation that could result from using the Latin word in speech, though the French *vertu* has not entirely lost the wide double range of meaning claimed by its Latin ancestor.

[79] Augustine was sufficiently familiar with the Punic language to explain Hebrew expressions that occur in the Bible by referring to the Punic; e.g., the word *mammon*, in *Serm.* 113.2.2 (cf. also *De Serm. Dom. in monte* 2.47, and the remarks by Dr. Plumpe *ad loc.*: ACW 5.205 n. 113). The language was fairly commonly known in Africa, though not by all; in *Serm.* 167.3.4, Augustine quotes a Punic proverb in Latin, because not all his hearers would understand the original. In *Epist.* 117.2 he gently reproves the grammarian Maximus for treating Punic names too lightly.

[80] There is here an indication that for Augustine the principal problem for the solution of which he proposes the doctrine of illumination by the 'Inner Teacher,' is how to explain why certain judgments are accepted by the mind as eternally and universally true. Similarly, in *De Trin.* 9.6.9 ff., he points out the difference between *believing* what someone manifests about his own individual mind, and *recognizing as true* what he says about the human mind itself; and it is only in the latter case that we gaze upon indestructible truth: *intuemur inviolabilem veritatem.*

[81] In a letter to a certain Gaius (*Epist.* 19.1), written shortly before his ordination, Augustine expresses the dependence on the internal light of truth with regard to the written word, as he here expresses it with regard to the spoken word: 'No one perceives the truth of what he reads in the book itself or in the writer, but rather within himself, provided a measure of the light of truth, shining with a brilliance beyond the ordinary and far exalted above the lowliness of the body, has penetrated his mind.'

[82] *Nescientes non se doctores potius laudare quam doctos:* the *docti* are the teachers themselves, who have received the same schooling from the 'Inner Teacher' as their pupils receive during the instruction.

[83] In *De immort. an.* 4.5, he had written: 'If art passes from mind to mind, departing from the one in order to abide in the other, then

no one would teach art except by losing it, or no one would acquire skill in art unless his teacher forgot the art, or died.'

⁸⁴ Quite certainly, this resolve was never carried out in any special treatise, nor to an appreciable extent in any of his other works; though in *De Trin.* 9. 7. 12, 15. 10. 17 - 15. 16. 26, where he treats of the Divine Word, the Second Person of the Blessed Trinity, he discusses human words at some length. Cf. M. Schmaus, *Die psychologische Trinitätslehre des hl. Augustinus* (Münsterische Beitr. z. Theol. 11, Münster i. W. 1927) 407-412. In *Serm.* 225. 3, where he uses the twofold element (meaning and sound) of words to illustrate the two natures of Christ, Augustine admits that words are vehicles of thoughts; and in *Conf.* 10. 10. 17, he grants that fundamental principles of judging might never be brought to the fore but under the influence of the words of others. But there is no retraction of his insistence that without the action of God and the divine guarantee of truth, words have no value at all. In *In Ioan. Evang. tr.* 26. 7 (written in 416-17) he says: 'Quid faciunt homines forinsecus annuntiantes? Quid facio ego modo cum loquor? Stepitum verborum ingero auribus vestris. Nisi ergo revelet ille qui intus est, quid dico, aut quid loquor?'

⁸⁵ Matt. 23. 9.

⁸⁶ Augustine insists on this very frequently in his various works, and his second publication, *De beata vita*, had this message as its principal theme; cf. especially 2. 11 and 3. 17; also *Conf.* 10. 22. 32.

⁸⁷ Cf. *Conf.* 10. 21. 31: 'Certainly, all of us wish to be happy . . . .' See also *De mor. Eccl. Cath.* 1. 3. 4.

⁸⁸ Cf. *De lib. arbit.* 1. 14. 30.

⁸⁹ When Evodius asks (in *De lib. arbit.* 2. 2. 4) why God gave us the power of free will, which is the direct cause of sin, and whether it would not have been better if we could choose only what is good, Augustine replies that the question is difficult, but he goes on: 'God, I hope, will enable me to answer you, or, rather, He will enable you to give the answer to your own question, by the instruction of that inner truth which is the supreme teacher of all.' The second and third books of this work were written after the Saint's ordination in 391.

⁹⁰ *Oraculum* (Gr.: χρησμός, λόγιον) is a favorite word with the Fathers when referring to the Scriptures, Scripture utterances and mysteries, divine revelation and inspiration, etc.: see the notes by J. A. Kleist, ACW 1. 117 n. 179, and J. P. Christopher, ACW 2. 104 n. 64.

INDEX

INDEX

Adam, origin of his soul, 194; transmission of his sin, 195

Adeodatus, disputant in the *De mag.*, 115, 221; Augustine's tribute to his talent, 115, 222

age, not a reason for growth of soul, 44, 46 ff.

Alfaric, P., 192

Allevi, L., 221

altitudo, 197

Alypius, friend of Augustine, 90, 211

Ambrose, St., 211; influence on Augustine, 3, 190
   De mysteriis 1. 2: 196; 2. 6: 196

Ananias, 176

angels, and human soul, 107, 217 f.

anima, animus, 200

animals, and reason, 75; and knowledge, 81 f.; and sense perception, 81; have souls, 100; have sensitive memory, 198

Aristotle, 121, 195
   De an. 2. 2: 213; *Nic. Eth.* 5. 3: 199, 211

Arnobius, *Adv. nat.* 2. 20-23: 203

art, 50 ff.; innate, 54, 203 f.; a level of the soul, 109; liberal, 231; does not pass from mind to mind, 239 f.

Auctor ad Herennium 4. 28. 39: 230

audibilia, 227

audibles, 140, 227

Augustine, St., conversion, 8, 192; notion of philosophy, 3, 189, 220; early Manichaeism and skepticism, 3, 189; early materialism, 3, 193; influenced by Platonists, 190, 191 f.; influenced by Plotinus, 209; differs with Plotinus, 213, 217; knowledge of Punic, 184, 239; knowledge of contemporary physics, 7, 91, 211 f.; enthusiasm for numerical illustrations, 7, 191; plays on words, 158, 230; disclaims authority, 63; friendship with Alypius, 211; letters to Evodius, 190 f.; had ecstatic vision of God, 214; desired understanding beyond belief, 199; doctrine on creation, 193 f.; views on world soul, 97, 212 f.; inconsistently defines man, 205 f.; views on pre-existence of soul, 123, 203 f.; on immateriality of soul, 196 f.; difficulties in defining soul, 196; his extreme spiritualism, 209

Conf., contain principal account of his mystical experience: 8; 3. 4. 8: 191; 3. 7. 12: 189; 3. 10. 18: 213; 4. 2. 3: 189; 4. 15. 24: 197; 4. 16. 28 ff.: 212; 4. 16. 31: 189; 5. 2. 2: 217; 5. 10. 19: 3, 189, 197; 5. 10. 20: 189; 5. 14. 25: 189, 231; 6. 3. 4: 190; 6. 7. 11-12. 21: 211; 7. 9. 13: 190, 223; 7. 10. 16: 214; 7. 11. 17: 216; 7. 17. 23: 206, 214; 7. 19. 25: 216; 8. 8. 19-12. 30: 211; 9. 6. 14: 211, 221;

the Light, 120; the Inner Teacher, 177, 186, 238; Augustine's devotion to, 189; authority of, 191; purpose of belief in, 192; dwells in hearts, 177, 234 f.; Wisdom and Power of God, 235

Christopher, J. P., 216, 219, 240

Church, Catholic, 106; writings of, 108; as Mother, 105, 216

Cicero, M. T., 150
Hortensius: 191; In Verrem act. 2. 2. 101, 104: 229; Tusc. disp. 1. 7. 14: 229

Circensian games, 211

circle, most perfect figure, 33 f., 46; centre indivisible, 34 f.

coelum, 164

coenum, 164

Colleran, J. M., 221, 224, 233

confirmation, sacrament of, 196

coniunctio, 143 f., 156

conjunction, not a noun, 143 f., 146; used as noun, 147, 151

consecration of infants, 111

consistency, and stubbornness, 78

contemplation, of God, 9; of truth, 106; a level of the soul, 109; mystical, 214, 215; impossible without moral rectitude, 218; prelude to eternal vision, 230; goal of philosophy, 230

Copleston, F., 223

creation, Augustine's teaching on, 9, 193 f.

credere, 233 f.

Cyprian, St., 216

D'Arcy, M. C., 194

deaf-mutes, 49 f., 136, 155

death, fear of, 102; the greatest boon, 106

definition, rules for, 71 ff.; difficult to form, 183 f.

depth, not found in soul, 41

Descartes, R., Med. 2: 197; Prin. phil. 2. 10 f.: 197

dimensions, in what sense incorporeal, 25, 198; third, see third dimension

discere, 239

disciplina, 231

discussion, requires words, 134 f.

docere, 225, 231

docti, 239

documenta, 179, 236 f.

Donatist heretics, 211

Douay version of Scripture, 233

doubt, exists in mind, 132

Downes, A. H., 206

ea quae vere sunt, 215 f.

Eggersdorfer, F. X., 221

elements, corporeal, 14 f., 89, 178, 195, 236

elephants, not intelligent, 42

emanation, doctrine of Plotinus, 9, 119, 193

ends, superior to means, 163, 165

Epicureans, 181 f., 223

equality, 30 f.

equity, 30

Ernout, A., 228

eucharist, 227

Euclid, 199 f.

Eusebius, Hist. Eccl. 6. 2: 222

Eve, first woman, 194

Evodius, 197; disputant in De qu. an., 4 f.; letters to Augustine, 190 f.

extension, not found in soul, 17

Nebridius, 4, 225
Neoplatonists, 197; influence on Augustine, 3 f., 8, 118, 190. See Platonists, Plotinus
nomen, 153, 227; etymology, 146, 228
non latens animam, 208 f.
noscere, 146, 228
nothing, meaning of, 132 f., 154 f., 229
noun, a sign, 139; definition of, 139; a word, 141; signifies realities, 140; and words, 141 ff., 144 ff., 228; constituent of proposition, 150 f.; one meaning of *nomen*, 227; general and special sense, 152
Νοῦς, Plotinic notion of, 119 f.

O'Connor, W., 195, 200
Olympic champions, 57
One, The, of Plotinus, 118 ff., 193
ὄνομα, 153, 157
opinio, 206
optima omnium disciplina, 231
oraculum, 240
order in universe, 110, 111, 213 f., 218, 219
Origen, 222
original sin, 195, 220
Ostia, 4, 190
Ott, W., 209, 221
Otto, A., 193, 231

pantomime, 136, 155, 227
parts of speech, 152, 229
passio, 208
Paul, St., 105, 120, 149, 150; *passim*
Pegis, A. C., 190, 206, 220

Persius, *Sat.* 3. 32-8: 167 f., 231
philosophy, Augustine's notion of, 3, 8; objects of, 189; purpose of, 192, 230; moral, 231
φύσις, 119
φωσφόρος, 212
physical strength, increases without increase of soul, 55 ff.; explanation of, 57-62
Plato, 122 ff., 235; Idea of Good, 118; held innate ideas, 238; *Meno*, 238; 20: 224; *Phaedo*, 18-22: 224; 39: 231; *Theaet.* 6 f.: 224; *Rep.* 6. 18: 118, 223
Platonists, influence on Augustine, 190, 191 f.; too lavishly praised by Augustine, 223; doctrine of pre-existence and reminiscence, 203; held the soul superior to body, 206; considered almost Christian, 214 f.; held illumination, 118, 223. See Neoplatonists
Plotinus, 122, 192; influence on Augustine, 3, 8, 209, 214; tenets of contrasted with Augustine, 9, 190; considered a second Plato, 118; considers imagination an imperfection, 213; counsels aloofness from society, 213; gives indications of ecstasy, 214; teaches merging of soul into the Absolute, 217; attitude on human body, 193; doctrine on soul, 193; admits world soul, 97, 212; considers soul the principle of life, 213; stresses separation from material things, 214
Enn. 1.6.7: 214; 1.6.8: 193; 1.6.9: 193; 2.9.1: 223;